AN UNBELIEVABLE LIFE

The Woman Who Became Vietnam Veterans' Voice Against Agent Orange

By:

Rena Kopystenski

DEDICATIONS

To my beloved husband, John Vincent Kopystenski, I dedicate this book compiled with the memories of a lifetime lived because he loved me more than I ever knew anyone could care for another person, and he never doubted me, no matter how much I doubted myself. For all the pain and illness that he suffered, but tried to hide from the world. I can only pray that, somehow there is a place where I can someday be by his side again because without him, I am truly lost.

To my son, Alexander Vincent Kopystenski, whose life has been so hard to live, but somehow he has survived and is still standing. You were always my gift to your father and taught us both the true meaning of the word pride.

To Giovanni Alexander Kopystenski, our little Angel who, hopefully sits at his grandpa's knee, waiting for your daddy and me to join you in a place where you can finally speak.

To the incredible Band of Brothers that created Agent Orange Victims of New Jersey from 1978 to 1988, and taught not only America, but the entire world that there truly was no greater group of men and women than the Vietnam Combat Veterans and their families. For trusting me to be your Voice and for following me with your hearts and your devotion, which still humbles me to this day.

To Charleen Davis, my editor without whose help and support I would not have been able to write this book.

CONTENTS

INTRODUCTION

How does someone, set down on paper, the story of a life filled with heartache and heart break caused by a corrupt and uncaring society that cost so many their very lives and destroyed the hopes and dreams of countless people? Can you write it, but yet never let go even for a moment of the reality that this is a love story between one woman, one man and 1.5 million Vietnam vets?

Is there any way to tell a story that spanned over nearly forty years, but feels like it all happened yesterday? Can you convey to readers that despite the sadness and the sheer mortality of the characters who were forced to play the game of life with both hands tied behind their backs, that those thousands of players could still find humor and reasons to laugh while working hard to try to end the pain of their circumstances? There has to be a way to describe all of these things just the way they happened because this is a true account of what happened to those who thought that they had survived the Vietnam War.

The thing that makes this story a love story, is certainly not romance, soft lights or even sexual tension. It is what one woman did to change an entire country's view and structure based entirely upon saving the lives of her husband and their child because of her love for them. That, and the realization that if she was going to be able to help them, she had to figure out a way to help everyone else who had been poisoned by the defoliant Agent Orange in Vietnam sprayed upon all those brave young men by their own government who were then ignored by not only that government, but by the majority of the American people as well.

This is not intended to be a statistical teaching tool or a textbook on that war, and most of the factual data included is done so to explain the circumstances which motivated the characters at that moment in time. The people and the facts are simply part of a population of boom babies trying to live the American Dream that had been promised to them from the day they were born, one that through no fault of their own was always kept at the top of an ever rising plateau just out of reach. It is what one family lived through. Yet, it is what they also shared with all the other families they met on the never-ending journey to that unreachable plateau.

The amazing irony of what was accomplished, by inventive initiative and in spite of the concept that the endeavor undertaken was unheard of without power and financing, was not realized until over ten years after it had already changed national perception, as well as laws and regulations governing entire governmental departments and finances. In other words, what was done on a shoestring was thought only possible by using millions of dollars, professional lobbyists and legislative scholars. It was not supposed to be accomplished by housewives, veterans and anyone of any influence who could be enlisted to work for free—nor through efforts that relied heavily on church members and especially on using incredibly creative shock and awe methods to raise awareness.

In keeping with the unorthodox methods used to organize and educate those who were not paying attention to the Vietnam

War or its walking casualties, this book's Chapter One relates to a trip to Paris, France in May of 2009, by an old widowed senior citizen who gave a speech in testimony before an International Tribunal investigating the spraying and long term effects of the chemicals 2,4D and 2,4,5T, also known as Agents Orange, Blue, White and Purple. The testimony in its entirety is included as an appendix to this endeavor, but this book is the story of what and who that old lady had become more than thirty years earlier, without ever knowing what the end results would be, not only to her family who and how without ever knowing what the end results would be, not only each effort, much less the end result of all the years, had never given up the fight no matter what it cost her, and cost her it did. This is the story of ME, of MY LIFE and of the incredible people that I met along the paths that life had chosen for me to "take on a government, and bring it to its knees," as many of the Vietnam veterans who are still alive, never miss an opportunity to quote when writing or speaking of what I had done for them.

My testimony should have been the end of a nightmare. However, for this writer, regardless of the findings of that Tribunal, which were that the United States was guilty of a war crime, this was simply the beginning of another nightmare of the destruction of American families that still has not completely played out.

CHAPTER ONE

REMINISCING THE JOURNEY TO TELL A LOVE STORY

MAY 15TH, 2009, SHOULD HAVE been the end of this story, the final chapter in a tale of a lifetime, with its closing scene taking place over six thousand miles from where it played out in the United States, and yet still very much alive where it all began, in South Vietnam. This was really supposed to be sort of my swan song, my time to let the whole world hear about who was responsible for the early death of my reason to wake up every morning and go to sleep every night, my husband of nearly forty years; the man I wanted to grow old with and the man that I had dreamed with about wonderful experiences we would have in our golden years. The man named John, who loved me and liked me more than any other human being on this Earth had ever cared about me.

I wanted to go to Paris, France and testify before the International Tribunal of Conscience, a worldly panel that was investigating and making a determination regarding the brutal and devastating destruction of over one million people and the inherited destruction of ten times as many children over the generations yet to come. My reason was really very simple. I WANTED TO GET SATISFACTION FROM THOSE WHO MURDERED MY HUSBAND AND DESTROYED OUR LEGACY!

What I did not know was that although my testimony made headlines across the globe and was a major influence in the findings of the panel; the story was far from over and what was yet to come would prove to be an even greater nightmare for my family, and moreover, total proof that the decisions made by our government from1954 to 1972, in first Korea and then Vietnam was going to destroy America by the 21st century. The speech that I gave, that unexpectedly put me not only back in the public spotlight, as well as back into the world of what is known as activism can be found is in the appendix as a guide through an unbelievable journey traveled almost incognito, at least to the inhabitants of our everyday existence. That trip to Paris, which was supposed to be the last battle of a war that lasted over 40 years, circa 2009, turned out to be not just simply the end of a great marriage, but the beginning of an even larger chapter in the lives of one family and over a few million of their friends and counterparts. It is actually a story without any end at all in sight.

The airline flight of approximately thirteen hours was actually the first time in weeks that I was allowed to be alone with my own thoughts to reflect on what brought me to what I thought was full-circle; ending with a trip to Paris, France, one of the primary sites on Johnny's and my "Someday" list. Now, I was going, but I was going alone to talk about what had not only robbed us of our Someday, but had made our entire life together a forty-year struggle created by a two-year experience forced upon a boy of twenty-one, that had cost him so much of what he could have been. My husband, my Johnny Weeble ("because Weebles wobble, but they don't fall down") did accomplish many great things. Yet, at what personal cost and in how much constant and crippling pain?

Throughout our entire lives together, my husband took the hand that was dealt him and did whatever he could to be a good husband, a wonderful father, a caring citizen and an exceptional son. And while I knew that he would have loved for someone to answer just one question, "what did I do to deserve this nightmare?" he carried on almost never screaming out or demanding an answer. The task of asking the hard questions, of storming the Bastille known as Washington D.C., of making people care about those who had served and making them take responsibility in any way that was possible to obtain was my job! *I* wasn't a Weeble! I was more like the toy called the *Bozo* and the harder I got hit, the faster and harder I came flying back. My beloved husband used to say to those who asked how and why I was the way that I was, "My wife grew up in The Bronx." like that explained everything.

Where I was raised and the times I was raised in may have had some bearing on my inability to feel fear of anything unless it was related to people I loved or cared about, because throughout my adult life, regardless of the education, the jobs, the awards and the accomplishments, within moments of meeting me, while the letters before and after my name may have remained unknown it was known that I was Rena from The Bronx. My Bronx was the full picture that comes to mind: raised in the Sedgewick Projects, the eldest of three but the only girl. Protecting my brothers was my responsibility and only my responsibility, for which there would be hell to pay if I failed. This was probably the source of my tenacity with regard to the Vietnam veterans who were so vulnerable when they came home to what should have been as safe a haven as their mother's kitchen.

Early in our dating relationship, Johnny and I were driving home after seeing the movie, *The French Connection* which told the true story of the biggest NYPD drug bust ever made and portrayed detectives that we knew in real life. It had a strong understory about having partners that could be trusted to "have the backs" of their counterparts. Johnny, who very seldom spoke about Vietnam, quietly said, "If you had been with me in Nam, I probably wouldn't have been so scared". I didn't know where this came from or what response I was supposed to have, so I just said "What?"

He took his eyes off the road long enough to look at me and say "because you have bigger balls than any man I've ever met" and just left it at that. Please keep in mind that this man was a fireman who had been a door gunner on a Medivac chopper for the Army's 1st AirCav. He stood 6'2" and weighed about 210 lbs with about a 52 inch chest and triceps on top of triceps, but he thought I was tougher than him and everyone else in Vietnam. Okay!! I guess that because of that affirmation, I was determined to spend the next forty years trying to prove that my magic bracelets were always working.

Growing up in the 50's and 60's was different than for any other generation, which makes it hard to explain the very unusual situation that a large portion of the population of Boom Babies were and are forced to endure. Our parents lived as children and teenagers through the Great Depression, where there was unemployment, hunger and homelessness rampant at all levels of the class system. Businessmen were jumping out of their high office windows in 1929, and entire extended families were cramming into tiny apartments; children were begging in the streets, and food lines for one hot meal a day, if that, were blocks long. My own mother related that even though my grandfather, being a pressman, had work throughout the Depression although at much less than he had been paid before; and her memory was that even though there was always something to eat at mealtime, she had begun to notice that every once and again she would notice that my grandmother's wedding band was missing from her finger, but there was meat on the table.

It may have been our parents' childhood experiences or the need to give their own children all of the things that they had wished they could have had to play with instead of worrying about hunger. Whatever motivated the Boom Baby Generation, we seemed to have it all. For many of us, being born after WWII, and for reasons that went from where our immigrant families came from; our fathers' service in the war zones; the rationing of gasoline and food in this country; or the insidious and totally evil actions of The Third Reich, we were raised to be patriotic and patriotic meant strong. We were pushed hard to get an education and for some of us whose families had been annihilated, we were taught to never be bullied and to always stand tough. Or at least, that's how I grew up. I was raised "New York Strong" and with Jewish heritage by agnostic parents using the term "Never Again" when it came to anti-Semitism or bullying.

As a generation, we wanted "Our Own". Rock & Roll was something we had to fight for as our own music. We wanted our own styles and our own way of communicating too. But most of all, we wanted to have fun and not have to make ourselves crazy worrying about everything and anything like our parents and our grandparents did. We wanted cars as soon as we were old enough to drive and even though most of us were raised to know what a strong work ethic was, we didn't want to kill ourselves like our parents did. When it came to our Boom Baby generation, what we didn't know or have to contend with until we became closer to our old age, was that there were *more* of us than any other generation ever before.

Guys coming home from WWII and those who stayed home to work on the home front wanted three basic things from their country. Those things were: jobs, a home of their own and babies, babies, babies. What our parents never realized is that all those babies were going to grow up and create an environment and a whole new society of "Our Own". It was not until most of the early boom babies became adults that we, as a generation began to realize that the government of our country was not exactly what we had been taught it was.

Thinking back to how ridiculous our education was at the hands of our government there are things that we may laugh at today, but beginning in grade school we were taught to fear the "Red Devil" or the "Yellow Devil" or whatever devil could scare us into not noticing what was happening in our nation's Capital. We were taught in public schools that a flimsy little wooden desk, when climbed under and into a fetal position, could save your life in case of a nuclear attack; or that everyone leaving the classroom and congregating in the corridors would, in the case of an atomic bomb or nuclear attack would survive. While the building walls would collapse, apparently the hallways and corridors would magically remain standing and save our little lives.

For some reason that we never understood, children from every other nation of the face of the Earth hated us and at the same time wanted to be us; and that people in all of the other countries lived an impoverished and miserable existence. We were told that we had to finish all our food because the "children in China" were starving, as if somehow by osmosis if we gorged ourselves, those little Chinese children would feel full. We, the earlier born boom babies (1945 – 1952) were successfully fooled into thinking that our parents and teachers knew everything and were always right. We were raised to be people-pleasers and do as we were told especially since those elders were also very often "hitters", making us people-pleasers who could take a punch or slap on the back of the head.

Years later, my oldest son who was born in 1965, the last year of the boom baby generation, taught me the stupidity of sounding like my mother. One evening, at about seven-years-old, he came to the dinner table and when full, stopped eating. I repeated the statement that had made me throw up many times from overeating as a child, and he reached into his pocket and came up with an envelope that was addressed to "The Children of China" and he had even drawn a stamp on the envelope. Needless to say, that was the day that I stopped using that argument forever. I also believe that it was a sign of things to come about seeing nonsense for what it was and questioning authority. Some of us adopted that as our own rite of passage, regardless of the year we were born.

When I was in school and learning about the federal government, the President of the United States was Dwight D. Eisenhower, or as everyone called him, as if they knew him, "IKE". Ike was a general, a war hero which meant, unbeknownst to the unthinking, that he understood and loved WAR. What no one was yet to realize was that unlike the previous World Wars in which our country was attacked even if not on our own mainland soil things were now very different. Wars and conflicts after the Second World War were old men in power sending *young men with no power* to die for the economic gain of the few and the wealthy.

I had a cousin, Melvin Rosen, who was ten years older than me and his sister, my beautiful cousin Helaine, who was exactly five years to the day older than I was. My cousin Mel was so handsome and nice that he was the subject of my first crush and I would follow either him or his talented sister anywhere they went. But then I remember that for some reason and some way, Ike had found out about my cousin Mel and sent him to a place called Korea, for what reason I didn't know and was never given.

I do remember when Mel came home from Korea when I was about ten or eleven-years-old and we all went to my aunt and uncle's house for a Welcome Home party. Mel was sitting in a chair when we came in and even though he was still handsome, I remember, and in fact, I've never forgotten that besides the uniform, the neat hair and the physical build, not only did he look different, he didn't have that Bronx swagger and sense of humor. He looked very nervous; and when he talked he sounded nervous. But more importantly, his eyes kept blinking repeatedly and he had a sort of a tic in one eye. How bizarre that years later *I* would become the person who wrote the government protocol for Post Combat Stress, and started the Vet Centers that could have helped my cousin nearly fifteen years before. An even more recent revelation came to my attention first in 2009, in Paris, where I learned that the spraying of Agent Orange began in Korea in 1954 and didn't stop until 1975, which meant that my cousin, who was at the DMZ in 1955/56 was probably sprayed.

To my horror, in writing this autobiography I tried to reach out to my cousin Mel, only to find that he had passed away in 2005, from pancreatic cancer which his wife, Gloria told me she thought was from Agent Orange, but wasn't sure and she hadn't known how to get hold of me. Me, Mel's cousin, The Expert. To also learn that their own children and grandchildren suffered from everything from horrific health problems since birth and Autism, and that I'd never known about any of it is a cause of great sadness to me. As one reads this memoir they will learn that I tried to save a world full of strangers in an effort to try to save my own beloved husband. Learning that one of my favorite cousins might have had an easier time and maybe a longer life had I just been aware of what had happened in Korea before I went to Paris, is truly another undying sadness in my mind and heart.

In my last year of high school, the ugliness of an impending war that never happened cost me what was one of the biggest things in my life at age sixteen. I lost a trip to Hawaii. My boyfriend Charlie Munson was in the Navy, having enlisted right after his high school graduation (as many did back in those days) and his ship was stationed in Pearl Harbor. Charlie had written to ask me to see if my parents would let me travel to Hawaii for his two-week shore leave if he made arrangements for me to stay with the parents of one of his shipmates. I couldn't believe that he would ask me to do this, but was even more flabbergasted when my parents agreed. I had never been on an airplane and had never been anywhere other than summer's at Rockaway Beach or in the Catskill Mountains, and now I was to fly to an island over 5,000 miles away to spend time with Charlie.

Time seemed to go slower and slower as we got closer to my departure date and then as we were just days away, the world fell apart or at least as far as I was concerned. My two weeks in Hawaii with handsome Sailor Charlie was destroyed by three people I didn't even know. President John F. Kennedy of the United States, Fidel Castro of Cuba and Premier Khrushchev of the U.S.S.R. all conspired to rob me of this dream vacation, my first grown-up adventure. They called it the Bay of Pigs, but it should have been called, Busting a Teenage Dream. All leaves were canceled and all ships were sent to form an embargo barricade around the island of Cuba, because the U.S.S.R. (now just known as Russia) was moving long range missiles onto Cuba which was just ninety miles from the Florida Peninsula and they had picked this time in my life to have their muscle flexing exercises. NO TRIP FOR YOU!! I eventually forgave John Fitzgerald Kennedy, but not the other two.

In 1964, one year after my own high school graduation, the news was full of stories about how the French had been battling for over ten years in a foreign land known as Vietnam, and had pulled their fighting forces out a few years before, since it is almost impossible to win a war on foreign soil when the inhabitants of that soil don't want another country coming in, and while not conquering or taking over, to tell them how they should live. The cost of the French occupation was creating financial hardship for France and dissent amongst the French citizens and so after ten years of death and wasted effort, France pulled out of Vietnam, which should have been the end of that. It was at this point in my own life that I began to be fascinated with the political structure of our own country, which was, whether we were interested before or not, a source of confusion and concern with the murder of the young people's President John Fitzgerald Kennedy.

Before his death, President Kennedy had ordered the military to provide "advisors" to the people of South Vietnam in an effort to help these people to resist the communist forces of North Vietnam. Our generation had been raised with the belief that we had to lock up our food, toys and freedom to protect it from the menacing Red Horde, and that it was America's job and responsibility to mind the business of other nations and whip a little DEMOCRACY on them; whether they wanted it or not. We were taught to fear that the Communists would rush into Vietnam to make intellectuals and warmongers out of farmers and laborers. They could then somehow be able build giant warships, instead of the frail tiki and balsa wood fishing boats they had used for hundreds of years.

There was a law at the time in the United States that to a thinking mind is really not very democratic because it was the forced call to arms for American males; they called it "The Draft". There were quite a number of young men, who for whatever their reason would enlist directly upon graduation so that they could chose the branch of the military they wanted to join. There was a good education and there were careers available in a peacetime military with full benefits included and that was their choice and their decision. However, as soon as an American citizen turned 18, it was his legal responsibility to go to any government office and register with the Selective Service Board. They were subject to being drafted into the military where they would no longer be free and decisive young American citizens. They would be G.I. which stands for "government issue" and would do what they were told; go where they were sent; and after a two-year stint in this most subservient way of living they would be discharged and be **"free"** again and yet changed forever.

Unfortunately, within two years of the "sending of advisers to South Vietnam" the United States had embroiled itself in, not a war, but a police action, the difference being that an Act of War had to be declared by Congress while a police action could be called by the Executive Branch in an effort to help their friends.

Oh wait, I'm sorry, I must clarify that "friends" were not the people of South Vietnam, but the lobbyists and big business owners of companies that profited by the enormous amount of revenue involved with any military action, but especially not a declared war, which would have made products and services cheaper and easier to provide to the military by low bid contract and government produced (which is a subject for a different book).

By the last two years of the 60's, this entire country was divided by what the media deemed, "the Hawks and the Doves" to separate those who were for this blood bath, this undeclared war; and the protests in the streets turned ugly more often than not. The biggest antagonist was the fact that the only bodies being sent overseas seemed to be the minorities, the working poor, blue collar workers and those who were not going to college. It didn't even matter if a student's major was "the history of rock and roll" or "poetry reading 101". The key safe word was "college".

After a while, the talking heads on Capitol Hill, in their inability to see the forest for the trees, got rid of the Draft and replaced that method of body snatching with the Lottery System. My two younger brothers were of draft age, but they were both in college at Ivy League Rutgers, so during the draft years they felt secure. However, when the lottery was put into effect, one of my brothers had a very low lottery number, but the other had not only a higher number, but also very weak vision. The decision was made that although we loved our country, we loved each other more and so packed bags were kept in the hall closet in the event that their lottery number or numbers were chosen, we would quickly be on our way to Canada. We all were opposed to the Vietnam War and believed that our servicemen should be called home from this senseless conflict.

Intellectually we could not understand what the hell we were doing in a place where even the war weary generals were incapable of orchestrating a jungle war. And to be honest, in the beginning of my entrance into activism, I didn't even know anyone who was sent or went to Vietnam. I knew Abby Hoffman and Jerry Rubin and agreed wholeheartedly with their stand. I did not understand and still cannot fathom how the authorities in this country could justify events like the massacre at Kent State or the brutality of the 1968 Democratic Convention in Chicago, Illinois. I did know that they were not only wrong, but a direct violation of the Civil Rights that we were supposed to be running all over the world and jamming down people's throats. I knew that the 57,000 plus and the MIA-POWS were American boys and young men who were taken out of malt shops or stopped from drag racing on Saturday nights to be sent to a place where they were hated, unwanted and where they died. What I found out years later was that those numbers of the dead and the missing were a pittance of what was going to become casualties of Vietnam in this country, the nations of our allies, and especially Vietnam, Cambodia and Laos. The fact is that close to a million veterans, and just as many of their children and their grandchildren were killed in Vietnam, but the veterans came home and took decades to die. And die they did and will continue to do for decades to come. The phrase became "I died in Vietnam and didn't know it".

What this writer may have done or have, in some small way accomplished was never because of exceptional brilliance or abilities; but was and still is because of love of family and friends, as well as the realization that if I didn't do this, who would? More importantly, would they realize that in order to at least try to save or heal their husband or their child that the only course of action was to save as many as humanly possible? One of my shortcomings in life is that I have always suffered from an inability to feel fear or to give much thought to what other people thought of me (unless, as I learned, I needed them to be swayed my way). All too often, when being charming didn't work, I would become so assertive that I became intimidating, especially to men in powerful positions because they knew deep down that they didn't earn or deserve that power, nor were they really as bright as the women they had married.

What did happen is that my army of Activist Warriors turned out to be the wives and mothers who were fighting to save their own, at my side; and the men, the tough veterans, the males of the species in a time when men still thought they were running everything, became the numbers that followed our lead and bared their teeth on command. Because of what the war itself and then what their own countrymen did to make them feel that they weren't supposed to make it back alive, they were more than happy to stay back and let wives, children, extended family members, etc., sound the alarms, raise the funds to keep going and to speak out publicly. The vets on the stage answered questions and looked like the heroes that they truly were. There were some Vietnam Combat Veterans also, in the beginning of our fight for recognition, respect and representation who would stand up in-front of others and do their best to make students, seniors, politicians and anyone else who would listen, to care and learn what the schools weren't teaching and the government wasn't fixing.

Throughout this story, I shall attempt to honor many of those men, most of whom are now watching down from the DMZ in Heaven; men like my husband John Kopystenski, Frank Delaney, Stephen Drake, Frank McCarthy, David Cline, Melvin Rosen and so many more, now gone, but never forgotten. The true purpose of this book, however, is to give understanding of how one housewife can mobilize millions in an effort to honor the slogan of Holocaust victims of World War II, and then picked up by the families, veterans and generations still being destroyed by the dioxin of Vietnam: *NEVER AGAIN!!!!!*

CHAPTER TWO

THAT'S NOT HOW YOU "BE" ON TELEVISION: INFANTRY ACTIVISM

IT WAS MID-AFTERNOON in late spring of 1982, when the phone rang; and the voice on the other end was a teacher at the Yellow Duck Day School. After ascertaining that our son, Alex was okay, the teacher began to laugh; she was delighted to tell me about what had happened earlier in the day. She had brought in a large refrigerator packing crate with a cut-out picture tube sized opening in the front which she introduced to the class as a TV game. She explained that she told the class that they were all going to take turns climbing inside the box and putting on a "television show" for the other students. However, when it was, Alex's turn, he just sat there and looked at her with an incredulous stare, so she asked him if perhaps he was afraid to climb into the box?

His response was the reason for her call. He just sat there

and stared at her like she was "odd"; he finally said "that's so ridiculous, that's not how you be on television" and went back to what he was doing before she had bothered him. The teacher said that she had forgotten who our son was, and so she said, "Okay Alex, how do you be on television?" Alex stood up and explained with a flourish that, "Sometimes the truck comes to your house, and a guy with a camera follows as you ride your Hot-Wheels Cycle up and down the sidewalk, smiling and 'looking cute'; or sometimes your parents wake you up in the middle of the night and there is a big limousine on the driveway to take you to New York City. You go into a big room that they call the green room, even if it's not green and there's lots of food to eat. Your parents go to another room and someone puts makeup on them, even your dad, before they go and sit down to talk to a man or woman while a camera is taking their pictures. Then the limousine takes you back to New Jersey, but your dad tells the driver to stop at the McDonald's drive-thru because you didn't like the food in the green room. When you get home, you watch your parents on the news. That's how you do television! *Nobody* climbs in a box!" He just stood with his hands on his hips, looking at her as if he was amazed that she hadn't known this stuff (or so he told me, when I asked).

The teacher said that all she could say to this four-year-old child was, "sorry Alex, but the other kids don't get to do that stuff, so they have to get into the box."

As much as this memory brings laughter, it also makes me pause to think how that little boy got to these understandings because of what he had to endure, and it is the reason for this story to be told. The choice to have a child was because we felt that it was time to start our family, which would consist of "at least six kids". A big family was our plan, especially since

Johnny had lost a son through a previous divorce and he was a man who loved children. Family and a happy life was all he wanted, and was what he believed to be important above all else.

We had done everything right. We dated and shared our lives as a couple for four years before we decided to marry and to start a family. We bought and moved into our first home just six months after our wedding and Johnny had started his own business. The task of becoming pregnant was a bit harder than we had expected, and it was more than a year until we were blessed with the good news that we were going to finally be parents. Our baby was due in November of 1977, and the first few months were a very happy time as we shopped for and designed a nursery for our special angel, the child that no one could ever take away from his daddy.

One evening in mid-August, while waiting for Johnny to come home from work I remember watching the evening news and waiting to hear what the announcer had said would be a subject of interest to Vietnam Combat Veterans. What made this unusual was that, Johnny who had been an Army door gunner on a Medivac chopper out of An Khe Province in South Vietnam, was one of over 2.5 million servicemen who had, for most of the war and especially since the end of that War in 1975, been the object of silence, unconcern and even actual hostility from the American public. Figuring that the announcement might involve some sort of welcome home festivities, since there had never had been anything whatsoever; I sat down and listened intently. Suddenly, on the screen, there was a plane flying over what I recognized as the landscape of Vietnam with streams of what seemed to be some sort of spray or even some sort of fuel blow-back, coming from that plane and spreading across the jungles below. The words spoken by the commentator were unreal and confusing because he was talking about "poisonous herbicides sprayed on American Veterans".

The government of the United States of America would never be a part of any action that would indiscriminately spray poisons on their own troops, especially men who were willing to put their very lives on the line because their government said they were needed! No way could that happen to our soldiers, right???? Then, I heard the words that although sounding like sirens, were unfathomable, "SUSPECTED OF CAUSING BIRTH DEFECTS" and I remember feeling sick and almost faint before I realized that I was crying. I was sitting in the living room of my beautiful suburban home, pregnant with a planned and very wanted child; waiting for my loving and devoted husband to come home for dinner. Yet, I was watching a show on television that would change our lives forever with tears running down my face.

It is still a complete and vivid memory even thirty-six years later. I recall sitting on that couch, rubbing my stomach and talking to the baby inside me, saying over and over, "It's not true, you are going to be fine. We are going to be fine. It's all going to be all right". But, he wasn't; and so nothing was all right, nor is it still. When Johnny did come home that evening and saw the condition I was in, he listened intently and then as was his way, dismissed the idea because he was such a physically strong, seemingly healthy and intelligent man. A man who had suffered through what we later learned was Post-Traumatic Stress Disorder for the first couple of our years together, and we had beaten it, together by combined effort (an effort which later became our gift to all Veterans). He dismissed it because Johnny truly believed that if you worked hard and loved and took care of your family that everything would work out just fine.

Our son Alexander, was born on November 8th, 1977, ironically just days before Veteran's Day and almost six years to the day that his dad and I had our first date on Veteran's Day 1971. The birth was natural because I was terrified and wouldn't allow any chemicals or methods to induce labor or any of the birth process in order to protect the baby. We quickly learned our sweet boy was born in a severe state of jaundice for which he had to remain in the hospital for almost one month for treatment. He also had a deformed left ankle and foot, known as a "clubbed foot".

There truly is no worse feeling than to have a baby and to come home without that baby. I stayed in the hospital for nine days until the insurance company's time limit for my stay, forced me to leave our Alexander there. I had never felt such emptiness and devastating worry. Each morning I would wake up and drive Johnny to work, and then drive the twenty-five miles to the hospital where I would sit and tend to our son. I never left him for a moment, until a co-worker would drop Johnny at the hospital after work. He would sit while I went to have something to eat. The rest of our evening was spent together, with our baby until very late in the evening. Every day was the same, except for weekends, when we would make the trip and the vigil together until the doctor told us that we could finally take our little boy home.

From the first day that Alex was put in his own room, in his own crib, Johnny developed a very obsessive daily routine. He would come home from work, go into the nursery and check his son from head to toe, hold him and feed him his bottle and then come into the dining-room to have dinner. After dinner, without fail, he would return to the nursery, pull a chair up to the side of the crib and for hour-after-hour, he would massage Alex's left leg and foot sometimes until his own hands would go numb. There was never any discussion about what he was feeling, or what he was doing, and even though I would sometimes sit next to him, our conversations were always about work or other matters. We never discussed what now had a name, AGENT ORANGE, or the guilt that Johnny felt for what he believed was in some way his fault. In fact, it would be years before he would feel free to express those feelings and it never mattered how much I tried to convince him, even when that poison prematurely took his own valuable and precious life at age sixty-three, he never forgave himself for what happened to Alex and twenty-five years later, to Alex's own beautiful only child, Giovanni.

During the first months that we had Alex home, one of his problems was a skin condition that required constant applications of Vitamin E cream but the pediatrician, adding more concern and alarm, could not figure out what was causing the problem. The second thing that we noticed, but by far the most important, was that our child was having a very hard time and substantial pain in passing stools. It was often so extreme, that we had to assist him by using suppositories and massaging his stomach. Johnny and I had become ever vigilant of Alex's stomach size and would administer assistance if he seemed even a little distended, bloated or unusually fussy. Johnny's daily ritual examination now included running his enormous hand and fingers over the baby's sides and his stomach and he was able to measure any changes in girth.

One evening, during a terrific rain and snow storm, when Alex was about 3 ½ -months-old, Johnny called out for me to call our pediatrician, Dr. Faktor and tell him to meet us at the hospital. The doctor suggested that we were being foolish and shouldn't make the big trip in the bad weather. He suggested that we wait and bring the baby to his office the next day. Johnny grabbed the phone and told the doctor that we were leaving at that moment and that he had "*better* meet us at the hospital". When we arrived at the hospital, the doctor was there and seemed annoyed, but nonetheless he took Alex back into the examining room, instructing us to wait outside. That was the last time that ever happened. When the doctor returned about ten minutes later, he stated that we should take our son home, because it was "just gas".

I watched in horror as my husband, a very large man in his own right, lunged up and grabbed the doctor with one hand around his throat, lifted him off the ground and pushed him against a wall. This gentle giant was yelling "*IT'S NOT GAS AND WE WILL TAKE MY SON BACK IN THERE AND YOU WILL FIND* OUT WHAT THE PROBLEM IS!!!" Johnny returned the doctor to a standing position, picked up our son, and they walked with nurses and security in tow very quickly into the examining room. Fifteen minutes later, Johnny came out and told me that the doctor had taken Alex to an operating room and would be out to talk to us.

I had that same sinking feeling once again, and was amazed at my husband's previous action and the current obvious control that he was showing while I shook in fear. When Dr. Faktor came out to speak to us, he was red-faced, contrite and very apologetic as he told us that if we had left as he had suggested before Johnny "insisted on another action" that our baby would not have survived the half hour ride home. Our son was diagnosed with a deformed intestine that had telescoped back into itself and caused a blockage that would have been fatal. The intestine is supposed to lie like fire-hose, but Alex's was elongated and twisted, like soft spaghetti in a colander. While the cure was surgery our son was too young and small to have it; but the condition could be monitored and controlled while surgery came with only a 20% CHANCE of survival.

They were able to release the blockage with barium that time and ten more times in the first three years of his life. While he never had the surgery done, our son grew around the deformity and is aware of what he must be concerned about in the event of a problem. That first emergency room visit was also when Johnny and I discussed and made a vow that we were not only going to confide in our doctors about Agent Orange and what was suspected, we were going to study to become authorities on our own. We were determined to do something about what had been done to our family. Later we would come face-to-face with what was happening to my husband's body and his health, but this was ahead of us and for that time, our efforts were totally based upon our son, Alex.

CHAPTER THREE

ACTIVISM 101 – LEARNING FROM THE BEST

FROM ABOUT MARCH OF 1978, through all of 1979, trying to learn everything there was to know about chemicals used by the Department of Defense, or for that matter, any government agency, was quite a formidable task. There may have been some sort of early computers, but they were not available to suburban housewives; nor did the Internet even become a concept in that period. Our research efforts were especially difficult for me as I was never that interested in scientific studies. My major education was in psychology, which did indeed turn out to be very helpful, but not when it came to chemical poisoning, biological contamination and anatomical mutation.

The little bit of information we were able to glean led us to make a most heartbreaking choice: that the plan for a large family was out of the question and that Alex would be our only child. We confronted the reality that even if we had another child who was in no way effected by Agent Orange that the attention that

Alex's health and needs required were far too consuming to allow us to be attentive to the needs of another child. We also realized that if we had a child with problems, how could we possibly handle or afford two children with so many medical needs with some major needs possibly still unknown? As it was, when Alex was born, we had my twelve-year-old son, Edward, who was equally involved with becoming a teenager and being jealous and thrilled (not at the same time) with having a kid brother.

By the end of 1979, it was apparent that our son was suffering from an immune system disorder, which we found out later was the condition of Leukopenia, which meant that his immune system was compromised to the point that he had to be sheltered from anyone who had something as mild as a case of the sniffles and totally isolated from any childhood diseases or contagious illnesses. If and when he was exposed or showed any signs of illness, he virtually became, "the boy in the bubble" until his doctors decided that his white cell count was high enough for him to be exposed to other people again. It was a balancing act that combined with his intestinal problems made it very hard for this happy little boy to not notice that he was different from other children. Our goal became trying to teach him to enjoy and live his life as normally as was humanly possible. It became important for him to always know that nothing was impossible, although sometimes things were more difficult to achieve.

We would have become totally frustrated early on in our quest to figure out how to get the kind of information that we needed, had it not been for some very caring and supportive people, most of whom were not personally connected to what we were at the beginning of creating, and some of them were what others might consider "too powerful to care". At this point, we were searching for answers with regard to illnesses and conditions caused by what we learned to be the by-products caused by the mixture of 2,4D and 2,4,5T. Chemicals which had been contaminated by the inclusion of other chemicals not listed on the schematics or on any sort of labels, the end result of which was Dioxin. It was the worst chemical killer known to mankind, made even more lethal by who knew-what else that we had not uncovered.

One day while listening to the CBS News, I stopped everything to watch the woman being interviewed on the midday program. Her name was Lois Gibb, a woman about my age who described herself as an upstate New York suburban housewife in a community known as Love Canal. The words that stopped me in my tracks were, "DIOXIN, TOXIC WASTE AND CHILDREN WITH CANCER", and so, with this show my whole world changed once again. This time, however, it was because there was someone who was a housewife and mother, just like me. BUT, she had the answers that I needed. And she was taking the world on! Not one chemical company at a time, but every company involved with what was killing her neighbors, her family and causing an entire town to have to give up their homes. And to leave the lives they thought they had built without the knowledge that their town was built on a toxic waste dump that was one of the worst in the nation. By the time her interview was over, I had the television station and the show's producer on the telephone demanding that if they couldn't give me Lois Gibb's telephone number, they had to take mine and give me their names with their promise that she would be given my information.

Even all these years later, I still have a hard time with the realization that the producer, hearing the urgency in my voice and my words, told me to hold on. Within minutes I was talking to Lois Gibb, who was still in the studio. I guess that live television and a smaller, much more caring citizen media was the reason for that miracle. Suddenly, not only did I have an ally and a teacher, but I also had a New York City News staff, all taking my phone number and asking me to call them anytime I was ready to go public. My greatest memory of that entire experience was that I spoke to Lois for the first time and we exchanged information, as well as realizing that we liked each other very much. How could that be a surprise? We were the same people, with the same problems and we were fighting for the same things: our families, our children, our husbands and our very own lives.

Through Lois, I was introduced to a group in Newark, New Jersey, near where Johnny had grown up. This group was made up of residents of the Ironbound Area which was right next to the Diamond Shamrock Chemical Company and whose members were all suffering from the exact same problems as those from Love Canal. Even though there were very few and far between stories on the television news or in the papers about Vietnam Vets and Agent Orange, when there were, those reports were also the exact same illnesses and the health problems. My days became filled with trips to Rutgers New Brunswick Campus to do my own research with a two-year-old in a backpack. I talked on the phone, having long conversations with more and more people who lived in dioxin-contaminated areas. I spent hours too trying to reach out to the Veterans Administration to try to get any possible facts or information from someone there; although at that time that was the greatest waste of time imaginable.

I was trying to do as much as I could during my son's nap times, which were few and far between because at the age of two, there was a direct relationship between a toddler's naps and Mommy talking on the phone which I was grateful to know was a condition that had nothing to do with the subject at hand. I was dedicated to the work I was doing, covering a lot of ground and making connections, but often what I was learning was more frightening as my education increased. Although Johnny and I were determined to keeping our weekends as family time with housework on Saturdays and family stuff on Sunday, little did we know how short-lived such normalcy was going to last; or how much paperwork was going to start to overtake every flat surface that was too high for a toddler to reach.

Figuring out how to use what I now knew required me to become familiar with what my options were to get what was needed. In my mind, going public was not feasible unless I not only knew what the problems were, but what the possible solutions were as well. Lois and the other people she had introduced me to were pivotal figures in my education. The other people, who became instrumental in my new life as an Activist, were two women that I had known from years before. In the early days of feminism, beginning in New York City, I had been the "new kid on the block" in the fight for the ERA and had the distinct privilege to meet and work with women, such as Bella Abzug (my hero), Betty Friedan, Gloria Steinem and Geraldine Ferraro (my friend).

In the early 70's, having moved to New Jersey with Eddie, my son from a previous marriage, and while studying at Rutgers, I joined the New Brunswick Chapter of N.O.W. and became instrumental in the formation of the Women Helping Women Task Force, resulting in the creation of the first Battered Women and Children's Shelter in the State of New Jersey. In 1979, at a ceremony honoring feminist achievements, both Congresswoman Abzug and Congresswoman Ferraro were present and we renewed the friendship that we had begun years before. It was at that ceremony, that the Congresswomen introduced me to Congressman Jim Howard from New Jersey who became my friend, mentor and "go-to guy" in Washington D.C., until his untimely passing in 1988. He along with my original two female mentors taught me how to write legislation, be an effective public speaker, and lobby and influence politicians into caring about what I wanted them to care about. I really have never believed that the Vietnam Veteran Community realizes just how many local, state and federal politicians were in their corner and helped to make the many changes that were made from 1981 until 1990, when most of the changes were made with regard to the care, treatment and respect given, FINALLY, to the Vietnam Combat Veterans.

Throughout the years of 1979 through 1988, I had been known on Capitol Hill and in many State Houses, as "the only housewife with the best trained military in the world", and that was how Congressman James J. Howard introduced me to most of the people I have yet to mention. Moreover, there were some unusual trademarks that I became known for all over not only the United States, but anywhere that Agent Orange victims lived. One was that I always wore big hats and Agent Orange t-shirts that my housewife neighbors and I had designed and which made every news magazine in the civilized world. In cooler weather, I wore capes instead of coats; wonder where that style came from? It was always somewhat amusing in later times to see an article in the newspaper of whatever city I was speaking in or organizing demonstrations report in all seriousness about my message; but at the same time many never missed a chance to mention either what I was wearing and often referring to me as either "The Mother of Agent Orange" or the "Flamboyant Mrs. Kopystenski". This always gave me a laugh to break up the sadness of our situation when I stepped onto the speaking stage. Why shouldn't the Vietnam Veterans Spokesperson be flamboyant? Didn't I represent the greatest fighting force on Earth? The crowd would laugh and the tension was broken so that the speech I was about to give could be understood and related to by a somewhat relaxed room full of Combat Veterans.

No matter how many followers any Activist can encourage to join the fight, there has to be one person who provides a personal support system. For me the greatest was the actual wind beneath my wings and my biggest fan, my husband and life partner, John Vincent Kopystenski. When the child that he loved more than life itself was born as Alex was, and we both began to learn and realize what had taken place in that foreign land that we had no business sending our best and brightest to, he would bring up a problem and quietly say "Someone needs to do something about that". It didn't take me very long to realize that the "Someone" he was referring to, WAS ME! After all, he really didn't know that many other people well enough to suggest such things to. Except when around other firefighters, Vets or lifelong friends, my husband was a shy, quiet kind of teddy bear with big muscles. Quite candidly, my full understanding of what he was talking about had nothing whatsoever to do with activism, politics or anything other than "stuff" that needed doing; until new neighbors bought and moved into the house across the street from us and we went over on moving day, with a big casserole, as neighbors used to do.

While talking, Johnny very magnanimously stated, "Hey, whatever my wife can do for you, just let us know!" As I may have said, my Johnny got nervous around strangers; but after that little faux pas, I got the picture of who "Someone" was in Johnny Kopy Land! The one thing that was almost like a unspoken understanding was that as time went on and fighting the Agent Orange War, every time Johnny would make his "Someone" statement regarding something that I had both no idea of how one would set out to accomplish such a feat or what was involved that was alien to anything I'd ever done, I would say "I can't do that." And his response was always, without a second's hesitation, "Why can't you?" or "Why not?" It was not that I was the incredible Crusader Rabbit that people started to tell me I was, it was that I just never could come up with a reason why I couldn't do whatever it was we had been discussing.

The only thing that I started to understand, especially when in 1980, my husband began to suffer from some most unusual and debilitating health issues and I had come to terms with the fact that the only way that I was going to save the lives of my husband and child was to figure out a method and come up with the strength and the nerve to save as many Vets and children as was humanly possible. I also realized that I was always trying to live up to those words about my strength and "Big Balls" made in the car so long before.

Ironically, it was actually the Iranian Hostage situation in 1979 that opened up the floodgates for Vietnam Veterans regarding the MIA-POWS still left in Southeast Asia, and the feelings of anger as so many were getting sick and dying, that enabled us to bring awareness to all of the conditions that our comrades and their families were being forced to endure. It was at that time that I made those calls to the television and media reporters that had all told me to call them when I was ready to go public; and public is exactly where we went. Even all these years later, there are still some newscasters and on-air television personalities that are still available for a friendly chat or to hit ideas off of to this very day.

CHAPTER FOUR

WE'RE NOT CRAZY, WE'RE A BAND OF BROTHERS

THERE CAN PROBABLY BE NOTHING, There can probably be nothing more frightening than to be a young man, who is barely old enough to shave, and certainly not old enough to buy an alcoholic drink or vote in the United States, than being sent off to a foreign land that he really didn't even know existed; forcing him to go 9,000 miles to put his life on the line, and more often than not if he came back at all, it was either physically or almost always emotionally disabled. The inhumanity of this situation, was that these young men came back to a hostile and ungrateful country who blamed *them* for the political errors and financial greed of the government leaders and large business lobbyists that forced them to go, supposedly for the good of the U.S.A.

When Johnny and I first began our friendship and as it was turning into a relationship, it was impossible not to notice that there were times when this usually pleasant and intelligent man would seem to be lost in thought, seeming to hear or be aware of what was happening around him. There were also times while watching television and munching on chips, when all would be fine and he without warning, would lose his temper because someone was "chewing too loudly". It was times like those which would make me wonder where our relationship was going and what was causing these erratic outbursts. I did not know much about his life before we had met and his life after we were together led me to believe that he was a really decent and stable man. I knew that he had been married for a brief time and had a three-year-old son, but at that time in the late 60's and early 70's, didn't we all? He was supportive of my work, my studies and my interests and I enjoyed being in his company -- normally. It was not until we decided to move in together that things not only suddenly began to make sense, but also not to make any sense at all.

One night I was awakened by Johnny standing by the blinds of the bedroom window, peering out through a slightly lifted blind and saying "Incoming, incoming…." At first I wasn't sure of what he was saying, as it was not something I had ever heard anyone say before. Suddenly, he bolted out of the room, grabbed a broom and ran downstairs and into the courtyard of our apartment complex, staring at the sky and heading for the bushes. I don't know how or why I responded as I did, but I ran into the kitchen and got a big spaghetti pot which I put upside down over my head and ran after him, saying as loudly as I could, but not loudly enough to awake our neighbors, "All clear, all clear, stand down!" Once I got him back upstairs and had a moment to think about what had happened, I still didn't know what or why this had happened, but I knew that my reaction was straight out of the recent movies I had seen, for example, *Kelly's Heroes* and *The Dirty Dozen*. By the time I had calmed down and went into the bedroom to try and discuss what had just happened and before I started packing, Johnny was in bed and fast asleep!!! When he was awake in the morning, after a totally sleepless rest of the night for me, I asked Johnny what the Hell that was all about. I was certainly not ready for him to look at me like I'd imagined this whole thing and he had no idea what I was talking about. I did know that I wasn't crazy, and I related exactly what had happened in as calm and non-provoking way as possible. He looked away from me and quietly said, "I was in Vietnam".

My shock wasn't that he had been in the military or even that while we had never discussed the Vietnam War, he knew that I was very opposed to that war and had brothers with low lottery numbers that I intended to escort up to Canada if they were called up; but it was the way that he looked away, like he had done something wrong and was ashamed, that made me realize that not only wasn't I packing anything nor going anywhere, I was sticking with this guy and we were going to tackle this, whatever it was, together. I had been warned by his ex-wife, that he was "nuts and totally erratic" which I had originally discounted since that was my opinion of how she acted.

Something happened to our relationship after that night and it is still hard for me with all my psychological training to give it a scientific name. I think the only thing that seems to define it is the word "TRUST"; a simple word with a meaning that too many people never get to understand. The man who would become my husband, my best friend and the only love I ever really felt for and from another person, had been through Hell and back, both before and after his tour of duty in Southeast Asia. His marriage had been a terrible mistake, to a woman who resorted to our generation's trailer trash method of getting a husband with a good financial future, by getting pregnant after just a couple of dates and so Johnny married her and even bought a house under the GI Bill, as well as getting two full-time jobs in order to pay for that house. After the baby was born, his wife used all that free time to entertain men in the house that Johnny provided and made no secret of her behavior. Believing that marriage was forever and children needed a two-parent home, Johnny was lonely and miserable, but tried to make the marriage work. He was also a volunteer fireman, having been a fire department EMT in Newark, New Jersey before and after Vietnam, as the suburbs did not have a paid department. It was due to this service to others that his marriage came apart. In jumping out of a burning building, Johnny not only broke both of his ankles, but also developed pneumonia and was bedridden in the upstairs bedroom of his house; unable to climb down the stairs that his buddies had carried him up at Denise's insistence of not having him lying around downstairs "all day and night".

One day Johnny called down to ask his wife for something and realized that there was no one in the house. He reached for the telephone on the night table and was surprised to realize that the line was dead. For three days, he was trapped in that bed with no food, no ability to use the facilities and no help. His wife had packed up all of the furniture and whatever else she wanted to take and loaded it into someone's van, leaving this man to live or die unless someone found him. Fortunately, some of Johnny's firemen buddies showed up one evening and saw a totally dark house except for one window upstairs and started to call out his name, which he heard and screamed out for help. Six months later, Johnny was back on his feet, divorced and had moved into the apartment directly across the courtyard from a woman who thought that all the good men, if there were any, had been grabbed up until someone was stupid enough to throw this guy away.

From the time of our wild night running through the courtyard, we developed a rather unique way of living our lives. When Johnny returned home from work, I would keep my son occupied and quietly playing or take him outside to play for at least a half hour or so; giving Johnny a chance to relax and wind down from his day before we all sat down to dinner. Things were usually pretty normal, but every now and again, Johnny would go into a rage and complain about one thing or another. He even developed a jealous obsession if I went to the grocery store or anywhere. When I returned he would question me about who I saw, what I did and any other thing he could come up with. We were able to put an end to that surprisingly easily when I sat him down and explained in no uncertain terms that since I not only had my own income, which he knew was twice what he made (but I never said that to him), that if I wanted someone else I would not be sleeping next to him every night; and if I were interested in someone else then that is where I would be all the time. He got very quiet, looked at me and finally said "Okay, I understand"! Boy, was this transition going to be easy, or what? NOT!!!!!

He then decided that the way to stop me from going anywhere without his knowledge, was to remove the lead distributor wire from his car's alternator and since I rode a Harley Davidson to-and-from work since my own car died, and I wasn't going anywhere with a six-year-old kid on a motorcycle. Imagine his surprise to find out that in high school I had no interest in domestic sciences and took automotives instead? This meant that we were the only couple either of us ever met who each had their own lead distributor wires. At least we were the only ones until we started hanging out and working with only Vietnam Combat Veterans and their equally resourceful wives. As a group, we would have a good time laughing at how many different crazy ways we came up with during those early days just to get things done while working around what I had started calling Post Combat Stress, for lack of any other name. There was a sort of comfort then in knowing that other wives spent as much time explaining why all those insecurities were only in their husbands' minds.

Most of the healing time for Johnny's emotional and stressful times was at night when it became apparent after that first night, that it was not unusual for him to start shaking or waking up abruptly with a cold sweat or anxiety attack. He had bad dreams especially in the spring and summer months and once in a while driving in the countryside he would become disoriented and forget where he was. For about six months he would go to sleep at night with his head in my lap and I would just sit with my arm over him and either read or watch television. If he started to shake or call out in his sleep, I would slightly tighten my arm so that he felt safe or rub his head and lull him back into a peaceful sleep. I would sleep after he left for work and we just lived like that, without ever discussing our nightly ritual until we both realized that his sleep was almost completely undisturbed and peaceful. If he woke up, he would wake me and we would either talk softly, get up and play gin-rummy or if he was really tense, I would just hold him until he fell back to sleep. I also introduced pot to Johnny, who had to be the only guy to serve in Vietnam who had never experienced the relaxing pleasure of "wacky weed". He was "straight as an arrow". There was no way that we could have known that every experience that we went through, from holes in walls, to spaghetti pot hats, to dual engine parts, etc. was going to become a nationally celebrated protocol developed by the spaghetti hat wearing, motorcycle riding woman and used to help veterans from 1981 until forever (as the same protocol is in practice today). We couldn't foresee either that the term Post Traumatic Stress Disorder (PTSD) would not only be suffered by everyone in military combat, but would become the national battle cry of any personal injury lawyer who wanted to make a fast buck.

Of all the PTSD stories I have ever heard about, my favorite is not our shared duck and cover in the courtyard; but happened years later, after we had created the first private Vet Center in the United States, in Freehold, New Jersey. It opened in 1980, based upon the concept of peer group counseling and many other Vet and family involvements in creating comradeship and a place where Vets felt safe and not alienated from others. One of the group members, was Joseph (Joe) Belardo, and just like Johnny and most of the others, he was a married suburban family man with a business of his own. He was a caring and great guy (as most of them were and still are). Joe had been a Quad 50 operator in Vietnam, which is a single-occupant APC (anti-personnel carrier) similar to a mini tank and about the size of a motorcycle sidecar. It was a deadly contraption for the enemy to encounter and Joe rode throughout a battle zone usually ahead of soldiers (grunts) who were walking the area.

One spring day, Joe was driving on Rte. 9 So., in an area known as Howell, N.J., which was an overgrown, wooded area and as mentioned before, spring and summer months are very treacherous for Combat Vets in wooded areas or forests in full foliage. Along the side of the road there was a VFW Post which had a Quad 50 as a lawn ornament in front of their wooden building. Joe suffered a flashback and somehow got himself inside the Quad and began to imagine himself shooting at the passing cars on Rte. 9. He must have been there for some time because we got a call from one of the VFW members that when they had come to the Post for a drink after work, they found Joe sitting inside the Quad in a terrible state.

This was in the first or second year of the 80's and there were no such things as cell phones yet, so Joe had given the men our phone number and asked that they call Johnny and me. We didn't know what had happened and the man who called just gave us the location and hung up, but since this was way before anything resembling caller-id, we just took off running. When we got to the VFW Post, we couldn't believe what we were seeing and it practically killed us to keep from laughing. It seems that after leaving Vietnam and his Quad days in the late 60's, Joe had added a wife, some kids and at least 100 lbs. in weight. We couldn't figure out how he had gotten into the little APC but we were sure there was no way he was going to be able to get out on his own!!!!

Johnny ran to his truck and came back with a can of WD-40 and poured it all around Joe's middle, but nothing was moving upward and we were afraid of two things: the first that if Joe tried too hard to get out he would hurt himself; and the second that if we attempted to dismantle the equipment, the VFW members would hurt us. There was a supermarket about a mile down the road, so Johnny drove there and came back with about ten cans of Crisco shortening. It took about two hours and most of the Crisco before we were able to slide Joe out and get him on his way. As soon as he drove off, Johnny and I fell on the ground laughing. Surprisingly, at our next Friday evening group meeting, Joe related the story to everyone and we all had a great laugh, which I still have every time I think about it. After almost 24 years, I spoke to Joe Belardo to ask his permission to relate the memory in my writings and once again we giggled like children as we relived the event as if it just happened yesterday.

In returning to the natural progression of how my unbelievable life played out, Johnny and I spent the first four years of our relationship building the strongest friendship and love match of any I've ever seen. At least, my encounters with other people have continued to amaze me that from the day we met, until the day he passed over, and even through the years since he's gone, Johnny was someone that I always liked being around and trusted with my every thought and secret. He never let me down or ever tried to stop me from being me.

We both worked hard and saved as much money as we possibly could with the intention of being able to buy our own home. Johnny started a small vending business while working a full time job and I worked and went to school to finish up my education, as well as becoming one of the first "coupon queens" and feeding a family that consisted of Johnny and me, my son Eddie and Johnny's son, John Jr. on approximately $40.00 each week. Our idea of a date night, was to pick up a pizza and watch television on a Saturday night after the kids were asleep. I think that our efforts to take aim at our future created a bond that would keep us focused and strong enough to survive some of the hardest and worst times that any couple could ever have to endure. It certainly made the scrimping and saving worthwhile when we had put away $10,000.00 in one year and were able to buy a beautiful home in a safe suburban neighborhood. The reward we gave ourselves and the boys was to never have to put more breadcrumbs than meat into the meatballs ever again.

Johnny still suffered from bouts of depression and even some erratic temper problems, but they seemed to be happening less and less as time went by. Still, it was impossible to make any type of family or social plans without being aware that, more than likely our plans would come to an abrupt halt about ten minutes before we were ready to leave the house. The cause of our never making it out the door, would either be an argument that, when reflected back on, would basically create a sort of constant conundrum of "What'd I say? What'd I do?"

A few years later, after we had started working with and socializing with other Vietnam Veterans and their families, it was somewhat comforting to know that whatever was scheduled would be shy at least a couple or two and the following day, over the telephone, wives would call the missing spouses and say the same thing, "What'd you say? What'd you do?" It really was much less frustrating to know that you were not alone in this dilemma, and that you weren't actually losing your mind as you had always thought you were.

Since Johnny and I had a large house with a pool, in the warmer months we were usually the ones who entertained, so I never had to worry about whether I was getting all dressed and made-up for no good reason. But, and this could only be understood by other Combat Vets, when Johnny got tired he would stand up, say goodnight and march himself into our bedroom. In a non-Veteran suburban situation, this would have been considered rude or as a loud sign that the party was over and the guests were dismissed; but not where Vietnam Vets were involved. The other guys would acknowledge his departure with a pleasant "Night John" and then continue on with what they were doing. My husband was not the only one who did this, just the only one at our house! It was hard not to notice that until we became involved with the Veteran Movement in the mid 70's, Johnny would go out of his way not to mention that he was a Vietnam Combat Veteran to anyone but myself and a small group of friends that he had known since childhood. In those early years, it was not really something that bothered or confused me to the point of needing an explanation because I understood the trauma and the fright of being in a constant state of fear as an unfortunate consequence of one's employment. Especially if it was a situation that was without any respite for twenty-four hours a day and in a foreign land. However, as a psychologically trained professional I thought I had a better understanding of why there was such a marked kind of shyness surrounding my husband's personality, until I started to notice that when we met other Vets, they would talk to each other, but usually never about what happened in Vietnam and they never told "outsiders" that they had been "in country". It was not until that night in August of 1977 that we found out about Agent Orange and put on the "Activist hats" that the reality of what my husband, this really good man, and all of his counterparts had been forced to contend with, but never had a voice until from what they told me, they got mine!

CHAPTER FIVE

TURNING BOOM BABIES INTO CANNON FODDER AND LOONEY TUNES

AS STATED EARLIER, my first date with my beloved Johnny was on Veteran's Day 1971, and our son, Alex, was born just two days before the same holiday in 1977, so it seemed strange to me that Johnny never wanted to go to the parades or any of the service organization parties to celebrate the day that was earmarked to honor those who served. Eventually I, who normally paid very little attention to state or national holidays, started to realize that not only did Johnny have no interest in the day, but neither did any of his brother Vietnam Vets. Before being a Veteran became a medical matter of life and death interest to us, especially where our baby was concerned, I am embarrassed to admit that this lack of interest (or that's what I thought it was) really didn't concern me very much. I guess that, as weird as it is to say, the Vietnam Veteran and the Agent Orange Movements, as well as all the changes that were made in respect and services, can be credited to the Ayatollah Khomeini of Iran.

In 1979 the American Embassy in Iran was invaded by the radical Muslim fundamentalist party that had ousted the Shah of Iran, a ruler of horrendous cruelty who had been the puppet of the American government; and all but six of the Embassy personnel, who managed to escape to the Canadian Embassy, were taken hostage and kept in captivity for 441 days. Nothing like this had ever happened to American citizens before and our entire country became enraged and engrossed in patriotism. There didn't seem to be a tree anywhere that wasn't adorned with at least one yellow ribbon and for the first time, since Vietnam, television news was all about foreign soil and demonstrations, both in the United States and in Tehran. My husband who had always been politically informed, but never really seemed all that interested in any politics except local concerns such as education, property taxes etc., started watching the news even during dinner, which was a practice that we had never made a habit of doing except during this crisis. He would stay up later than usual to watch the late news and he would grow quiet though obviously annoyed.

Very early into the hostage crisis, while watching a demonstration in front of the Capitol Building, Johnny jumped up, yelled "SON OF A BITCH" and threw his plate at the television set. Although I was grateful that his aim was off, I decided that it was a great time to shut the television off and before I could even ask him what his problem was, he looked at me and, for the first time since that night at the hospital with Alex, I saw tears. He was crying! Then came the tirade of words that changed our focus, our lives and I daresay, our country's entire concept of what it meant to be a Vietnam

Combat Veteran. From that night on, Johnny and I also gave birth to an organization that became an international game-changer, A.O.V.N.J. - Agent Orange Victims of New Jersey. His angry words were: “What about the 2,500 guys left in cages in Nam? Where the Hell are their fucking demonstrations?” This was also the last time that my husband showed any interest whatsoever in the Iran Hostage Crisis. It was also the last time that we gave any thought to being politically correct.

What we did begin that evening was our entrance into the realm of the “politically powerful”. The number 2482 became almost a battle cry for Nam Vets, and as if we were all simultaneously taken over by the Pod Veterans, who, within a very short time, started writing letters to the editors of every newspaper in America, asking why the hostages were more important than the MIA-POWS. It was as if these men, all strangers to each other from all over America had gotten a subliminal order to “Take Capitol Hill”. Conversations began to take place in any forum available and suddenly men who had, just as Johnny, never bothered to mention that they were not just veterans, proudly told all that they were “NAM VETS”.

Up until 1980, Veteran’s Day Parades, Memorial Day Events and even the Fourth of July festivities only seemed to feature and pay homage to veterans of the two World Wars. The guys from WWII liked to refer to their war as “The Big One”, while almost never mentioning Vietnam or even Korea. Veterans in full regalia would march and be cheered and would then have massive drunken parties at their official service organization clubhouses. Groups like the VFW, American Legion, AmVets, etc., were crowded and noisy with revelers who all shared one unspoken rule with its own understood slogan, “NO VIETNAM VETS WELCOME.” By the mid to late 70’s, the animosity between the established service organization members and the Vietnam vets was so strong that it was usually impossible to find even one Vietnam Vet who was willing to step foot in a VFW or AMVET meeting hall or sit at their bar because the more the aging Veterans who "fought in the The Big One" had to drink, the more insulting and obnoxious they would become toward their younger counterparts. The concept was that the guys who served in Nam "lost their war" but not even one of these blowhards could ever explain how the Vets themselves did anything other than be courageous and try to make it home. Nor could they explain how the Vets had any kind of authority or leadership involvement in the making of so many bad decisions or the faulty planning of how the battles were to be fought.

To make matters even worse for those who fought in Southeast Asia, there was an advanced technology and quick-fix method of returning the warriors home to Main Street, USA usually less than 48 hours after leaving the firefights of Vietnam. In all previous wars and even conflicts, especially those battlegrounds in Europe or the Philippines, the soldiers were there for the long-haul, they stayed for the entire time of the war unless they were wounded or killed, in which case their injuries would get them returned home, as would the body bags that brought home their remains. When the war was over, the forces would be returned home on Navy ships for a leisurely sailing journey which could take as much as a month. During that trip across the oceans, early to mid-20th century, there was little to do other than playing cards, talking or whatever other simple ways that these men had to amuse themselves. The biggest advantage that neither the veterans nor the military brass realized the lesson to be learned, that being able to communicate, debrief and wind down with people who were your lifeline in battle, were also your partners in psychological counseling.

For the Vietnam combat vets, there was a DEROS date, which basically stated, if you weren't killed, captured or wounded, the day that you landed in Nam, you knew the day you were leaving to go back to the United States; not to a base to be debriefed or counseled on what to expect, but back to your hometown and whatever you were going through was your problem. If a car backfired while you were walking down the street or your uncle came up behind you to give you a hug, you were either diving for cover or turning around and hitting your uncle in the face. What was even worse for these guys, was that they had just left a place where everyone and anyone either just hated them or would be trying to kill or blow them up, because that was what they were told to do. Then they returned to a town where not only were there demonstrations by other Americans that didn't separate the soldier from the unpopular war; or people that you knew were either embarrassed because they didn't know what to say to you, or felt guilty because they were fortunate enough to have been able to avoid what you had been through. Add to this some of these people actually had hostile feelings because of their own inability to rationalize their anger or their embarrassment. So, they internalized it as a reason to be mad at the person who needed supportive friends, not humiliation at the hands of others.

The natural progression that began to take place for a large number of Vietnam Combat Veterans, in their quest for companionship and understanding, was to create their own organizations and social associations, like VVAW, Vietnam Veterans Against War; VVA, Vietnam Veterans of America; BOVV, The Brotherhood of Vietnam Veterans; AOVNJ, Agent Orange Victims of New Jersey; Black Vets for Social Justice and many others, all of which, within a few short years from their inception, began to affiliate and work together for the rights and the common good of Vietnam Veterans and their families. AOVNJ became the representative spokes-group and the driving force of this network which also included Vietnam Veteran groups from Australia, New Zealand, South Korea and every state or country where Veterans organized. As the matters that effected them all began to become better known and recognized by all the Nam Vets, AOVNJ became the clearinghouse for every different way of dealing with these problems and communicating with everyone to share information and compile data.

What was most amazing was that not only the members of our New Jersey organization were aware of the fact that everything was being accomplished and organized in a dining room, turned office of a suburban home in a yuppie neighborhood by not only the Vets and their wives, but by my friends and neighbors who would meet for coffee or play dates for our kids and they would volunteer to help with whatever tasks were needed by Vets they didn't even know. What still amazes me, forty years later, is that as our efforts multiplied and our notoriety became international, television news personalities, newspaper reporters and magazine writers all were aware that the legislation we were getting passed in states and on the national stage, demonstrations and public events we were controlling was being done from my dining room table and the telephone on my kitchen wall; but not one ever made these "grassroots efforts" public knowledge or really ever even mentioned it at all.

It was not unusual for a reporter, even a well-known news reporter from the large newspapers or television news shows would on their days off do whatever they could do to help out. It became common practice, for a reporter or news personality to call me immediately if there was some story or facts of interest that came over their news desk that pertained to the work we were doing. After we would act on whatever it was, from a government agency holding a sort of secret auction to unload tons of Agent Orange from one of their bases or storage depots, or whatever the appropriate action was, those same reporters, who gave us the heads up, would ask for an interview and cover our actions like they were totally surprised. Whoever was giving the talking points would just automatically thank "the unknown source" or "one of our affiliate organizations" for providing us with the information that instigated the action we took. One reporter from a very large New York newspaper showed up unexpectedly at my home, an hour-and-a-half drive from the City, and told me that he was "in the area" and the editor wondered if we could use the practically new FULL SIZED COMMERCIAL COPY MACHINE that was being carried into my dining room and secret headquarters of operations!

By the beginning of October, 1979, we decided that it was time to go public and because of the upcoming Veterans Day holiday, I called the editor of the local weekly newspaper, whom I had met on a couple of occasions and talked to him honestly about how there were a large number of Vietnam Combat Veterans living in our county, owned their own homes, had jobs and families, but every year when the day that was supposed to honor Veterans came around, the media covered all of the parades and festivities and then there would always be an addendum showing some group of men standing in front of a shelter or hanging out on a street corner in a dilapidated neighborhood in the poorest area of the city and the commentator would advise the viewers that these were Vietnam Vets celebrating their holiday. The editor agreed with me that especially in the upwardly mobile town where Johnny and I lived, the paper should do a story about our family and that we should introduce our efforts as far as Agent Orange was concerned.

At this point we had not given any thought to the fact that the problems that Johnny had suffered and that we had worked through together, were an overall and vastly overlooked problem for most of the Vets we were to meet. The reporter came to our home and interviewed both Johnny and I at length and then the newspaper sent over a photographer to take pictures. We talked at length about Alex's birth defects and health problems, and even discussed not only some of the beginning health issues that Johnny was starting to experience, but we also talked, quite openly, about his problems with anxiety, stress and his discomfort with going to crowded places or hearing loud noises, especially fireworks and cars backfiring. The article became a two-part piece which ran for two weeks, making the front page and going on for two more full pages in both issues.

After the first article appeared, we began to receive letters that, since the paper had not put our address, had gone to the main post office in the town next to ours since our town had no post office and were delivered to our home by the postal truck. By the time the second article had been distributed, the postman showed up with boxes filled with over a thousand envelopes. We were flabbergasted because somehow even though we knew the problems we were dealing with, it really never occurred to us that we were just one family of so very many. Days before Veterans Day, we received a telephone call from a

New York television news show asking if, since they read the article, which we didn't even know had been picked up by the Associated Press, they could send a news reporter and a camera crew to our home to interview us for their V Day show. Their concept was to do an interview based on the fact that there were plenty of Vietnam Veterans who, as typical Boom Babies, had returned from Nam and were going after the American Dream. That they were living, working, married and mowing their lawns on weekends, just like everyone in our generation was supposed to do.

We held the interview in our backyard, on the patio and next to our swimming pool, with our son playing on his swing set, all very normal. It was a lovely day and the interview went very well, and we were sure to explain that we would not be going to the holiday firework show because as a door gunner on a helicopter and having been shot down once, Johnny preferred the tranquility of home, family and having friends come over instead. As soon as the crew left, we called all of our friends and our neighbors and told them to watch the News at Six on CBS. There was really no way that we could act nonchalant because we were GOING TO BE ON TELEVISION and representing the "real Nam Vets". Our closest friends showed up at our house to watch with us and we were feeling really excited. At 6:00 p.m. we turned on the television and there was film of the major parade and then they announced that after the commercial break, there would be footage depicting the special showing of Vietnam Veterans on this special day. After the commercial, as promised, the commentator set up again that the next coverage would be the Vietnam Vet celebration; which to our shock was THOSE DOWN AND OUT INHABITANTS OF THE NYC BOWERY WALKING IN A RAG TAG LINE, which the announcer gleefully noted was their concept of

Vietnam Veterans on parade.

From that humiliating experience we learned quickly that if *I* was going to be the voice of the vets, when it came to the media, I had to exact a promise before I would open my mouth or even agree to talk to media, that if they did anything to disparage the image of the REAL Vietnam Combat Veterans, that would be the last time they would ever get the opportunity to talk to anyone about anything related to Vietnam. How ironic that over the next forty years, throughout the entire United States and elsewhere, the media has kept the promise that I circulated all over the country as the Movement grew and not only our group and affiliates refused to give interviews to that national network, most still don't.

CHAPTER SIX

TALKING IS THE TREATMENT, LAUGHTER IS THE CURE

THE SHOCK OF BEING INSULTED, The shock of being insulted, as mentioned in the last chapter, quickly subsided because as I mentioned, the original newspaper serial about Johnny and I created an incredible amount of mail. As novices, it never occurred to us that we did not have an unlisted phone number and the name Kopystenski was an easy one to find. It may have been pretty common in Poland, but in Central Jersey, there was my husband, his father and a maiden aunt. Honestly, in all of New Jersey, we were it. The phone would start ringing first thing in the morning and sometimes wouldn't stop until nearly midnight! This presented a *major* problem because although innovations such as cordless phones and answering machines, may have been invented and in use in the big businesses in the cities, in suburbia, if those things existed, we knew nothing about it. The second and most insane situation caused by a constantly busy telephone is that in a house with a two or three-year-old boy-child, there is direct correlation between Mommy picking up the phone and all bedlam breaking loose just out of the reach of the phone cord. I got really good at sounding welcoming and concerned while taking names and numbers and promising to call back shortly or at least within 72 hours. I did feel that it was important to respond personally to everyone, even those who contacted us by mail. If they sent their number, I would call them; and if they didn't, I would drop a short note (no time for letter writing) and ask them to send me their number. Once again, we were in the Stone Age, so there was no caller id. I learned very quickly to not just give my number to anyone who hadn't thought of the White Pages.

My biggest reason for feeling so strongly about direct contact was because about a year after our son was born I read about a group known as Vietnam Veterans of America and its founder Bobby Muller. I was impressed with how he was building an organization dedicated to all the guys who served in Vietnam. I sat down and wrote him a very long letter pouring out my heart regarding my husband's anxiety problems, his health concerns, and of course, our son and my need for more information which I foolishly thought he might have. I mailed the letter and every day I would check the mail as soon as it came, hoping for an answer. I only knew that if someone wrote me a letter like that, knowing the type of person I am, I would hurry up and respond. Approximately a month later I finally got a letter from VVA and rushed to open it. To my shock and then anger what I had received was an application to join and a request for nine dollars.

It was on that day and at that time that I swore that if I was ever in a position to help someone about what I was studying constantly at that time, they would either hear my voice on the phone or if there was no number, they would get a response and request for their number *within 72 hours*. It is a promise that I and those many Vets and their wives have always kept. This is still true even though we became the fastest growing and most active force to contend with in less than one year's time of any group yet seen. Still, forty years later, a family with an autistic child or one with birth defects, gets a call and a referral to another Vet activist in their area. A sick Vet or the wife who has just lost her husband to Agent Orange not only gets a call, they get whatever assistance they need and we refer Vets in their area to go to them. I suppose that we all can thank Bobby Muller for setting our goal to never do what he did.

What can be construed as hilarious, is that after my being pulled back in by my testimony in Paris in May of 2009, and my return to the world of Agent Orange activism, not only did I return to the fold. I also returned to the secret clubhouse which is not in my dining room anymore, it is in my family room where million dollar research grants are discussed, applied for and then turned over in their full dollar amount to the best research departments on the face of the Earth. And this is in spite of the fact that Agent Orange is what cost me my beloved Johnny and then our beloved grandson, Giovanni.

In the beginning of our entry into the public eye, with each couple that we would speak to, the husband was not the one that usually initiated the conversations. It was the wife. Their concerns mirrored all of mine when it came to both their relationship with their husband and how unpredictable and often volatile they could be. So many wives told me the same story. Each was actually afraid to go to bed for fear of waking up to find either his hands around her throat or him cowering in a corner and unresponsive to her voice. The other major concern was the children and in far too many instances there were birth defects from cleft palates to holes in the heart and many other conditions which weren't genetic to either parent's family.

I had been interning a couple of years earlier with a clinical psychologist named Isaac Schladovsky PhD, and so I called him to hit some ideas off of him. He was well aware of what Johnny had been going through and how we had handled relieving quite a bit of the stress he was suffering from. Isaac knew, as well what efforts we made to be sure that our home was to my husband his comfort zone, the place he could hide from the rest of the world and just relax and enjoy his family and his life. While these transitions were happening, Isaac was constantly telling me to "keep notes and write it all down," but I always felt that Johnny would feel more like a study subject than the most important man in my life, if he saw me keeping journals. Fortunately, I had every day and every situation fresh in my mind, so that once we started hearing from other families, I wrote a journal of theories and exercises. By that time, Johnny would read and add things I may have forgotten. That he was able to do this told me that we had perfected a way for others also to make it back from the horrors of Vietnam.

One of the most wonderful feelings for me is that even now in a new century, I will hear from Vets who came to our group as far back as the very early 80's, who took the trouble and the time to search me out. Most of them just want to tell me that they didn't remember if they ever said "thank you." They say that we saved their lives, their marriages, and allowed them to live the lifestyles that they thought they'd never have all those years ago. I always tell them the same thing, and each time there is roaring laughter from the other side. I remind them each of how much I loved to wear hats and that if I didn't figure out what needed to be done, I would have been condemned to a life of wearing a spaghetti pot upside down on my head!

I guess that those who read this now will understand that while I have always been grateful for the trust they put in me, it was my husband's life, my marriage, and our forty years together that was my real motivation. Everything else that happened afterward was just destiny and situations falling into place. There are innumerable stories to be told and maybe this book will give Vets or their wives or children the incentive to tell theirs. I want to share my story about my unbelievable life and the events along the way that relate to Agent Orange. With yet more battles and wars now and ahead, people need to be aware of the past and understand that the damage that befell the Vietnam Vets cannot be allowed to happen again.

One July evening, right around the Fourth, a couple came over to our house and the men were sitting in lounge chairs in the backyard and talking for hours about the problems they were having and their feelings about not only Vietnam, but the treatment they were not given when they came home. It was a calm night in a quiet neighborhood. Just after a veteran told Johnny how grateful he was for the time spent and how much better he felt about things; somebody in one of the adjoining backyards, set off a bottle rocket and both men scrambled under the picnic table. I ran downstairs just in time to see them standing back up and Johnny, visibly nervous was trying to joke that the blast was a "pop quiz"! The guys all looked at him as if his head was on fire and then they broke up laughing which was something that they never could have done earlier in their impromptu peer session. The one thing that my husband and I had set up very early in our relationship was laughter, trying to find some humor in whatever booby trap we were tripping over at any particular time. It was that ability to laugh at ourselves or the situation that kept us sane. We laughed over details or aspects of some pretty horrendous experiences related to our activism or even more importantly in our daily lives. We were fortunate to have the same humorous view of life and it was both a weapon and a shield.

When we started holding weekly peer group meetings, there were three things that we felt were important enough to post on big signs at the door and in clear sight on the walls. The messages were self-explanatory and taken extremely seriously. It was a rule that personal criticism was never allowed:

1. What's said here stays here.

2. There is work to do inside; please leave your ego outside.

3. Talking is the treatment. *LAUGHTER is the cure.*

By early December 1979, we had a pretty good idea of what we had to do next. The telephone was a one-on-one experience. While we could ask questions and even provide some answers or information could be shared, it was a slow and non-productive way of getting any real momentum. The reporter who had done the two-part story on us had become a friend. It was through her editor that we were able to get a large meeting hall donated. The newspaper also ran a large advertisement of the meeting which we held on a Sunday afternoon. Neither Johnny nor I had even the vaguest idea as to what we were going to do at this meeting and we really didn't think that anyone would even attend. It was quite a shock when by the time arrived to call the meeting to order the room was standing-room only and there were approximately 300 people waiting anxiously to listen and to speak. Johnny, being much more parliamentarian than I, stood up and introduced himself. He told them that he was an Army Veteran, a door-gunner on a Medivac Chopper, and that he served in An Khe in 1965/66. This created a deafening round of applause and hollering; then he introduced his wife, *me*. For many more years to come, it was like pulling teeth to get him to talk on stage again.

I spoke about that evening when I heard about Agent Orange on the news and how absolutely nothing was being done about what so many of us were living through. And how I believed that if we were going to get anything done, we had to mobilize, organize, and fight like hell. The response was very positive and many people wanted to volunteer to work or do whatever we wanted them to do. I sincerely had been hoping that on that day one person would walk up to the front of the room, push me out of the way and just take over. I envisioned that person with the surety of what needed to be done appointing everyone to do the thing that they could do best. But, no one jumped up and took over. So, I guess we were playing a game and I was *IT*!

The second thing that I talked about was a total leap of faith because I was enough of a psychological professional to know that I was treading on dangerous territory. It was possible that I was going to open up an avalanche of emotions and maybe even some angry denial on the part of those who really needed the most help. I talked about my relationship with my husband who sat very quietly and nodded in agreement, looking the vision of mildness and patience. I spoke about the holes in my walls and then found out the importance of laughter. All of the women looked nervous, although it was very obvious that they knew what I was talking about. The men, however, were beginning to look very uncomfortable, for the most part, because how could this woman know about what was happening in their houses? I nonchalantly said that my husband went from Genghis Khan to Clark Kent, when one day when he was striking out in anger at a wall, *he found the beam*!

For just one moment there was stunned silence that I would say something so embarrassing about my husband whose nickname in Nam and in the Fire Department was "TANK" because of his physical size and strength. But everyone could see he was smiling as soon as I said that, and then the entire room was in a state of roaring laughter. The more I talked about what we had gone through, the more heads were nodding, and then I noticed that quite a number of these couples who had been sitting next to each other and nervously fearing what was going to be said or done at this meeting, were holding hands. Some, or I should say, *quite a number* of men and women had tears running down their faces and were making no effort to wipe those tears away.

Most meetings of any sort usually never last more than an hour or maybe two, but this meeting went on for over four hours and even after it was declared over, no one seemed to want to leave. I knew that we were on our way now. We would finally have volunteers, help, and comrades to share the monumental work that we were going to have to accomplish if we wanted to save our children and our own lives. We had to undertake whatever we needed to get done since no one else seemed to notice that the government and then the citizens had broken the backs of their best and brightest of the early baby boomers. It was also painfully obvious that the Establishment couldn't care less. Our job was going to be to make them care, and to make sure that they all knew that everything about Vietnam was *wrong* as far as the American Servicemen was concerned. I still remember walking out of that meeting and thinking first of all just how successful it was, and then the thought hit me: "Okay, so what are you going to do for the Second Act?"

Life has a way of happening the way it wants, as opposed to what one plans or wants to have happen; and that is what happened to our lives. We very quickly put together a working group of Vets and their wives, girlfriends, even their moms. Just like everything that we wanted to create, the first thing we needed was to have a name. The organization that we created was given the name Agent Orange Victims of New Jersey, which made perfect sense at the time since we all lived in one of Jersey's 21 counties, right? The shortening to A.O.V.N.J. took hold almost immediately because the media seemed to have a problem with the amount of time, space, and ink that writing out the whole name more than once in an article or saying it in a three-minute time spot.

The reality though, was that within six months' time of its inception, AOVNJ had nearly 600,000 members from all over the United States, Australia, New Zealand, Korea, and many other places. That doesn't mean that 600,000 active members were running around doing stuff like crazy. To be honest, like in any group, association, or organization there were usually maybe fifty to a hundred, or approximately 10% *active* worker bees throughout. A couple of years later, those numbers all worked. It was the membership book (and since there were no computers this was an actual book) with over one half million names, addresses, and phone numbers that scared the bejesus out of everyone who was elected from townships, states or national political arenas.

At that initial meeting, there was a reporter from one of the two major newspapers in the state of New Jersey. The paper was the *Asbury Park Press* and the reporter, who didn't even let us know she was there, was an incredible writer and a woman who turned out to be the Vietnam Veterans' best friend from that day until this one so many years later. Her name is Colleen Dee Berry and even though I have not seen or talked to her since 1988, when I think of professionalism and those to whom we must always be grateful, hers is the first name that comes to mind.

Colleen was not an obnoxious personality like we learned some media people could be, in fact, she was reserved and quite humble. So much so that when I would try to shower her with praise or gratitude, she would always tell me that following me and the organization we built was a reporter's dream, a career maker. Without her tenacity, talent, and support I really don't think that we would have accomplished even half of what we did, and certainly not within the time frame we got it done.

Throughout this memoir there will be many efforts, trips, stunts, and successes that included Colleen quietly in the background, writing and writing, regardless if it was New Jersey, Washington D.C., New York City, or elsewhere in the United States. I think that when Johnny and I had to move West for the climate and Johnny's health, the Movement not only lost us, but its greatest advocate in Colleen. That loss surely slowed it all down substantially.

AOVNJ had other media friends whom I am sure will come up later on, and we were very fortunate to get as much media help as we did, but the unbelievable Bella Abzug taught me well and the more outlandish my hats, capes or attire were, the more coverage we would get. I used to talk to all new media people and explain to them that I would be happy to give them as much coverage as they wanted, but they had to promise one thing and one thing only and if they broke that promise, exposure was ended and over. The promise was: "The Agent Orange Vets and their families have more problems than anyone can imagine. So, if you can't be supportive, be silent. If you do that, I will make sure that you have gossip about anyone else on this Earth, even if I have to make it up." That always got a laugh and I suppose that there was some validity to my threat because we never got bad press. Fortunately, no one ever asked me to make up any stories about any other citizens either.

Approximately one month after our initial public meeting, we were invited to a meeting at the Middletown American Legion Post in New Jersey to discuss the Agent Orange situation. The speakers were: Wayne Wilson, a Veteran; Peter Kahn, a scientist from Rutgers University; and a VA representative named Eddie Corbett who was also a Nam Combat Vet. Dr. Kahn spoke about research that he wanted to do with regard to Vietnam Vets. Wayne Wilson talked about trying to establish a New Jersey Agent Orange Commission. Unbeknownst to anyone in attendance, he also wanted to be the person to run the Commission as his own little kingdom; and Eddie Corbett spoke about the "new Agent Orange exams" that the VA was going to perform on any vets who signed up. The only people who weren't trying to pull a fast one on the attending Vets were the Vets themselves, not the two non-veterans on the stage.

The best thing that came out of that meeting was not the fact that AOVNJ wrote the position papers on forming a Commission nor the legislation that we wrote to get the Commission. It was also not the Commission itself which gave Vets a whole lot of hope and sometimes an even larger lot of frustration. By the way, of course Mr. Wayne Wilson became the Executive Director of that Commission, expense account and all. Regardless of what their needs might be, the greatest gift that the Vietnam Combat Veterans and their families received was Governor Thomas Kean, the only Republican I ever would have fought like a tiger to make President of the United States. Unfortunately, he never ran and I have always believed that although he was a terrific Governor, politics was not a good fit for him because of that crazy honesty that he insisted upon living his life by.

There wasn't anything that we went to Governor Kean about that he ever turned his back on. He also did everything he possibly could to ease the way for Vietnam Vets and their families, and that included changing a whole list of New Jersey laws and regulations. Governor Kean was and still is an incredibly intelligent and caring human being, while nobody's fool; which is why, as I just mentioned, I was always shocked that he became a politician. However, he was too smart and involved with the people to play the political games, as evidenced by some years later. After the horrors of 9/11, it was Thomas Kean who was asked to co-chair the 9/11 Commission and come up with conclusions to insure greater safety to the American people. He did just that and his findings were ignored by the Bush Administration as well as the entire Republican Party.

One of the Governor's first changes to help the veterans was to change the civil service regulations regarding Veteran's preference. In New Jersey, if there was a civil service employment opening, on a percentage basis a Veteran was given a ten percent advantage with regard to any testing or registration requirements. One of the major problems confronting a large number of Vietnam Veterans was that those who were already suffering from dioxin poisoning or the problems associated with combat stress syndrome could not work outside the home or very often, with other people. In addition, those who were already employed, but needed a two-salary household in order to survive, could not take advantage of the preference being afforded to them. Governor Kean understood that in cases where a Veteran's spouse was capable of working a state, county, or municipal job in order to support their family, it would be of immeasurable help if the preference could be transferred. Accordingly, New Jersey became to our knowledge, the first and only state to allow veteran preference to extend to spouses.

Governor Kean was instrumental in the creation of the New Jersey Agent Orange Commission. However, just as the VA, as announced by Eddie Corbett, who passed away from Agent Orange related illnesses in 1989, was conducting Agent Orange exams, we found that there really were no such tests! All that the VA was providing was a perfunctory simple physical examination and then placing an *orange sticky disk* on the paperwork! The Agent Orange Commission kept AOVNJ extra busy trying to straighten out the misconceptions and ridiculous assumptions that the Executive Director was passing out like cheap cigars. At first they were telling Vets that the dioxin was being stored in the fat cells of the body, so they should try not to lose or gain weight. This of course, was nonsense; common sense tells us that many different things are first stored in the human fat cells until they can be broken down and absorbed by the other parts of the body. Therefore, any veteran who served in Vietnam effected by the spraying, was back in the United States anywhere from 1966 to 1975, so that by the early 80's fat cell absorption and systematic dispersing happened a long time before the Commission started giving dietary advice.

The Commission would hold meetings throughout the entire state and explain that the half-life of dioxin in the soil was twenty-five years. This lie was as true as the fat cell supposed facts. Since the soil they were talking about was in Southeast Asia and no one from the Commission had gone to get soil samples or investigate, one can only assume that the number twenty-five seemed far enough off in the future that it sounded good. The only problem with that statement was that now, fifty years later, the dioxin contaminated soil in Vietnam, like the toxic waste dumps in this country, is just as volatile as they were originally. We have seen this evidenced by how many birth defected children are still being born not only in Vietnam, but anywhere the poison was sprayed. The half-life theory can only be attributed to how many families are still being cursed by half of the life span they should have, or half of the limbs they are missing.

Fortunately by the end of 1983, the Agent Orange Commission had become just another government agency and no longer held their dog and pony shows all over the state. So, it became unnecessary for our group to have any involvement with correcting the erroneous information they were giving out. AOVNJ since the end of 1980, was operating the only privately-run Vet Center in the entire country. We started with weekly peer group meetings for Vets and had also created groups for significant others, and for the children who were coping with a parent suffering from combat stress. The Governor's office and some local governments found ways to financially assist with either grants or payment for projects we had previously just volunteered to take part in. These were of incredible help since the only monies that we had were what we could either glean from donations or fund raising activities. All too often the same percentage of members who did most of the work were also the first people to reach into their pockets or to pull out their credit cards; Johnny and I not only helped with the expenses, but were often writing checks to help Vets who couldn't pay their rent or needed a place to stay.

In the warmer months, we were able to setup for free game booths and an information table to sell t-shirts at all festivals, fairs, and carnivals. The guys would construct the most elaborate booths for everything they could think of including tossing ping pong balls into little fish bowls. It became known that the smaller the child, the better chances that if the kid couldn't get the ball into the bowl, someone behind the table would toss a ball and give the kid a live goldfish in a plastic bag. All in all, those days were hard work, but loads of fun. The Vietnam Vets' image in New Jersey was different and better than anywhere else that we heard of at that time. This was rather sad considering that those young men who fought for their country in Vietnam were heroes, and should have been treated as such by a grateful nation just because of their service and not because they worked hard to change the negative image as A.O.V.N.J. had deliberately set out to do. What we found out was that at least in New Jersey, the population for the most part welcomed our efforts with generosity and total acceptance.

Freehold Regional Hospital was a beautiful new private hospital and their Administration gave us a small wing that they named The Wellness Center which we could use whenever we wanted and even went so far as to convince some of their attending staff and doctors to come in to assist in everything from psychology to answering any medical questions that our members had. The hospital provided all of these things, free of charge and was always asking what else we needed. It was great that they recognized that our Vets had significant issues, but all that they offered was just a beginning.

The problems of Vets suffering from combat stress did not begin and end in their homes and the majority of guys who came home after the war changed into a political farce in 1969, were coming home with even greater problems than emotional stress. Alcoholism and drug addiction were rampant and it was figured that one-third of the homeless in this nation were Veterans. One day I was reading in the newspaper about an attorney who had defended a Vietnam Vet on a murder charge and had been able to prove that the crime was due to flashbacks to Vietnam and PTSD, which got the Vet care and treatment instead of incarceration. Consider that in relation to the fact that about 70% of the inmates in American jails at that time were Veterans of something, but usually Vietnam. Less than one week later, I had called the attorney, who as it turned out was one of the best criminal attorney in the United States. I made an appointment with him and convinced him to join the AOVNJ Advisory Board, something we didn't even have until he agreed to be on it. The attorney was John R. Ford, who because of his work with AOVNJ and our legal programs and services, spent so much time on television that CBS ended up offering him a job as their legal commentator. Then in 1989, he left the legal practice and shortened his name to Jack Ford.

He spent the next few years as a prime time commentator on everything from legal issues to sports (since his Yale education was covered by a football scholarship) and even had a full-hour daytime show called Jack & Allie. AOVNJ and John Ford, Esq. made some extraordinary changes in the New Jersey legal system, which became a model for other states in record time. If the police were called for what was an assumed or was an obvious incident involving a Combat Vet who had done something that could be either stress or flashback related (in other words, bank robbery or holding up a store was out), the police would call the AOVNJ member who had registered in with them so that the Vet had someone with him when he went before the Judge. The local judges offered the Vets the option of being escorted to Lyons VA Hospital for mental evaluation or going to jail; the choice was theirs to make.

It was a great program that would have worked very well if

it were not for the fact that we couldn't get the VA on track with what we were trying to do. The end result was that Lyons VA Mental Evaluation was a voluntary admission and so while the police, the judges, our members all worked together in perfect harmony, there were a couple of times that the Veteran, after being taken to Lyons, actually refused testing and signed himself out, sometimes even beating us home. Jack finally came up with a great idea and we made the Vet sign a form that stated that he would stay at Lyons for the entire 72-hour evaluation. If he was found to be in need of admission, then we had to find that out and get a court order from the judge. Otherwise after 72-hours of treatment and evaluation, the Vet could leave.

The best part of this voluntary commitment agreement was that it had no legal teeth whatsoever, but nobody told the Vet that. So, we found a solution because anytime a lawyer or someone in authority tells you to sign an agreement, especially if you don't want to go to jail, you take the words as gospel! Meanwhile, every move we made and every program we came up with ended up as a feature in the Sunday papers or on the evening news. One of the reporters used to constantly tell me that we were wasting our time and we should be starting a cult. The problem with that plan was nobody knew how to do that and we didn't want to wear sheets. The greatest deterrent to turning what we had all created into a cult was (not that anyone gave it much thought) that the reasons we had been so successful were the very standards that we lived by, all of which were totally un-cult-like. They were truth, democracy, camaraderie, shared responsibility and friendship; all of which came under two simple words: Semper Fi. It was, and still is for many of us, a dedication to what had become a family and a Veterans' community, regardless of what state or even continent where one might now live. If one was in trouble, we were all there to try to solve the problem whether it was medical, legal or psychological. If a Vietnam Veteran passed away, which happened much too often those first years since the dioxin created cancers, attacked the guys early and spread fast. Vets like Stephen Drake of Long Branch, New Jersey; Frank Delaney of New Haven, Connecticut; or Eddie Caubett of East Brunswick, New Jersey were diagnosed with this strain of carcinogenic disorders that the doctors could not recognize and for which they knew of no cure or treatment. All while the VA was still refusing to even recognize the cause, much less the illness, the veteran was overrun with visitors and his family was given any and all that they needed to survive. Babysitting, cooking, housework and taking the kids to whatever activities they were signed up for or just out for the day to give mom a break or time to be with her husband never had to be requested, things just happened and money was always there if it was needed. Grieving widows, who were women in their late 20's or very early 30's were never alone or left to feel abandoned by friends and family, which has always been one of the major problems in trying to figure out how to handle everything that was new for a woman, and/or a mother, alone for the first time since she married. I always called it the "Where'd everybody go?" syndrome. In the Veteran world where each of us knows the cost and the consequence of military service, even if it is something unbelievable like Agent Orange poisoning, our friends, who are most likely dealing with the same fears and experiences, do not disappear. However, in the non-vet world, the death of a young husband and father is so alien that friends, neighbors, co-workers and even family members feel uncomfortable not knowing how they are supposed to react or what to say. Though in reality, nothing needs to be said or reacted to; just a warm body, a listening ear and a held hand is all that is truly necessary.

In our world, especially in our younger years, when a grieving family was up and moving on their own again, in their new reality, sometimes it became necessary for the widow to let us know that they were ready to maintain the sense of community without feeling smothered by our attention. One of the funniest experiences that I had was after one of our members had been gone for about a year, his widow called me and we were chatting. I felt there was something though that was not being said, so finally I said to her, "You sound like there is something you are trying to tell me, just say it", and so she did. Her question really gave me pause and made me realize that we all needed to set some ground rules or a way to know when we should let go of the back of the bicycle seat; she said "I met someone and he asked me to go to dinner, which I did and had a very pleasant time, but now he's asked me to go to a dinner and a movie and I was wondering if it was all right?" I started to laugh with relief that she wasn't telling me some horrible news regarding herself or her kids and then realized that she was in serious confusion. "I'm not your mother, I'm your friend and unless you don't feel ready to date, then I hope you are not asking me for permission." I also told her that even though I was called "The Mother of Agent Orange" her name wasn't Agent Orange and I was way too young to have a child her age. After that, whenever there was a similar situation, I made sure that either myself or the member who was closest to the bereaved family made it their business to wean themselves away slowly in the closeness department.

CHAPTER SEVEN

ATTACKING THE HILL, SURVIVING THE MALL

EVERYBODY WHO CAME of age in the Sixties knew that if you are going to be "Activists", you had to plan on "Demonstrations", but if I am going to be honest then I have to explain right off that nobody told us. We, as you recall reading, were predominantly in our beginnings, suburban yuppie/boom baby homeowners. Before we started our group, we lived our lives by working and then hiding in our "hole in the wall" homes. One of the guys brought up the subject at group that we really needed to do something to demonstrate the fact that the VA was not taking Vietnam Vets seriously. Most of the guys were terrified of going near a VA Hospital because of the stories they had heard about what could happen there. Being honest again, since most of our members were working, most of us had health insurance from work anyway. Our very first public demonstration was scheduled for a Saturday at the VA Hospital in East Orange, New Jersey and we all met at the gate of the hospital. Besides not realizing that if we wanted attention, we had to send out a press release, we didn't know that we were supposed to march to an appropriate cadence that one of us had composed. We organized and began walking on the street in front of the hospital fence; across the driveway entrance to the hospital; and halfway down the sidewalk on the other side. Then we turned and did it back the other way.

Something was wrong! We probably looked like about fifty people who couldn't decide which side of the street they wanted to be on. After about twenty minutes, a security guard from the hospital came out and asked us what we were doing. When we explained in detail what and why we were there. He just looked at us like we should have taken our show to Lyons VA *Mental* Hospital, and then told us that he had been in Nam too. He paused, and asked us the $64 thousand question, "*Where are your signs & placards?*" Try to imagine about fifty people all standing and staring at him like Moe, Larry, and Curly. Half of us didn't take our kids to soccer practice in order to stand and stare blankly at his question. The security guard suddenly changed his facial expression and just said to us, "Wait here". He ran back toward the hospital and then drove out the gate yelling again, "Wait here". After about fifteen minutes, he drove back to the entrance gate, opened his car door, and threw out two big bags. We watched him return to the hospital parking area (who knows what he told his boss). We just stared at the bags for a minute and then picked them up and saw construction paper and a whole lot of markers! *We had signs*!!! We were still there when the guard got off shift. While we knew he couldn't join us, we did insist that he come to our meetings. We knew this guy was not only a Vet; he was a very valuable Vet. To this day, remembering how we had been when we started out and how methodical and influential we became, it is amazing that we were able to accomplish all that we did.

In September of 1981, I was invited to a massive national Vietnam Veterans event in Washington DC, which was organized by the largest group in the United States, Vietnam Veterans Against the War. Johnny had been a member of this group. Then I joined later on, after I met Johnny of course. Most of the scattered Vietnam Vet groups in the United States and even some groups from Australia knew who we were, but we didn't know much about any of them. The reason that they all knew who we were, and went with us to this four-day event was Colleen Dee Berry, representing the *Asbury Park Press* and the Associated Press.

This event turned out to be the turning point, in most of our lives. But, for me it felt like a cross between a coronation and an inauguration that was going to end up with world recognition and some incredible awards. Invaluably, it resulted in a national program to treat Post-Traumatic Stress Disorder (PTSD) and laws to recognize, treat and compensate Agent Orange victims; and we did it all in just four days. The preparation for what was going to happen, or should I say, what we hoped was going to happen, took over a month of planning and even then I never expected what was going to take place or the outcome for the Vietnam Veteran/Agent Orange Communities. This adventure was going to be the first time I had ever left my husband and children for even one night, much less what would be five full days counting traveling time. Originally, I had been trying to convince Johnny that he needed to go with me, but his normal excuse of not being able to leave his business gave way to the reality that someone had to stay home with the kids too.

The real reason that I gave up quickly was because even though Johnny was much better than he had been in those first years, he really was uncomfortable around strangers. One of the things that made us an unusual dynamic duo was that while I would talk to anyone about anything, my husband, brilliant as anyone I had ever met or even more so, was probably the shyest man I had ever met in my life until he actually got to know some-one. He seemed to be most comfortable letting me be the voice just as long as I didn't commit him to do anything public or go anywhere without discussing it with him first and privately. So, I was leaving my family and going away for the first time since I spent nine days at the hospital when our Alex was born. I don't think that I ever realized just how married I was until I had to start thinking about being totally alone except for strangers in a strange city, hundreds of miles from home. Had I really changed that much from an independent person who was proud that she was capable of being on her own and alone, or had I just realized that trust was a particular feeling that I had never really been able to have in another human being before?

The trip was going to be shared by four Vets and two Vets' wives, one of whom was flying in from Indiana to go as part of the AOVNJ contingency. It nearly came to an abrupt stop before it started when we found out that the host group V.V.A.W. was very big on camping out and had already secured a permit to camp on the Washington Mall. Let's try to remember that our organization had its roots in suburbia, and not just suburbia, baby boom yuppies with puppies and mortgaged homes and kids who played Little League, Pop Warner Football and soccer. My idea of roughing it was a hotel without cable or room service. These people planned on sleeping on the ground in tents! One of our members, Kenny Larsen, who was very good looking, with a trimmed beard and camis that were always pressed with a sharp pleat, looked like someone had outlawed hair gel when he heard about the sleeping arrangements. Then he came up with a wonderful plan. He and Johnny took a walk outside and when they came back they announced with gusto, “We’re going to rent an RV!” Johnny told me later that it was Kenny’s idea and it was a good one. But he was laughing like a schoolboy when he told me that when they went outside to talk, the reason that Kenny had given was that because of his appearance, he was the Vietnam Veteran that we stuck in front of the television cameras all the time. Without an RV he couldn’t keep his hair perfect or his clothes clean and pressed. Johnny was laughing so hard that I thought he was going to pass out, but all he kept saying was how far they had really come from the jungles of Nam, especially since our Calendar Vet was a Marine!!!! So the Jersey Vets rented an RV, shopped for provisions like steaks and shrimp, beer and wine, loaded our RV, and hit the road to demonstrate and complain on Capitol Hill.

As much as Johnny and I would joke and try to find the humor in all situations, the fact that never left our minds was that my husband had already started to lose his ability to walk because of the osteoarthritis that had eaten about 75% of his spine in just over five years. In 1974, he had undergone a full Teamsters Union Physical complete with x-rays and he had no signs of any arthritis or inflammation problems at all. Johnny and I had learned to live with the medical problems of our son Alex and his orthopedic deformities, but we had just found out that his leukopenia required constant monitoring and that he might have some neurological problems that were yet to be tested. The woman who came from Indiana was the wife of a Vietnam Veteran who had a brain abnormality and lesions that had rendered him unable to speak or function, and the doctors couldn’t figure it out how to slow down or stop the rapid degeneration of his physical condition; Danny Doyle had a son who was born with hydrocephalus (water on the brain) and had to have shunts from his ears to his brain that had to be changed as he grew; Jimmy

Burdge had chloracne so badly that his skin looked like he was a space alien; and Kenny had two children with serious health problems as well.

So, we all made jokes and were fortunate enough to be financially upwardly mobile though we really didn't know for how long our good fortune would last. For us, our good fortune was not measured by how many toys we could buy to entertain ourselves, but how many doctors we could pay to keep our children alive. For me and the other wives, it was also a measure of how long our husbands were going to be able to function or maybe how much longer we would have husbands. One day years later, while talking to a friend, I began looking at our original membership book and realized that in the first two years of our activism, Johnny and I had gone to more than 134 funerals for men under thirty-four-years of age, most of them having died of weird and unusual forms of cancer unheard of for such young men.

The drive from New Jersey to Washington DC should have been a relaxed sightseeing journey. Surprisingly though, just like the East Orange demonstration, we hadn't taken into account that of the seven of us, no one knew how to drive a large recreational vehicle. The only truck driver we knew was my husband and we had left Johnny waving goodbye to us on the driveway of my home. We made it to Washington DC, in six hours instead of the four that it should have taken. When we parked next to the Mall, we couldn't understand why the refrigerator and the running water wasn't working until one of the Vets already set up with a tent came over and explained that the vehicle was parked on an incline and so, nothing would work. Now, keep in mind that most of us were college-educated, albeit some from the GI Bill, and we were all employed, but this activism thing was kicking our collective asses!

As we left the RV and walked over to the Mall, Kenny and Jimmy stopped dead in their tracks and whispered to our group, "Dear Lord, they built a perimeter and a base camp!" There had to be anywhere from 750 to 1,000 people and they put up tents, had generators and military radios called Prick 25's, and everyone was wearing camouflage and bush hats. I, who had never been to Vietnam (except for that one night in the apartment courtyard, with the spaghetti helmet) started to have flashbacks! The aroma of weed, which at the time was still called "grass", permeated the entire Mall and there were coolers full of cold beer every couple of feet. We didn't know any of the people who were there except for some whose voices I recognized from the many hours we had spent on the phone sharing information and making strategies for how each of our groups would deal with different problems. Within about an hour, though we were all like family.

Luckily, we were all still young enough to remember names and faces because there were so many new names and faces to put together. If that same event happened today, those of us who are still on this Earth would just be calling each other "Hon or Babe or Buddy" and hoping nobody asked us what their name was within more than an hour after they had told it to us. It was surreal to be inside the chicken wire fencing that had been put totally around the entire encampment. I saw two Vets stationed at the opening, but at least they were sitting and talking, not standing like sentries. I noticed that DC Police were driving slowly past the Mall though never stopping or getting out of their cars. In fact a couple of them seemed to keep their eyes trained on the road ahead of them, never looking sideways to check on the big bad Vietnam Vets. It really felt kind of uncomfortable for many of us who were supposed to be heralded as America's heroes, which still had never happened, to be eyeballed as if we were some sort of foreign terrorists in our own country's Capitol.

That entire night, no one got any sleep and it was almost as great as Woodstock (yes, I was there), without all the mud and the loud music. The only music that was playing over the radios was from before 1975, which made me miss Johnny, because he was always quick to advise anyone, especially kids, that "nothing written after 1972 was of any real importance". Here I was with a whole bunch of guys who obviously felt the same way. Everyone was talking, laughing and telling crazy stories, but not even one of them that I met ever talked about being "In Country" or in "The Nam".

That night I met a woman named Annie Bailey, who was the wife of one of the Vets from Milwaukee. She wasn't like anyone I had ever met before. I'd been around activists since the early days of the ERA in New York, and had been preparing to change the world for the Vets and our kids, but Annie was this larger than life person: and for the next almost ten years, according to most of the Vets in the United States, the two of us "*rocked America*". Annie was so bossy that she actually made me look like a pussycat! I was the one with the big words and the ability to fit in with everyone from millionaires, politicians, medical, legal, and psychological professionals, *and* Vietnam Vets, but she was the one who could rattle off statistics and facts that I had never found any information on. So, I was the spokesperson. Annie, who weighed a whole hundred pounds sopping wet, was the terror, and the muscle, as well as the game planner.

Years later, after we moved to Nevada and I hadn't spoken to anyone in the Movement for a long while, a movie came out with Tom Hanks. The movie was *Forrest Gump* and suddenly our phones started ringing off the hook, as did those of other activists who knew us. Annie was a Board Member of V.V.A.W. which had been very active since the late 60's, and was the first anti-war group in this country. Two of its founding members were John Kerry, now Secretary of State to President Obama; and Bobby Muller who very few admitted to knowing anymore. John Kerry had set the Congress on end with his Winter Soldier Testimony right after he returned from Vietnam as a decorated hero, but I digress.

In the movie there is a scene where Forrest is awarded the Congressional Medal of Honor by then President Tricky Dickie. He then stumbles upon an anti-war demonstration and is pushed up on the stage to speak about the War. The group was immediately recognizable as VVAW because of their banners and their slogans, but that was not why the phones were ringing. One of the activists who was ushering Forrest and the others up onto the stage and the following day was lining them up to get on the buses that were leaving DC, was a skinny pretty young thing with very curly hair and tie-dyed clothing. *It was someone portraying Annie Bailey*!!!

There was another scene where a military officer got on the stage and tried to disperse the crowd of demonstrators by yelling into the microphone and trying to intimidate them. Suddenly, the cameras went to another young woman in fatigues and a cowboy hat with orange roach clips stuck to it. She jumped off the side of the stage and cut the power to the microphones. *Annie Bailey & Rena Kopy*, the dynamic duo were actually characterized in that wonderful movie! Ironically, unless you were a part of the fight for our lives, no one in our separate, home owner, shop and cook world knew that was us!

I saw Annie again the weekend of April 6th, 2008, because out of the blue, she called me and said that she was coming to Vegas to see Johnny and me since she hadn't seen us in over twenty years. It was quite a surprise because Annie would never fly on an airplane if she could travel any other way. Nevada was a *long* way from Wisconsin. Determinedly, she took Amtrak from Milwaukee to Kingman, Arizona, and then took a bus to Vegas.

Two of our close comrades, Dave Cline, who had become the driving force behind the Agent Orange Movement even before we had left the East Coast; and Bill Davis, one of the original VVAW founders had just passed away due to Agent Orange illness. Somehow, Annie told me, she heard that Johnny was much sicker than I had let on over the phone. I picked her up on Friday evening and before we even had a minute to relax, on Saturday morning Johnny had to be rushed to the hospital where Annie sat with him all day and all night. The next day Alex and I took Annie to dinner and back to the bus station and went right back up to the hospital. My Johnny passed away at 6:00 a.m. On April 6th in his sleep and it was almost like Annie knew she needed to say goodbye.

When Dave and Bill passed, Johnny, who believed that death came in threes, told me that he was going to be the third. I wouldn't listen. We had plans and things we had talked about doing for nearly forty years and had never gotten the time to do. We had so many things left undone and our grandson, Giovanni, needed his grandpa; but it didn't matter. Johnny had been in severe pain and was extremely sick for over five years. He had already had one leg amputated which for my TANK was the ultimate betrayal by his body. Johnny had stayed much longer than he should have because his sole reason for living seemed to be taking care of his children and making sure that his wife was taken care of and that she was going to be provided for. He was just that type of man, father, grandfather and mostly husband.

What we had no way of knowing was that our precious and autistic Giovanni, who was his grandpa's world, would pass away a little over a year after Johnny, and exactly two months after I returned from testifying in Paris in 2009. The circumstances of Giovanni's passing (I still can't say the D word about either of them) are too much to explain right now, but my theory has always been that because Giovanni really had no mother or anyone except his daddy, Grandma and Grandpa, that being non-verbal and comprehension delayed would have, if anything happened to Alex or I, left Giovanni alone in this world, so his grandpa sent for him to keep him safe and to wait for us. I only wish he had waited a bit longer so we could have spent more time with Giovanni and the Radio Flyer red wagon that his grandpa traveled all over to find for their last Christmas together, so he could pull it with his electric wheelchair.

Of everything I have ever written, I swear that the last two pages have been the hardest thing I've ever had to face doing; but Johnny's health, Alex's inherited mutated DNA and then Giovanni's neurological problems were the reason I started this whole thing, wasn't it? Hopefully now you have returned to the picture in your mind, to the beautiful Washington DC Mall fully consumed by tents, and fences. Since campfires were a no-no, hibachis were in front of every tent, and all of the people congregated on the landscape gave off the illusion that the Capital of the United States was under siege and by the music, somehow lost back in the 60's and early 70's. The amazing thing about that first night filled with strangers was the peace and harmony felt by everyone, and the good times being shared by people who would end up being friends for the rest of their lives.

The morning sun came up and most of us had forgotten that we hadn't slept at all. We had gotten there Wednesday evening and so we had Thursday to organize what was going to be a lobbying effort by some of the group. They were just going to walk the Halls of Capitol Hill and try to talk to any politicians they could corner. We set up tables on the Mall and covered them with pamphlets and copies of scientific reports. We included as well, pictures of not only our own children who were suffering, but also of children left behind in South Vietnam with the gift of death and disfigurement that our planes had showered upon them. There were a number of Vets who had returned to Vietnam, some on excursions and some to live out their lives. Because of them, we were always getting updates of just how horrendously the poison that was still very potent in the water and the soil was effecting the born and the not-yet born. Our children had health problems: some had spina bifida, some had missing limbs or holes in their hearts; but these Vietnamese children were born without eyes, without faces, and too many without any limbs at all. It was even worse than what was caused by the thalidomide that some of our parents or their friends took during their prenatal years and then had children born with flippers where arms or legs should have been.

Those of us who were used to speaking out, started the day running public speaking pitch sessions and dispensing talking points to those who were going on the Hill. Annie and I, along with the Board members or leaders of groups were going to the Veterans Administration Building. We were to appear by invitation to speak to then VA Director Charles Hagel (yes, the same Vietnam Vet who would later join me, Tom Daschle and John Kerry on the activist trail) and the men in charge of trying to help those Vets who came back with all the nightmares and flashbacks. Some of our Vets had been back from Vietnam for ten to fifteen years, but now these government officials finally wanted to help.

The truth of the situation was that AOVNJ had been contacted by Director Charles Hagel, now Secretary of Defense Chuck Hagel under President Obama, and I had been invited to come speak with him and the psychological staff at the VA with regard to the work that we were doing in New Jersey and were soon to be starting in Shelton, Connecticut. Since I knew Director Hagel when he was just Vietnam Veteran Chuck Hagel, I was well aware of how much he wanted to do all that he could (but quit after a little over a year because the Reagan Administration didn't keep even one promise that they made to us). When I knew the dates for the Dewey Canyon exercise, I scheduled my time to speak for that week. I also asked if I could bring about a hundred of my closest new friends!

We spent the entire day on Thursday preparing for Friday by talking to people who were visiting Washington who I guess had wandered over to where all the funny-dressed Army people were. After all, what good is visiting Washington DC, without witnessing at least one good demonstration? By the evening we were all tired and made big pots of spaghetti on the hibachis, ate dinner and then sat back to relax before going to sleep and getting up early to hit the Hill. However, all hell broke loose that night. It was really kind of nerve-wracking and about as scary as it could get.

What did happen, as a result of the bedlam was that by the time I met all these bigwigs at the VA, I had earned an immediate reputation, and they were informed that I had the night before brought "hundreds" (quite exaggerated) of cases of combat stress back from the brink on an average of one every five minutes!! That story and the fact that I just stood there with an "aw shucks" half grin and said nothing, gave them a reason to ask if I could stay after the meeting with everyone because there was something that Dr. Art Blank and Dr. Maurice LeBlau wanted to talk over with me. Because Colleen was there with us by the time we returned to New Jersey, the story had been repeated in not only the *Asbury Park Press*, but almost every newspaper in the country by the Associated Press.

In reality this big crisis was that a whole bunch of very over-tired Vietnam Veterans had essentially built themselves a Combat Zone Compound, complete with all of the noises, except for the helicopters, that they heard every day in Vietnam. As night fell and it was very dark, the bushes on the Mall seemed bigger than life to some of them. They were flashing back and even a couple of beers didn't help them to relax. I was sitting and talking to some of the guys when I heard one of the Jersey Vets, yell "Kopy, Kopy!" and I took off running. Kenny came up behind me, and to my surprise he had our favorite reporter, Colleen with him since she had flown down to cover this event.

We got to a spot where Jim Burdge was bending down and trying to talk to a Vet who had a wild look in his eyes and was cowering. I knew that look and without even thinking, I turned to Jim and Kenny and said "Oh fuck, I don't have my spaghetti pot". The guys from other groups that were gathering around heard what I said and just looked totally confused, but my guys were trying not to laugh. We talked the Vet out of where he was crouching and I got him over to our RV, opened the door, sat him down and closed the door with everybody on the outside wondering if he was going to go crazy and kill me. Kenny and Jim did what they could to assure everyone that I was okay with this, but told me later that they were scared too because "that guy's not from Jersey!"

Okay!!! Nobody had told me that different states or cities

have different Vets who reacted in some "other city flashback". Approximately ten minutes later, or so they told me, the guy, whose name was Ray, and I left the RV with him drinking a cup of coffee. We went back to the compound and within about fifteen minutes, I hear "Kopy, Kopy!" from one side of the Mall and "Medic" from other guys who didn't remember my name. I'm no medic, but I am a therapist and my name is Kopy, so I went toward the sound again. Once more, this great camping adventure named *Namland* was taking its toll. I finally decided that it was too strenuous to keep going back and forth, so I told my group that they were the catchers and I was going to stay in the bullpen. Besides, somebody had to make the coffee. This escapade went on for at least three or four hours and each time somebody got dropped inside the RV, I don't think my timing got shorter, but I think that the exaggerations got bigger.

My meeting with the VA psychological team was much livelier after they heard of my Super Powers. I was totally surprised when Dr. Blank asked me if I would like to assist in writing the protocol for the proposed VA Vet Centers that I knew nothing about, but tried to act like I did. They were very familiar with our private Vet Center at Freehold Area Hospital which totally surprised me as I didn't even believe that the VA knew that the guys came back from Korea in 1956, much less Vietnam in 1975. Then honesty prevailed when Art Blank told me that he had read about us in the newspaper. Director Hagel had been introduced to me by Senator Florio from New Jersey and was well aware of all of our New Jersey programs, since every politician in the state was jumping on the bandwagon. My concern was that I wanted three things, first I would not go to work for the VA, second was that I had to be paid by honorarium to AOVNJ, and third that I would be given professional credit for my efforts. And of course, my expenses to travel down to DC twice a month had to be taken care of too.

Little did I know that I would end up the following year, traveling all over the United States to not only help set up the Centers, but to attend speaking engagements at most of the service organizations to get the Vets to trust the VA when it came to the Vet Centers. The Shelton Vet Center which was opened by the Connecticut Veterans Alliance and the International Vietnam Veterans Network was born at Dewey Canyon and included every group that was represented at that event with others joining later on. It became the vanguard that the protocol was derived from, since AOVNJ's Center had too many other services that the VA wanted no part of there. Our group did, however, become the model for other private Veterans' groups who had joined our network, things like a jobs program, a food pantry, our statewide legal involvement program, and anything else that any member wanted to see happen if he was willing to spearhead and run it. Oh, and please let us not forget our fund raising booths at carnivals, our school speakers, our parade involvements, and our demonstrations *with* banners and placards. We were a very busy bunch and the guys were more than thrilled because they were vital, important, and appreciated. They got to spend time with each other and have fun with people who understood their possible mood swings. Johnny and I had the biggest backyard, so we bought a storage house and that is where all of AOVNJ's supplies and equipment were kept. So much to the chagrin of my yuppie neighbors, you never knew who was at my house or when, but they were all dressed like Vets and wearing Agent Orange t-shirts.

Even though we have gotten off the topic of Dewey Canyon and the exploding vets, I really would be remiss if I didn't finally explain that my Super-Therapist treatment was much easier than anyone could have known. About two years after losing Johnny and having gone to Paris to try to make someone take responsibility, I wrote an article for VVAW that I had been keeping inside for over thirty years and the response, after so many years, even for the guys who remembered being there that fateful night, was total shock. First of all I wrote in the article about my spaghetti helmet. Then I simply explained that with that first vet, Ray, I didn't know him or his wife or anything about him. Combat Stress was a brand new field, so I had to figure out how to wing it. As soon as we got into the RV with everyone outside and he still looked like a deer in the headlights, I started to pick up different things in the RV. I said to him, "Ray, it's 1981, and we are in the United States Capital in a very nice rented RV. Look Ray, see the television? Here's a refrigerator, a bathroom, and lots of light". After about four minutes of quietly just looking at things I was showing him, he got up and went into the bathroom. When he came out, he had washed his face and I said to him, "Want a cup of coffee?" and the rest was history. So you see why I said that "somebody had to make the coffee"! I am pretty sure that the talking heads at the VA would never have given us the funding or the respect of realizing that AOVNJ knew more about PTSD than they ever would, if they had heard that all they needed was an RV!

The saddest part of the problem of combat stress syndrome, now in the 21st Century, is that the government and the politicians still don't understand that other people's children are not put on this Earth to become cannon fodder. That if you send a young boy or girl into a combat zone where every day, in their mind is probably going to be their last; and then you send them directly home in a span of about 48 hours after leaving the firefight arena, with no debriefing or deprogramming for Main Street USA, you are doing them more harm than anyone can imagine.

What compounds the damage is multifaceted because as soon as they may begin to feel human again, they are being sent back to the IE-D's, the assassins, the terror and the fear, over and over again. Big business loves war and gives politicians all kinds of PAC monies for the right to keep those lucrative government contracts.

Politicians need to follow a very simple edict before sending anyone else's son or daughter into a war zone: *they* have to either send their own child or go themselves. I think that would solve the problem! The one thing that never changes though is that political wars are old men sending youngsters to die for economic gain. If the youngsters don't die in the war zone or come back maimed and broken; then they find out a couple of years later that they were killed in their war by either Agent Orange in Vietnam and Korea, depleted uranium in Desert Storm and Iraq, or chemical warfare and traumatic brain injury. *It is not right. It is not fair and it really is not necessary.* I, as a person and as a writer am not a pacifist or a flower child. I am a realist and until the American people refuse to let the government play Risk or Battleship with *their children*, we are doomed.

CHAPTER EIGHT

THE CHURCH OF THE ALMIGHTY DOLLAR (T.A.D.)

BEFORE LEAVING OUR Dewey Canyon adventure, we spent most of the day Saturday comparing notes, sharing information and then forming a loosely knit organizational network with selected spokespeople in each region for the network. We, as a collective wanted to concentrate efforts, as opposed to working separate group goals. We set rules and regulations so that no one group in the network could involve any of the others in any endeavors or, for lack of a better word "escapades" that would detract from the images and intellect needed if we were going to force our state governments, and especially, the Federal System to see the Vietnam Veteran community as it truly was. We needed them to see the Vietnam Vets as American heroes, not as the media and the uninformed had been portraying them. We also agreed that every group's newsletter would include either space or even a whole page to advise their membership about what was happening all over the country. It was that sharing of news and information that became the backbone of what was to come. In less than a year after our sojourn to Base DC we were able to mobilize and motivate the largest legal battle this nation ever seen even up until the present: The Agent Orange Lawsuit had signed on and actively involved hundreds of thousands of Veterans and their families, as well as every group dedicated to Vietnam Vets on the face of the Earth. Even the most mundane and boring motions and hearings taking place in Brooklyn Federal Court, in Brooklyn, New York, before Judge Jack Weinstein was standing room only, with the Vets lined up out the door and down the block either hoping to just get into court or to show support for those of us who were the Veteran liaisons and spokespeople. I don't know any of the groups in the tri-state area of NY/NJ/CONN, whose members didn't have their homes or apartments filled with wall-to-wall Vets who came from as far as California, Texas, Florida or just about anywhere. They came in cars filled and loaded to capacity with Veterans driving into Brooklyn.

Actually, those scenes did not happen until sometime around January 1, 1984. The amount of time, research, meetings and the compiling of data and information was immense. It included having to deal with some wonderful lawyers who were on our side from Day One. Unfortunately, the number of lawyers dedicated to our cause could be counted on one hand, with fingers left over, as opposed to the consortium of lawyers who could have cared less about whether the Vets or their children lived or died. Those mercenary lawyers came along later and only cared that they could turn the one-million dollar buy-in to the "CONSORTIUM TEAM" into hundreds of millions to which they would be able to split a 40% *plus costs and expenses fee*. *They* would be paid no matter what; right off the top and they didn't even have to have a chest cold or flu to make a fortune off of the Vets. Those valiant men whose illnesses had already contaminated the gene pool and DNA for generations, probably all generations to come would end up with less than the cost of a funeral.

From the last night of Dewey Canyon IV, or should I say, from the first time I'd ever heard of him at Woodstock in August of 1969, and through to this day, the honorary member and songwriter for the Vietnam Veterans has been Country Joe McDonald. He was front and center, so we ended our weekend long commitment event singing "Next Stop Is Vietnam" and even some of Dylan's and Marley's anti-war lyrics. It didn't seem the least bit strange that we were still singing songs to stop a war that ended in 1975, just as it is still common practice for those of us still standing to get all warm and fuzzy if we hear some radio station playing the lyrics "What're we fighting for?". Some of the Iraqi Wars and the Afghanistan veterans still sing it now, although they adjust the lyrics to suit America's latest military attempts. The songs work for them as they too see their wars thinning the herd and getting our youngest and strongest killed for no reason whatsoever. I have never expected and still don't that everyone has to agree with me on my views about political wars or for that matter privately run prisons. I believe both are being built on the greed of few to maim, kill or imprison the many for their own religious idol, *The Almighty Dollar* (hereinafter named T.A.D.). However, what is amazing to me is that there are still some men or families who suffered or are still suffering because of the actions not of the enemy in Vietnam, but by the government of the United States, who are fighting proudly *to defend the reasons that anyone was sent to Vietnam.* Whenever a Vet would tell me the old adage that we were in Vietnam to keep communism out of the United States, he could never explain to me, unlike the attack on 9/11/2001, how the Vietnamese were ever going to get to the shores of America. They had no Air Force and hadn't anyone noticed what their boats looked like?

The only way that they could acquire the artillery, transport technology, planes, etc. would have to be *from* the Americans. The high end cooking in Vietnam had become a cross between PHO (soup) and French cuisine because the French had occupied ten years of wasted time trying to take control of that country and the French loved good food.

Cooking is one thing and quite honestly, the best part of that military involvement that I do enjoy right here in America, is Vietnamese restaurants run by original Vietnamese nationals who came here legally and started businesses. But that even further makes the war supporter's argument moot, since the successful Vietnamese businesses here are because of Capitalism and what they wanted to escape was Communism. The United States of America for many years now has had a passion to swoop down on other countries and "Whip a Little Democracy Up on Them". Another problem with stupid thinking is that it has a habit of repeating itself when the majority refuses to learn from it.

So, let's go back to my original theory regarding our childhoods being filled with scary stories about the great Red or Yellow Menaces and their intentions to destroy us. Let me ask those who see where I am going with this; exactly how free are you as an American citizen now? Answer this as opposed to the compilation of information for the supposed Y2K that never happened? Or the imposition of the Patriot Act and all the freedoms that are no longer ours? The only thing that those who love war can take comfort in, is that here in the good old USA, you will always be free to bear assault rifles and firearms no matter how many little children die senselessly. The actual Vets who served in combat in Vietnam were very often wounded and killed because they didn't have the stomach to shoot a child even if they suspected that some grownup had made the child a walking bomb. I do not know even one Vet who sympathizes with the gun-happy non-vets who just want to arm everyone from five-years-old and up.

Fortunately, when AOVNJ, now a part of a national network, finally had a script to follow in keeping up with the other groups throughout the country and making sure that those groups were keeping up with us, the action took place in a much more politically receptive time in the American psyche. Those of us who grew up in the 50's and 60's had not yet come into political maturity. While we were still subject to the ruling class of a generation before us, these were the same everyday people who made sure that their kids had more than they did. They were family-oriented, but they weren't aware that there was a sinister and power hungry movement taking place in the White House and Capitol Hill.

In fact, it wasn't until a few years after the Iran Hostage Crisis that created so much anger and motivation for the Vietnam Veterans to take control of their own lives, that the entire nation was shocked to find out that the great hope of the Republican Party, Ronald Reagan had almost certainly manipulated President Jimmy Carter's loss of a second term. This is true because ironically, as soon as Reagan won the election in 1980, the hostages were released after so many hundreds of days in captivity. It was some time after he took office that all hell broke loose when the country was informed that our political machine, the Reagan Administration was found to have provided hostage takers and America haters with weapons. They had put the Shah of Iran in his figurehead position as main tyrant and terrorist of his own people, after he was overturned by the religiously insane Ayatollah, who made himself the real Ruler of Iran. Secretly from the American public the Reagan Administration also involved our country in sending money to the very brutal and murderous drug cartel armies who were indiscriminately killing the peasants of Nicaragua in the fight between the Contra and the Sandinista. The monies in the millions paid for the massive weapons and methods of destruction being sold to Iran under the darkness of lies. A young Colonel named Oliver North threw himself on the Congressional hearings grenade to try to protect his President, who we now know had early onset Alzheimer's. Thus began the nightmare of politics based upon that great religious idol T.A.D.

The majority of Vietnam veterans and their families were realizing what was happening in our government before any of the rest of the citizens. We were busy trying to teach the elected officials to understand that we did the one thing that so many Americans gave no seriousness to; that We Voted, not only in Presidential elections, but in off years too. And we encouraged our people to vote as well. President Ronnie the RayGun as he was known to the Vets never really understood that our generation was part of his Bedtime for Bonzo world, because in a town filled with incredible memorials paid for by the government the Vietnam Vets had to raise the monies for their own memorial.. We were busy fighting to make the VA take our Agent Orange illnesses and combat stress problems seriously as something other than "malingering". We were getting legislation passed that made sure that Veterans' benefits were not stripped from the roster, were made available justly, and that eligibility did not require bringing back to life an enemy combatant to testify that you killed him in Vietnam to prove that you had actually been there.

The excuse for needing more proof was always blamed on a "fire in St. Louis" that no one ever knew anything about until Vets started filing claims. While this was all going on, we raised enough money to build a granite wall engraved with 57,000 names of those young Americans who died for T.A.D., and then we had to pay for the security of the monument for years because the DC Park Security would not provide any services. When the original Vietnam Veterans Wall Monument was dedicated right there on the Mall with the White House within walking distance, you will never guess who never showed up to thank or address the greatest fighting force this country had ever created and then had sold out. Yes, you are correct if you guessed Ronnie Ray-Gun. The man who insulted the Vets not only once, but a second time once again when the Veterans, again raised the monies on their own to have a statue of three combat soldiers built within view of the Wall. This time for the dedication the President decided that he should get up on the stage and thank the Vets for their service. However, for this second event, the Veterans who had served in Vietnam, along with their families and loved ones were not allowed onto the Memorial area without everyone going through metal detectors; diaper bags were checked for weapons and a chicken wire fence was erected to keep ALL veterans and their families at least 1500 feet from the staging area, or they would be arrested if they tried to either move or go over that fence. The only other time that Veterans were treated like felons and enemies of the state was when approximately one thousand members of the Bonus Army of WWI veterans were mowed down by soldiers on horseback on the DC Mall when they tried to demonstrate for payment of the $1,000 bonus they had been promised if they stayed in the European theater until the war was over. Incidentally, they never got a dime of that money, but I never could decide which act of stupidity and un-American vulgarity was more insulting to those who had served.

Our government scorned the Vietnam Vet and portrayed a flawed and disparaging image of them that they encouraged average citizens to believe. This, of those who gave their lives, for even if they made it home, we now know that they were killed in Vietnam. But we kept our heads high and took pride in what we were accomplishing in our own right and for our own kind. When we did return to DC for the unveiling of the three soldiers statue, there was a "Welcome Home Parade" down Constitution Avenue, although it was almost ten years after the war's end. It was the fall of 1982, and our son had just turned five-years-old. The biggest reason I remember the image like it was yesterday is because Alex insisted upon walking beside his Daddy for the whole parade route, and he did so with incredible pride. It was a very chilly and windy day, so I had put my fatigue jacket on this little boy and one of the guys placed an Army hat on his head. The headline in the *Washington Post* and our local NJ newspapers (I don't know about any others) showed this handsome little boy in a very long jacket marching with his dad and the caption was simply: "*Welcome Home, Dondi*!" After that experience, an exhausted Alex slept on my lap in the hallway under the Lincoln Memorial for about two hours. This also made it a special day because I'd never met, or have yet to meet anyone who slept under Abraham Lincoln's chair, but not in the White House.

Johnny and I visited a meeting hall at one of the DC service organizations in the DC area that had opened their facility to any Vietnam Vets or groups who wanted to sell, trade or give out everything from t-shirts to memorabilia or brochures of information. It was fun to meet Vets from other states and laugh at some of the outrageous slogans that they had to come up with to put on shirts and bumper stickers. Our AOVNJ t-shirt was unique and quite honestly the only one ever featured in *Time*, *Life* and *Newsweek* magazines. It was a bright orange shirt with black ink which across the top of the front said "SPRAYED AND BETRAYED". Right below the words was a crude map of Vietnam, with a characterization of Uncle Sam on one side and a 55-gallon drum labeled Agent Orange on the other, but joined by shaking hands across the map. Under the map there was a picture of a GI bending over and holding his back while looking up at the map in pain. My reasoning for that detail was to show how many of the Vets had problems with a type of rapidly spreading arthritis. However, when the shirts were done almost every Vet would chuckle and swear that my intention was that they were being sodomized by Uncle Sam. The back of the shirt had a bulls-eye with the words Agent Orange Victims of New Jersey inside the circles of the bulls-eye and A.O.V.N.J. in the center.

Like the prior RV confession, what no one affiliated with our cause knew was that while I had designed the idea, I have never been able to even draw stick figures with any ability. So, early on in my activism while having coffee with two of my neighbors who had children the same age of Alex, I was telling them about my idea for a shirt design and also my lack of artistic abilities. Neither of these women had any involvement or concern with Veterans or the war and the only common bond was that we all lived on the same street and all had kids. Johnny and I had the only swimming pool in the development and so that made us very popular in the warmer months. So out of friendship and the need to swim, one of the women, Karen Sass said that she could draw, and Ellen Stein said that she knew some calligraphy. Karen, like me, was an economic coupon queen before it became a television reality. She collected magazines for the coupons, and ran home coming back with a bridal magazine. She proceeded to draw the picture I had described using a picture of a groom in a long coat tuxedo as her model for Uncle Sam. It actually turned out so terrifically that early on in the formation of our group, I showed it to the members and they loved it. At the time, however, we didn't even have a name, so the back of the shirt was blank. A couple of the guys came up with the name and then suggested the bulls-eye as they considered themselves targets of the spraying that was not supposed to be used anywhere near American or Allied troops, much less directly as it was *on them*.

When we went to the DC Welcome Home Parade, everyone from our group and the national network was wearing those shirts while they marched. We all wore them again at the American Legion Hall. While we were perusing the different booths, we noticed a crowd starting to gather and as we got closer we came face to face with General Westmoreland. He was the Vietnam War General who sued CBS for claiming that he had lied to the Pentagon about the troop strength of the enemy, stating that he did not require additional troops in an effort to make the government and the American people (who were getting pretty hostile about the war) think that we were somehow winning. The end result was the massacre and deaths of thousands of our own troops at the Tet Offensive and the Battle of Caisson. The lawsuit against CBS ended up proving that he had lied and that he was just as guilty of warmongering as any of the major businesses and politicians who prospered by the blood of our own youngsters. There were many Vets at that Hall, who still believed the lies that they had been tricked into giving up their own lives and their buddies for. So many were there that the General thought he was amongst friends *until* he put his hand out to shake my husband's hand. Johnny took one look at his face and said loudly enough for the whole room to hear, "You've got to be kidding; I don't shake hands with murderers!" The General and his entourage looked horrified and took off quickly through the exit, nearly knocking over one Vet in a wheelchair whose legs were still in Vietnam. My husband started to walk away when he was suddenly being hugged, applauded and slapped on the back; the cheers were deafening. And the guys who still thought of Westmoreland as if he walked on water just looked confused.

My husband was never a radical; he was a working class, blue collar self-taught intellectual, who had radical ideas that he could convince the radical he had married to carry out. I remember once that someone was giving him a hard time about something. All I remember and never forgot were his words to them, "Keep it up and I'll sic my wife on you". I don't even think that Johnny realized what he had said to the General or what he intended to say until after it came out. Even then he wasn't sorry or embarrassed by anything except the reaction of the vets because he was such a private man. He was much more comfortable with helping out our cause from the financial end and being one of the group in public displays. So I did understand just how much he hated that man.

That hate and anger came from the job that Johnny ended up doing when he landed in Vietnam. His job description or what he was trained for, his MOS was a teletype operator, but there were no teletype machines in An Khe where he was stationed. He was asked whether he wanted to be a "grunt" which is a foot soldier. Grunts traveled through the jungles and fought for their lives or at least had to be prepared to do so every minute that they are out there. They were in danger, not just from the enemy, but from the booby traps, mines and wild animals. Or, he could be a door-gunner on a Medivac chopper since An Khe was similar to what was seen on the television show M.A.S.H.*. Johnny's decision was an easy one for him because he was almost 6'2" tall and a very largely built man, so the idea of being concealed by bushes and trees did not appeal to him at all. He had, however, been a volunteer EMT from the age of eighteen and was not squeamish around injuries and blood. More importantly though, he figured he would be above the war for the most part and that would be safer for a man his size. Also, he was an incredibly strong man, so to him Medivac was a better fit. What Johnny hadn't counted on was that the injuries would be so severe. Very often too the chopper was flying into a zone where fighting was still going on. Though the troops had been told that Medivac choppers and medics and trucks marked with a red cross as in the previous wars were not to be fired upon, this was nonsense. The problem with that theory is that nobody bothered to tell the enemy! As Johnny would always say later on when watching an old war movie, "Those medics and medical vehicles were the biggest targets."

His job was to watch for snipers when the chopper was coming down if they were flying into a fire fight to try to clear the area so they could reach the wounded. With his assault rifle in one hand, he then had to carry the wounded back to the craft to be flown to the base. This is why later on when we spoke at any Veteran function, the Vets would line up to hug him, shake his hand and a few even kissed him on his cheek or his forehead. He represented whoever did what he did in Nam and got them back to base and on to survival. I was always amazed at how embarrassed he was when that would happen because my husband was an exceptionally good man who loved to help others. Nevertheless, he could never take credit for what he did without getting red-faced and shy. I used to ask him if he had any idea of how many people, both in Vietnam and in Newark, New Jersey he had saved. He would just get a half smile and shrug his shoulders which was his way to tell me to stop talking about it. He really had no ego that needed feeding or insecurities regarding the man that he was.

The reality of the emotional world for those who served in combat in Southeast Asia was that, just like my husband, they did not talk about what happened over there. They were noticeably different than the men who served in World War II, who at the service organization bars and meeting halls seemed to only come alive and be animated when they relived every battle and every event, or even made some up. It wasn't even the fact that the old timers and some of those who worked hard to avoid the draft thought they had the right to judge the warrior for the errors of the war that made the Vets feel uncomfortable; it was because what they had been forced into seeing, being a part of, experiencing or were led into, was so traumatizing and overwhelming that to repeat it was to relive it. Someone should have realized that if they were going to use Americans to fight a war that wasn't really a war that deprogramming and the provision of counsel, might have been a humane and a smart move on the part of the government.

For the most part, the enemy wasn't really an enemy, it was another youngster who was equally as scared and as traumatized as the face they were looking at. The only actual difference was that the Vietnamese lived on that land and most of them on the South Vietnamese side were also told as our men were told, that the enemy from the North was trying to force Communism and thus, a form of slavery, on them. The North Vietnamese were taught that they were going to become Capitalist pawns. The ARVN, or South Vietnamese that we were supposed to be there to help or "liberate" were the only people who were really fighting to save their homes and their land. They were trying to keep both sides from wiping out all the men, women and children who were just trying to survive. How bizarre does it seem that while America was supposed to be insuring the freedom of the South Vietnamese, they were not only spraying poison over most of the land, the fields, trees, water and crops, but also all over the people of South Vietnam and the soldiers of America and the Allied Forces? One has to wonder, even all these years later. Maybe especially for so many of us, those words first sung by Country

Joe and the Fish back in 1969 capture it: "What're we fighting for? Don't know, don't give a damn. Next Stop is Vietnam". Those words and what happened over there have haunted our lives, their lives and the lives of our offspring, our children and their children for all time to come.

CHAPTER NINE

WHEN ALL ELSE FAILS, READ THE DIRECTIONS – OOPS!

JOHNNY AND I MOVED INTO our first new house, in Manalapan, New Jersey on August 1st, 1976, and as stated, we had almost ¾ of an acre of beautiful wooded property with a big swimming pool in the backyard. We had scrimped and saved for about two years to be able just to afford the down payment and except for the kitchen, family room and my son's bedroom, we could have held dances in the other large empty rooms, but we didn't care. Things would come in time, and it was summer. We had always driven far to the Jersey Shore because my husband loved to swim and loved the water; but now all he had to do was go downstairs and out the back door to the pool. We had a small hibachi grill that we had used on our apartment terrace and when we put it in the backyard, Johnny advised me that he was going to find a 55-gallon drum and saw it in half just like the guys did in Vietnam. He raved about how great you could BBQ on one of those base camp grills. Neither of us knew where to get a 55-gallon drum and we forgot about it. At that time, we did not know that those grills used by the soldiers and marines in South Vietnam, were instruments of death and it was not until almost three years later that we made it a point during speaking engagements to warn every veteran who could hear us that if that was what they had constructed at home, to get rid of it and get rid of it fast.

It was approximately one year after we had moved into our home and were expecting what we believed was going to be our first of six children, that we learned that the chemical herbicides that I learned about on the television news had been shipped to Vietnam in those 55 gallon drums, the contents mixed with water and then the drums were labeled with different color duct tape, orange, white, blue… While they may have been colors of the rainbow, Agent Orange, Agent White, Agent Blue, etc., they were the carriers of death, devastation, disabilities and decades of generational destruction. The military draftees and enlisted men as well as the nurses, doctors and everyone else were told that the constant mobile spraying around the base camps and the aerial spraying over the jungles was a sort of pesticide to protect them from carnivorous bugs, stinging bugs and disease carrying bugs. Since most enlisted men and even draftees after WWII were the sons of Veterans, as that is who historically fights the wars, they had heard their fathers and grandfathers talk about malaria and dysentery, so it made perfect sense. The guys figured it was like military-sized containers of Raid and thought nothing of it, until they began to notice that everything around them was dying, except the bugs. The trees, the grass, the crops of the family farms, everything except those damn biting bugs. The grunts in the bush didn't pay much attention to the pesticide spraying right on top of them and over the water that they drank, swam and bathed in because their government was taking care of them getting sick from bugs.

The other advantage was that after an area was sprayed, the enemy couldn't hide in the wild bushes and jungles because it was turning into twigs and dead trees with no leaves. Tall grass couldn't hide any of the snipers or other Vietcong, so it was all good, right? Besides, those pesticide drums made great BBQ grills and holders to fill with ice for their Tiger beer. People always try to find an upside to every situation, if they are hell bent upon surviving that situation. So if the only time that they could at least try to relax from the constant fear of being in the middle of some God Forsaken country they'd never heard of before, was at base camp then the handy drums were part of their sacred, and not as scared recreation time.

Years later we would learn the true meaning of those duct tape rainbow colors on the drums and that meaning was more frightening than that jungle had ever been. As American citizens who were always taught that our country was the best and the safest place in the world to be especially in the

time before we had to teach little children about "stranger danger". Most of the GI's in Vietnam weren't even old enough to buy a glass or can of beer in the United States since most states had raised the age to twenty-one. These kids were just a couple of years out of high school, if that long and still believed that they belonged to the Land of the Free and the Home of the Brave. When it became an actual "mission" for AOVNJ, and with the assistance of a "concerned friend" who worked for one of the politicians on Capitol Hill, to get a General Accounting Office report and some confidential "Herbs Tapes" alleviated from their cabinet space, somehow the great democracy didn't seem so "Free or Brave". What we learned was that the DOD had requisitioned the purchase of herbicides, for which the exact specifications or schematics were supplied to the bidding chemical companies so that the military, which had little to no previous experiences in jungle fighting, could spray and destroy the jungle and the plant life which would not only make the enemy easier to find, but, would also starve the livestock, the plant life, rice, and the people of South Vietnam. Weren't those the very people that we were pouring young American bodies into Vietnam to help?

The exact components of this herbicide were 2,4D and 2,4.5T, which when used together put out the most deadly poison known to man – DIOXIN. It was also one of the best kept secrets that was known only to the government and the very large and profiting chemical companies. Where the colors and the problems came from, was that because when a company has a government contract, if all goes well, that or those companies get rich, but, if the manufacturing provider cannot keep up with the demand, they must pay a non-compliance fine that can be from tens of thousands to hundreds of thousands of dollars per day. Unbeknownst to the chemical companies was that the DOD was either not able to "read the instructions" or chose to ignore the dilution parts per million and that the solution was "NOT TO BE SPRAYED ON OR ALLOWED TO COME INTO CONTACT WITH PERSONNEL." Or they decided that if a little bit is good, then a lot has to be better and when it came to personnel, these weren't persons, these were GI's. Subsequently, the military was using much more herbicide than they were supposed to *and* not diluting it enough. It was being used at least 200% more, and stronger than it was supposed to be, which explains why supplies were diminishing very quickly.

All the DOD knew was that the orders had to be filled and all the chemical companies knew was that if they didn't fill the order on time, it was going to cost them big time. What to do? What to do??? What they figured out is that when they were running low on the spec'd solution, hey, chemical companies make all different kinds of chemicals and so they changed the tape on the drums to reflect additions of whatever they had plenty of. While we found out that they did write it down somewhere, they didn't advise the DOD. And when the Vietnam Veterans sued the eleven chemical companies involved, almost all of those notes disappeared like Houdini had just entered the room.

The end result was bad enough when it was just plain old, worst poison known to man, dioxin, but by adding in everything including probably their leftover morning coffee, what was being literally poured upon the American military and the South Vietnamese "friendlies" was "poisoned" poison. For this, there was never really any chemical input accounting to try to find some antidote, if any such thing even existed. The basic reality was that not only was the DOD, in cooperation with the chemical companies, raining down death upon their own military; the birth defects created by the gene mutating potions upon the offspring of anyone who was effected has in essence destroyed entire future generations. This is true not just for those who had a blood relationship to the poisoned Vets at the time, but also for whatever families their offspring married into.

Just as those Veterans who returned home from WWII and created the Baby Boom, the young men and women returning from Southeast Asia, and Korea before that were ready to begin their lives as grownups, looking to marry and start families of their own. The saddest thing that could have happened, according to thousands of Veterans, was that no one felt it was necessary to tell anyone what had been done to them. Quite to the contrary, they were denied any knowledge and then when the questions came up, an entire population of patriotic Americans were lied to, blatantly lied to until it was too late. The first problem was the number of children born with birth defects, such as spina bifida, holes in the heart and other catastrophic defects; and then as the children started school, it was realized that seven out of every ten children born to Vietnam Combat Veterans, suffered from mild to severe learning disabilities. It did not matter if a Vet had been raised on a plain in the midst of Montana, an urban area in a major city, or anyplace else in this vast nation, the only common factor was that they had each served in a sprayed area. In fact, the only other citizens that they could compare themselves to were those who lived in toxic landfill areas like Ironbound or Love Canal. Still, for the longest time, questions went unanswered and demands for answers were either ignored or lied about. Even the unusual number of Veterans, who were in their early 30's, dying from the rarest forms of cancers, wasn't alarming anyone in society except the Vietnam Veterans. Soft tissue sarcoma, leukemia and untreatable brain tumors were not normally a healthy A1 Combat Veteran's diseases of choice.

From about 1982 to 1985, Johnny and I went to over 134 funerals of Vietnam vets who either died from incurable malignancies or suicides and that was just Vets from the Northeastern United States, people that we knew or knew of. What does one say to a widow with two or three small children, who has only been married for five or six years? Who is responsible? How will that family survive, since they were too young to think of or to be able to afford large sums of life insurance? The government was still lying to the American people about what had transpired in Vietnam and were still saying that there was nothing to worry about. The only information given was that any absorbed dioxin was "stored in the fat cells" and so there was nothing to worry about. The problem with that theory was that it was as nonsensical as believing in the Easter Bunny since even if there was a scientific chance in Hell that it all began with the fat cells of a human organism, at what point does this mutating poison enter the blood stream and destroy the genetic pool?

In 1982, I had the great privilege to meet and really get to know some incredible and brilliant people, most of whom I could never forget and still think of often. The first person was a man of thirty-four years of age, Frank Delaney, who was a very successful, educated and bright man, an executive with the Liberty Mutual Insurance Company; married to a nurse, Carol Delaney, an equally wonderful person. Their lives were blessed by two children and Frank had used his GI Bill to get his college education and then to buy their home. They were incredibly decent and hard-working people who just loved their life and their children like they were supposed to do and life was good. I met Frank when he had been admitted to Yale Medical Center in New Haven, Conn., and a Veterans group from Shelton, which I was working with to start their own private Vet Center similar to the A.O.V.N.J. Center in Freehold, N.J. asked me to go visit one of their members, Frank Delaney. Frank was dying from a malignant brain tumor that was inoperable and the cause of which was baffling even to the great doctors of Yale and its in-house VA Hospital wing. Frank had private health insurance and the best doctors, but they could not figure out what had caused this tumor and why when he had already had surgery, the tumor regrew with vigor. The Veterans Administration was using Yale Medical Center as an outreach facility and Frank's specialists had tried to find out from the VA doctors if they could shed any light on the facts that we were giving to the doctors with regard to dioxin poisoning, but there was no information being shared and the Yale doctors were getting very frustrated because they felt that they were being lied to by the VA.

The only scientific studies being done at that time that the public and the Veterans knew of was conducted by the New Jersey Agent Orange Commission, which was set up by legislation signed by Governor Thomas Kean and written by A.O.V.N.J. The efforts were taking place at Rutgers University under Dr. Peter Kahn and being compiled by the Commission for the Veterans' Health Problems and our organization for the children's birth defects and other abnormalities. However, the Commission was looking at the same fat cell myth and the probability of doing liver biopsies which at their best were inconclusive. The only other known methodology was autopsy, which there was no funding for by any government entities, nor were any of the concerned living Veterans, willing to volunteer as candidates! Basically, the only information of any value was what was compiled by the Vietnam Veterans Network questionnaires that all of our groups would send out to members and the medical data provided by member Vets; except for the information and statistical data coming from the Aussies. Australia and New Zealand had embraced and honored their Veterans of our Allied Forces by compensating them as soon as the facts about the spraying were made public and the Veterans from Down-Under were very quick to try to assist our network organizations with any information or facts they could get documentation on and share with us.

Frank Delaney became my inspiration and my dearest friend. His personal strength even when the cancer had spread throughout his entire system and his intelligence were as much an incentive to me as was the plight of my own family, and there was nothing that I, or the other members of A.O.V.N.J. wouldn't do for him. We spoke at least once a day on the telephone and I would drive the three-and-a-half-hour drive from my home to

New Haven at least twice a month to spend time with Frank and Carol at the hospital.

One day while Carol and I were in the hallway of the hospital, she confided to me that Frank was afraid to ask me if there was any way that he could go to Washington DC to visit the VA and to speak to some of the Congress or Senate people because he wanted them to know who he was and why he was going to die. It was very important to him, but even though he knew how we all felt about him, he knew it was asking a lot of those of us who made the trip to DC on a regular basis from New Jersey. This would not have been a major request except that the trip from New Haven, Connecticut to Washington DC would be an eight-hour drive, just one way with a man who had been given no more than three more months to live; not to mention the logistics of getting him in and out of the Capitol buildings and the VA which at the time were not handicap feasible. My problem was that there was no way that I could turn down Frank's dying wish, so I told Carol to give me a chance to try to work it all out.

Besides making all the arrangements to have the Connecticut Vets drive him to my home in New Jersey and then drive to-and-from DC with a man who needed someone with medical training to make the trip with us; I would have to make sure that I had set appointments for him to meet with whichever politicians we wanted him to talk to, not their aides or their secretaries. This was going to take some doing. The first thing that I needed to do was to talk to Frank's doctors and make sure that the trip would not hurt him and to find out what we needed to take with us to provide in case of any emergencies. Carol arranged for me to speak with his specialists and his charge nurse, all of whom were very supportive because they were as fond of Frank as we all were, and wanted to do whatever was necessary to give him the opportunity he wanted so badly. One of our members, Betty Baker whose husband Bruce had like Frank, been a Marine, was a head nurse at Freehold Area Hospital where we had our own Vet Center, and she agreed to make the trip with us to take care of Frank if it became necessary. The guys from Shelton agreed to drive him to my home the night before we were going and then come back and pick him up the day after we got back, so that Frank could get some rest at our home, before and after the long trip. We were going to do this; and scheduled it for the same day that the Veterans Administration was having an Agent Orange Task Force meeting, so that Frank could be a part of it. We were also very careful not to tell anyone that Frank was going to be talking to just how sick he was or what his prognosis was. He needed to be heard, not to be pitied, and of course, Colleen Dee Berry from the *Asbury Park Press* and Jeanie Most of CNN made it their business to be in DC to cover Frank's pilgrimage, both well aware of just what his condition was. Frank's doctors even went so far as to contact the hospital closest to where we were going to be and speak with the oncologist as well as send copies of his file just in case we had any problems.

On the drive down to DC, Frank was like a kid on his way to Disneyland, he was so happy and animated. He was telling us jokes, not very good jokes, but we laughed uproariously just the same and he kept thanking us to the point of our having to tell him to "shut-up already". If I had any trepidations with regard to doing this for Frank Delaney, they disappeared just seeing what this meant to him. The first place we went was to the Task Force meeting at the VA and we sat Frank's wheelchair right up in the front row of chairs which made sure that if he raised his hand to speak, he would be seen and responded to without any problem. When he did speak, I think that the VA personnel were very surprised at his level of intelligence because they seemed to think that Vietnam Vets were not that bright. Then he hit them with the bombshell that coming to see them was his dying wish and explained *why* he was dying and probably when. For the rest of the meeting, it was hard for the Task Force members sitting at the head table facing us all, to not keep looking at Frank sitting right there, front and center in their faces. At the close of the meeting, the officials each came over to Frank to wish him well and ask if there was anything that they could personally do for him. I never forgot that his response was to introduce me, whom they already knew, as his "voice" and that what they could do for him was to do whatever we needed from the VA.

We know that never happened, although, for the next few years, I really had no problem getting hold of these people or getting them to help individual Veteran situations. It was almost like they never forgot Frank or the fact that he was looking down on them and making sure they kept their promises to him. Frank Delaney passed away approximately three weeks after our trip and I had spoken to him just the night before he died and he was still giggling then about the looks on everyone's faces in DC. If there is ever anything that I had to pick as one good thing that I accomplished in my years working with and for the Vets, that trip and spending those days with Frank Delaney would be the thing I would call upon.

At Frank's funeral, Carol was overwhelmed by how many Vets showed up from every surrounding state. Johnny and I had made sure that everyone in our network knew that Carol needed as much financial help as we could give her because although we knew that he had worked for an insurance company and had left some insurance, his illness had kept him from working for over two years. So Carol had been the only one to support their family, which left nothing for the final expenses. Frank's illness was not recognized as "service connected" until years later, which meant that there was no VA disability pension and nothing for funeral expenses at all.

I have also never forgotten the last time I spoke to Carol, about one month after his funeral because it was a rather bitter-sweet conversation. She called me late one evening and she was in tears. I had been aware that during Frank's illness, money was so tight that Carol had sold Frank's car and the only vehicle she had was her older station wagon. By the end of Frank's life, she had put so much mileage on that car driving back and forth to work and then to the hospital and home again every day that not only were the tires worn and the engine going bad, but someone had hit the side of her car and the passenger door would not stay closed unless it was kept tied to the frame of the car. She never complained and wouldn't even accept another vehicle from one of the Vets who knew the situation.

So, when I received that call I was very surprised to find out that the reason she was so upset was because she had done something that she began to think was an insult to her beloved husband and what he had been through. I didn't know what she was talking about until she reminded me of the condition of her car and then she "confessed" that the insurance monies had come in and she had bought a brand new car! Her anguish was because Frank had always dreamed of someday buying an Audi before he got sick and now she had bought a brand new Audi and thought that he would be upset. I wanted to laugh at what she was saying but knew that wasn't the right reaction. I asked her, "Now wait a minute, did you have a choice between buying the Audi or getting Frank back on Earth, all healthy and fine?" She got very quiet and all of a sudden my outlandish question hit her and she started to calm down and even laughed a bit. I reminded her that she and Frank had done all that they were supposed to do, the things we had been raised to believe were important, like getting an education, getting married, working, buying a home, having children and that Frank loved her so much and had wanted to live his life with her and provide for his family. He had been very troubled, but felt so helpless that she was forced to drive around in that broken down car. I then reminded her that the one thing that she and Frank had worried about was driving their children around to school or soccer in that beat up station wagon. These were the problems that families like ours worried about when we weren't worrying about our dying friends and our birth defected children.

It was also around this time, that our son Eddie, who was sixteen, fell in love for the first time in his life with his fourteen-year-old first girlfriend. She was a pretty and petite little thing which was funny in its own right because she was about 4'4" and Eddie was about 6'5". To kiss her goodnight, she had to stand about five steps up on the staircase of her house. I happened to notice that there was a problem with her left hand, but she actually tried to keep it out of sight. One day she overheard us talking about Johnny being a Vietnam Vet and she exclaimed, "My Dad was in Vietnam"; which sort of startled me when I remembered her hand. I waited a couple of days and when she was at our house, I asked if I could see her hand and she showed it to me reluctantly. May only had four fingers, no pinky finger, and all of her fingers were slightly gnarled and twisted. I complimented her on her ability to accept and learn to operate that hand as it was and commented on how pretty she was, but I knew what I was looking at and later when discussing it with Johnny, I was working myself into a frenzy because I had seen pictures of children, especially those living in the South of Vietnam. How insane was it that as a first responder and a Veterans' advocate, regardless of the severity of the situations I could remain cool, calm and collected, but when it came to my husband and my children, while I was capable of controlling my outward emotions and my ability to react, inside I was a basket case. What if they ran off and married? What if they became sexually active and there was yet another generation affected? Even though Eddie's biological father never served anything but drinks, May's father had reenlisted and done two full tours in dioxin soaked Vietnam. Fortunately I had waited to talk to my husband who reminded me that neither of these children were old enough to drive, didn't have a car, and Eddie already was planning on college; as well as the fact that this was going to be the first of many girlfriends in our son's life. I won't pretend that I was really laughing inside when they broke each other's hearts by realizing that they really weren't as madly in love as they had thought four or five months later, but I did pretend that I understood my teenage son's short-lived grief.

All I knew was that my family had dodged an Agent Orange bullet at that point in time. Since our youngest son was only four-years-old, I wasn't thinking about the far future of when Alex became a grown man with a child of his own. I was also, at that time of my life being Super Activist. I was going to change the world in a short time and never doubted that Johnny, myself and A.O.V.N.J. were going to solve this problem and force the government to test, treat and compensate our vets and our children in the very near future. There was no way back then that we *weren't* going to win the Agent Orange Sweepstakes, except, just like every other lottery, unless you buy a ticket you don't stand a chance to win it. If the Veterans Administration and the Department of Defense owned up to their actions and their responsibilities to the Vets, much less to their children, how could they possibly afford any more of the "great for big business" wars that they had on the drawing board? They couldn't, so they didn't and now, in 2013, Vietnam Agent Orange Veterans who survived the horrendous cancers of the first few years, are dying at the average of 285 per day, across the country or wherever they have moved. The average life expectancy seems to be approximately sixty to sixty-five years at most. So that by the year 2020, the name of the first book written about Vietnam Vets, "Waiting for an Army to Die" will be a completed American task.

CHAPTER TEN

THE SAINT OF THE VIETNAM VETERANS, OUR HOLINESS MAUDE DEVICTOR

IF YOU RECALL, in an earlier chapter, I related that the very first time I had ever heard the words "Agent Orange", was in August of 1977, which was the beginning of what would become an unbelievable life. However, in June of 1977, a woman, a Veteran herself and an employee of the Chicago Office of the Veterans Administration; a person who I had never heard of before would become my dearest friend and the most important human being on this Earth, with the exception of my own family. Her name is Maude DeVictor and if I lived an unbelievable life, then the only way I can describe her life would be the closest thing to sainthood and suffering, because of her love for her fellow Veterans, than any person I have ever known to exist. This woman, a devout Buddhist and the most private human being I've ever known, changed my life and changed history through me because without knowing her and everything she stood for, no one would have ever known what the government had done to such a large portion of our generation. Maude was not a very vocal or extroverted person, but she was one of the first "whistle-blowers" in government history and eventually what was done to her by that government did create and change the laws to protect those who came forward. No one, however, was there to save or protect Maude DeVictor except for people like myself, Annie Bailey and our respective Veteran followers. I have always considered it the greatest honor that Maude, because of her quiet personality and understated ways, chose me to speak out for her and lead the way down the path that she had cleared before me. So, it must be understood that whatever I have been credited with accomplishing, had it not been for Maude DeVictor's intervention, Vietnam veterans and their children would have died unnoticed and without anyone ever knowing the truth.

Maude's journey began on June 11, 1977, when she, as a VA caseworker received a call from a woman, Ethel Owens, whose husband Charles, a Veteran of twenty-four years was dying from cancer that the Veterans Administration was denying was "service-connected" and this woman needed help. It was Ethel who told Maude about the "chemicals sprayed in Vietnam" and that her husband had consistently told her that if he died, those chemicals would be the reason. Because of Maude's tenacity, when Charles Owens passed away, she actually forced the VA into compensating Ethel for her loss, which was totally unprecedented at that time. Maude had become the foremost authority on Agent Orange at that time and while the VA did everything that it could to discourage her and finally fired her in 1982, leaving her without any medical coverage or income while she was fighting her own cancer at the time. For as much as the VA and the "system" wanted to stop her in her crusade to help the Vietnam Veterans effected by Agent Orange, the Veterans themselves made her their hero, and those of us who were very organized and had set up a strong network after our Dewey Canyon IV collaboration in DC, we were able to raise the monies needed for Maude's surgeries and her welfare, thereby saving her life. Because of the 1982 VA firing, Maude was virtually blacklisted and was not able to return to the workforce. In 1983, Maude came to New York for the Agent Orange Lawsuit hearings and moved in with Johnny and I until late in 1984 when she decided to move back to Chicago, and then on to California, where she still lives. Maude DeVictor was very involved and instrumental to the Agent Orange Lawsuit in Brooklyn, New York Federal Court and never missed even one court date, cancer or no cancer.

At the same time as Maude was taking on the Agent Orange fight in Chicago, a Vietnam veteran named Paul Reutershan who lived in Connecticut, was diagnosed with cancer and he also blamed the spraying in Southeast Asia. He, with another vet, Frank McCarthy started a group known as Agent Orange Victims International which was instrumental in the filing of the Agent Orange Lawsuit against the eleven chemical companies that manufactured the contaminated dioxin death that was sprayed in Vietnam. Unfortunately, Paul Reutershan died from his cancer in December of 1978, but before he passed away, Maude had already interested Bill Kurtis of the Chicago CBS affiliate station to do a documentary called "Agent Orange: The Deadly Fog", featuring both Paul's situation and Maude's efforts. This was the first legitimate acknowledgment of what had been done to those of us who trusted in our own government. As soon as it aired, the VA Headquarters in Washington DC issued an order to their Chicago office at the Lakeside VA Hospital where Maude worked stating that she was to be kept far away from Vietnam Veterans and to "limit reporters and the media" from Maude, "as much as possible". So much for the Land of the Free and the

Home of the Brave.

While Maude was living in our home in New Jersey, on November 10th, 1984, on Veteran's Day, there was a television movie, titled "Unnatural Causes", starring John Ritter as "Frank" and Alfrie Woodard as "Maude DeVictor". It was done with such caring and talent that the Chicago VA which had terminated Maude two years earlier, received so many phone calls from all over the United States, that somehow, someone inside the VA was able to not only find out that Maude was now living with the Kopystenski family, but started giving out our unlisted private home phone number and address to anyone that called. Just in case our ongoing paranoia about the government watching us since Johnny and I first came out publicly in 1979, was actually "all our imagination" as we had been told when we complained to the government, the fact that within hours of the broadcast, our private address and home phone number were made public by the Veterans Administration proved the fact that "just because you're paranoid, doesn't mean that they're not out to get you" theory is not a valid one. For me, the best part of that television movie was not only the cameo of Maude in the film, but the fact that Aunt Maude had given our son Alex, a stuffed alligator with a logo patch of a man on its shirt, and Alex had given her a small stuffed piggy in a suit and hat, with a briefcase and the initials "VIP" on his jacket, and both toys were panned onto by the camera during the movie as they sat on a shelf behind Alfrie Woodard's (Maude's) desk. Two very strong women who were taking on the entire government, all teary eyed and touched by two stuffed animals, displayed repeatedly by a television camera, who could believe it? Nearly thirty years later, that alligator still sits on the top of my dresser. Even though Alex's puppy had gotten hold of it years ago and chewed off an arm, we bandaged it and made a sling on which we placed and Agent Orange button which it still brandishes for authenticity, as a constant reminder of our dear friend Maude. During one of our infrequent telephone conversations last year, when I mentioned that I had the alligator, Maude told me that VIP Piggy is still sitting on her dresser as well.

In 1981, Frank McCarthy, on behalf of his friend, the late Frank Reutershan, made it his life's mission to convince a Long Island, New York attorney, Victor Yannacone to file a class action suit against Dow Chemical Company and the other ten companies that made the Agent Orange that was used in Vietnam. In order to file such a lawsuit, there had to be "unnamed plaintiff Vietnam Veterans" from all over the country and there also had to be at least one "named plaintiff" from each state. One of the New York television station reporters gave our names to Mr. Yannacone and Johnny agreed to become the named plaintiff from New Jersey. Victor Yannacone and his wife Carol, for reasons no capitalist could ever understand, took on this lawsuit of all lawsuits and became our champions.

These two people bought the vacant house next door to their own and set up an office to house the truckloads of papers that were being sent in to them from Veterans, widows and other lawyers from all over, not just America, but from the members of the Allied Forces all over the globe. Both of the Yannacone's were unlike anyone in the legal profession any of us had ever met. They never dodged a phone call and if they didn't have the answer to a question about what was causing, or what could be tried for an Agent Orange child's health problem, they would tell people who to call. Or they would offer to check on the question and call back; which they always did. They also wouldn't accept any offer of financial help from any Veteran family, stating that this was a Tort case which meant that they would be paid if and when they won the case. It was their belief that the Vets had given enough and done enough to be asked for anything more. Eventually, however, the costs of the lawsuit became so high that Victor had to bring in other attorneys who didn't have the Yannacone's high moral values, a subject to be covered later on. The Yannacone's also supported my desire to study Tort Law and civil liberties with regard to the Feros Doctrine and being poisoned by one's government. They sent A.O.V.N.J. copies of every piece of paper filed in the case and a list of law books for me to study. Annie Bailey took it upon herself to become one of the most accomplished "high school graduates" as she liked to call herself, to have infinite information regarding the herbicides, their effects and cases from all over the world. We were a formidable group, if I do say so myself.

In 1982, our son Alex, was recommended by his Day School for early enrollment in public school because he was very precocious and had been speaking in grammatically correct sentences from the age of two. Johnny and I were concerned about the fact that as bright as he was, he seemed to be an auditory learner who we couldn't seem to teach how to read. He could retain anything he heard or saw, including being able to give directions to go anywhere in the car after just being taken to that destination one time, regardless of whether it was in our town or even when we drove up to Boston. But being able to visually read letters, words, numbers, etc. was a major frustration for him. At a Veteran's event, I was talking about our concern over Alex with Victor Yannacone and a colleague of his, Dr. Waxman who was a doctor and an attorney. Dr. Waxman asked me if we had ever had our boy tested for any neurological problems, which, we hadn't and then he suggested that he arrange for a pediatric neurologist friend of his to examine Alex. His friend's name was Dr. Bennett Shaywitz, the Head of Pediatric Neurology at Yale University and, as I would find out later on, was considered by his peers to be the finest in his field in the entire country. We asked Dr. Waxman if he would set that up for us and figured that it would take weeks or maybe even months to get in to see such a specialist.

There was no way that we could have expected that four days later, I would be driving my son to Yale University to meet with not only Dr. Bennett Shaywitz but also his partner and wife, Dr. Sheila Shaywitz, the second best pediatric neurologist in the United States. The doctors spent an entire day testing and examining Alex. When we went back the next morning to get the results which, had we perhaps gone to lesser professionals, would have been devastating. We learned that Alex had a very high intelligence quota (IQ) however, he had at least eight different types of learning differences. We have always said "learning differences" because both Drs. Shaywitz explained that our son could learn everything and anything, he just had to learn it differently.

They also had taken it upon themselves to arrange for a second and third opinion within the jurisdiction of the State of New Jersey, because that was where we lived and where his education would be taking place. The first visit was to St. Barnabas Pediatrics and the third was at Princeton University Medical, all three concurred, and we then went to the school system and asked them to run their own testing procedures. Even though the school wanted to accept the Yale findings as well as the others, Johnny and I explained that those facilities were not going to be teaching our son, so we needed to have them test him and give us their findings, as well as how they intended to provide him with what he needed to get a quality education. Then and only then would we share the findings of the experts. There are no words to adequately express how angry we were when the school system, which was supposed to be one of the best in the state, came back with a finding that our son, was "High IQ Ineducable", What Did That Mean? We just sat there and stared at them with our mouths open until finally Johnny stood up and said "Our Kid, Our Problem!"

We had already discussed the idea of homeschooling and were comfortable with it. I had joined the ACLD which is the Association for Children with Learning Disabilities, and had spoken with a number of educators who ran private schools in other cities across the country to get their input on what steps I had to take and things I had to learn in order to create an effective educational program for our son. Hundreds of dollars were spent buying and reading books written by supposed professionals each of whom had their own ideas about what worked best for what conditions. It was from these books that we built an educational profile for home schooling and created varied methods to teach a child with a magnificent intellectual ability and eight different forms of learning disabilities to master every subject he needed to succeed.

Before we could get busy with our own educational programs, we had to contend with a school system that had just told us that in their estimation, our child could not be educated, but when we filed with the system that *we* were going to teach Alex at home, we were informed that we had to adhere to their curriculum. That made absolutely no sense to us because if he was not educable according to their expertise, how were they going to provide the lesson plans? Since one of Alex's weaknesses was dyscholcolia which was dyslexia with math or numbers, I had seen a method of math that was being used in Korea, known as Chisanbop or Finger-math, which used fingers like a computer or even an abacus. Complex math could be achieved by using just ten fingers, with the left hand being singles and the right hand representing tens. So I found a bookstore that had the textbook and the workbooks and bypassed the dyslexic "crossed wires of the brain". There were so many different ways to teach a multiple dyslexic, one just had to find the one way that the child could learn and that was what made learning easy.

I had even taken a course with a special education expert who would turn an entire room of educators and parents into dyslexics so that they could understand how our children saw the world and faced life and learning. But, first Johnny and I had to take the Board of Education to court because we were refusing to follow the district's rule of having to follow their curriculum for a child that they had basically told us to throw in the trash. We won, but more importantly because we were constantly in the media as Agent Orange activists, the amount of publicity given to the shortcomings of the special education capabilities because we dared to bring it all out into the light, not only helped to make changes in the way special education was handled, but also brought out publicly thousands of Vietnam Veteran families who had children with learning differences. The funniest part of the local situation was that a PTA for Special Need Kids was founded and for the first year of its existence, I, who didn't have a child in the system, was the president since it had been the big fuss that Johnny and I had made that woke up other parents to the fact that things could be changed.

There were some very serious upsides to homeschooling because Alex's luekopenia was a constant source of concern when it came to his involvement with too many different normal germs especially in a classroom setting. A child with a common cold, could innocently create pneumonia or influenza if Alex's white cell count was stressed, and we were relieved not to have to make him feel like he had to stay away from other children, or to feel like he was different, even though he was. There was also an incredible educational advantage because homeschooling is basically a 24/7 process, while the normal school day provides approximately twenty minutes of education for every forty minute class, which means that those twenty minutes must be divided amongst however many children are in the class. Because homeschooling means that the child or children are at home most of the time, Alex spent many hours listening to Mommy lecturing in auditoriums, classrooms and on college campuses about a multitude of different subjects. He didn't even realize how much more he knew by age ten about world history, world geography, social studies and environmental biology until he was a grown man who was having a conversation with some other young men. The subject of Iran-Contra and Oliver North came up and he was amazed that at age twenty-six, these young men didn't have a clue about what he was talking about. We had to fight everyone in order to provide Alex with the best teaching we had to give, and he completed his studies by age fourteen and started his higher education. Today, he is an entertainer on the Las Vegas Strip who still has health problems but has an incredible education.

As much as I would like to say that having gotten to know Maude DeVictor, Victor Yannacone and so many other "door openers" were wonderful strokes of luck as far as helping with bad situations, there is no way that I could ever say anything about meeting and knowing those people and all the others, other than "we were blessed to have gotten some help". But, life probably would have been so much easier if Vietnam had never happened to us or to them. Since then we probably would never have needed the help to keep people alive, educated, medically cared for, financially compensated, and on, and on… Finding out about Alex's learning problems after so many health issues was always a sore spot with me when I realized that seven out of every ten children born to Vietnam veteran families have similar or worse neurological problems. As much as I would like to believe that all parents had the ability, the finances and the patience to live as Johnny, Alex and I did for so many years, I would be fooling myself and that makes me sad. Not because I think that any parent was somehow lacking if they couldn't do what we did, but because especially from what we saw in the Veteran family community, they would have if it were at all possible.

After 1982, the Agent Orange lawsuit was taking up much of my time and effort doing research, helping compile data and running into court in Brooklyn or meetings all over the Eastern Seaboard and Washington DC. Since Alex was either always right next to me or he would go to work with his dad and do his studies in the truck while Johnny drove, I was always surprised that Alex didn't become a lawyer by the age of twelve. Back in the early 80's, involving children in demonstrations and civil disobedience efforts was not something that protesters did. Not because it was "no place for children", especially in situations where the results being fought for involved matters which effected children; but because very often grownups thought that children had no opinions about the subjects at hand. Or that they would be in the way somehow. A.O.V.N.J. was probably one of the first dissent organizations whose members saved money on babysitters by incorporating their children into the fight for research, testing, treatment and compensation based upon the belief that it was the child's life that was being fought for. When Alex was being diagnosed by the school system, one of the tests that was required was that he be seen by a school sanctioned "optometrist" in case his stupid professional parents didn't think to have his eyes checked. And so I took him to the doctor picked by the team. When the doctor came out he acknowledged us, and held his office door open for us. When my five year old son walked behind me, the doctor stopped us and said that Alex could wait in the waiting room. I was perplexed, how was he going to check my son's eyes without my son's face being in the examining room? He responded to my look of confusion by telling me that he "never talked in front of a child". I must admit that I have a very short fuse when dealing with the "stupid-factor". I said to this mad scientist, "You seem to have a problem with problem ownership, doctor! I don't need an eye exam and I'm not a dyslexic. My child is, however, required to be examined and he is dyslexic. I am merely his assisting grownup and quite honestly, I could die tomorrow and he would be very sad, but HE WOULD STILL BE DYSLEXIC. So, he needs to be present when anyone is discussing him and if he has any questions or needs any other information, he will tell me and I will make sure that you advise him so he can learn how to deal with people who are supposed to be helping him!" I also gave the doctor the ultimatum of either rethinking his policy, at least where my son was concerned or I could go to the school board and insist that they stop wasting my property taxes on fools.

Our involving our Agent Orange effected children was based on the same logic used on the eye doctor, it was their lives and they needed to understand what was going on, in a way that was in keeping with their age and ability at processing the information as well as learning how to deal with strangers who held the key to doors they needed to be opened. One of the perks of involving our children was how much fun they seemed to have in marching and posing and yelling out slogans! Some families go to the playgrounds and some march down Fifth Avenue in New York City. Hey, whatever floats your boat, right?

Earlier, I related how our son marched down Constitution Avenue with his dad at the Vietnam Veterans Welcome Home Parade in Washington DC, and there was also the New York Welcome Home Parade where Alex again wanted to march with his dad, but the step off was on the Brooklyn side of the Brooklyn Bridge with the Veterans walking over the bridge and then through Manhattan. Johnny insisted that I take Alex to the Manhattan side via taxi because the walking path of the bridge was steel slatted with large separations between the slats through which one could see the water of the East River and he was nervous about Alex's little feet getting stuck in between those slats. I teased him for years that it was his fear of heights that could only be handled from the open side of a Huey with an AK47 in his hands! Alex vowed to never forgive us for not letting him march over that bridge, but he eventually stopped complaining about it after about ten years! My greatest memory of that New York Event was a gift to the Veterans from, of all people, Donald Trump who provided the most incredible firework show

I had ever seen and have yet to see anything to compare. The fireworks were shot from boats in the Hudson River while we all assembled at the 23rd St. Sea Port, a brand new open-air area at the time, with a glass wall filled with letters to Veterans encased as a monument. The firework show went on for over forty-five minutes, with music being played and simulcast on all of the New York radio stations. As much as I have never been a big Trump fan, I have to give the man his due for what he did for us all that night. It was magnificent and there was the most incredible feeling of closeness and joy amongst the thousands of veterans and their families in attendance, however, one could not help but wish that it had taken place ten or so years earlier when the last Combat Vets actually came home.

A.O.V.N.J. in cooperation with the Ironbound Residents Association, had arranged a joint demonstration at the Diamond Shamrock Chemical Plant in Newark, New Jersey, in 1984, and the turnout was terrific. Even our kids were psyched up because one of the members had told us to make sure that all the kids brought either their very trendy Cabbage Patch dolls or favorite stuffed animals with them to the demonstration line. We had become much more professional from our original efforts at the East Orange VA Hospital, and there were not only banners and placards for all the grownups, but someone had made little picket signs on long straws to be attached to the hands or paws of the children's dolls depicting discontent with Diamond Shamrock. The kids were very vocal and were bobbing their dolls up and down while demonstrating which made a really great photo event for the media.

About a half hour after we had begun, all the cameramen and the media trucks quickly packed up and just left in a hurry. The agents sitting a half block away that we weren't supposed to know were there, but they were always just a half a block away from everyplace we all went. Maybe not always the same two guys, but they were all like clones in the way they just sat and dressed while trying to look nonchalant and invisible. It was always puzzling to me that these "agents" whether they worked for the government or the chemical companies or even Santa Claus never stopped to think that the people they were supposed to be "watching without being noticed" had spent time in a jungle constantly watching out for snipers and enemies hidden in the strangest places because that was the only way they could stay alive was by being vigilant and aware. How could they figure that if they sat in a car, in plain view no one would notice them?

It was after the demonstration was over and we all went home, that we heard on the evening news that Freehold Race Track had caught fire and burned down. Freehold, where our Vet Center was put the kibosh on our demonstration 45 miles away. So the topic of laughter throughout the entire Movement was based on the fact that the government burned down one of the oldest horse racing tracks in the entire United States just to take the news watching eyes of the citizens off the demonstration of Cabbage Patch dolls at a major chemical plant.

In March of 1983, A.O.V.N.J. made headlines and the front page of all of the Central and South New Jersey newspapers by simply taking part in a St. Patrick's Day Parade in the town of Keyport. It was also the last time our organization was ever invited back to anything in Keyport, New Jersey. Keep in mind that our mission was to bring awareness to the plight of not only our effected Combat Veterans, but to our entire families because of the number of birth defects and the mortality rates of Vets and their children. We also wanted attention to the fact that neither the Veterans Administration nor any other agency was even recognizing what was happening to us. So, when we were invited to join the parade and told that we were expected to create and display a float, Johnny and the other guys came up with one Hell of a float and worked hard on evenings and weekends to build their creation. They also had decided that we, their wives, would not be told anything about it until the day of the parade. The response to what they had come up with was almost as shocking to us, as it was to every other person at the event and then to everyone who watched the news or read the newspapers.

It was a beautiful day and the float was built on a full size trailer which had been filled with plants in planters, flowers and a real look of spring, with Vets, their wives and small children all standing and waving to the crowds, with our organization name spelled out on full banners on both sides of the float. Onlookers smiled and waved as we went by. But then, right before the float was getting close to the reviewing stands and the television cameras, the truck pulling the float slowed down to an almost stop, moving very slowly. Suddenly, the vets reached over the side of the float and pulled an incredibly large tarp over everything, like a caterpillar climbing into a cocoon. Just as the float got to the beginning of the reviewing stand, the tarp was removed and on the float, the pretty bushes and flowers had turned into planters with just leafless twigs and dead flowers; the men and women were wearing gas masks and Scot Packs and in the women's outstretched arms were children lying very still, like corpses, while their mothers looked down at them in despair. The signage on the tarp side was no longer Agent Orange Victims of New Jersey; it spelled out in bring red letters "AGENT ORANGE KILLS". The vets pulled out plastic spray bottles which were filled with orange liquid (water with food coloring) and started spraying the onlookers with the spray bottles!!!!

People looked horrified at the float; the television cameras and newsmen were filming and taking pictures as fast as they could and then when the spraying started, everyone within reach was turning and running or putting their hands up to their faces and moving backwards as fast as they could. Still can't figure out why they never invited us back, but we certainly got everyone's attention on that day. If memory serves me, that effort was what put an end to most of the claims that we were making it all up and that Vietnam Vets were malingerers because when we were interviewed by the media at the end of the parade, we just all said the same thing, "What was everyone running from if they say that we have just been making up stories about our illnesses and our children's birth defects?" After that even those parades and events that we *were* invited to take part in, knew about Keyport. Every one of the people inviting us made us promise "No Floats!" We had made our voices heard, our message was out and none of us wanted to do all that physical labor anymore anyway.

These were the kind of things that we needed to come up with in order to bring attention to our cause and our reasons because we were very well aware that when groups or organizations make a splash, and then do nothing else, their cause is soon and easily forgotten. The Vietnam Veterans were fighting a war caused by a war that they were forced into fighting and that was the big difference. For every imaginative stunt or creative effort we came up with to stay in the public eye, our reality was that if our membership dwindled, it wasn't due to anyone quitting the group. They were dying and our children all needed each other because too many citizens looked at a child with no arms, a cleft palate or an obvious shunt, like he or she was some sort of freak. Whether our children had outward signs of defect or, like our Alex, except for the fading limp, looked perfect and healthy, the beautiful thing was that none of our children ever looked at each other as anything but friends. They not only understood when a child had a seizure or an emotional meltdown, or needed to stop playing to take their meds, but they took care of each other like the littlest Vietnam Veterans that they were.

CHAPTER ELEVEN

SACRIFICIAL LAMBS, MALINGERERS AND OTHER OUTCAST HEROES

SINCE MOST OF THE PEOPLE who serve in the military come from the part of society that is the majority of the population known as blue collar, the working poor and the lower middle class often children of those who served before. Of course, as in any society, there are generals' children and other high ranking officer's kids who are admitted to military academies such as West Point, Annapolis. Or students are only getting in if Dad knows a senator. Those places are basically just institutions for the families of the 1%. However, no one in the general population, when thinking about Veterans, ever thinks about West Point cadets, they think of Cousin Joey or Uncle Bill's son (or daughter now) who either couldn't afford college or didn't have the grades or the ambition to spend four more years in school. Once the draft was over and there was no war, the military was a good place to get some type of training and a steady paycheck, even though it wasn't a very large paycheck. Besides, girls really liked guys in uniforms, so enlistment was a sort of win-win for a couple of years; as long as no fighting broke out anywhere that our government could find a reason to stick their two cents in. After a day's work, there was always beer and the camaraderie of hanging out at the bars or doing guy-stuff with one's buddies, so what could be bad?

Up until the mid-60's, most veterans could be found at whichever service organizations their buddies belonged to or were closest to where they lived. Places like the V.F.W. Post, the American Legion, the Elks Club or the D.A.V., etc. were where "men could be men" and talk about "their war", making up stories or pretending to be heroes and getting drunk. But, when the guys came home from Vietnam, most of them never wanted to talk about what they had been through. Very few of them made up stories either because the real stories were more frightening than anyone could imagine; and besides, those Veterans Clubs were never a place where they felt welcome.

The other, but more telling reasons that they didn't feel comfortable or welcome at the V.F.W.'S etc., was because the older vets, the guys from "The Big Wars I & II" were, very often, hostile to their younger counterparts and their reasoning was always an insulting insinuation that somehow, the new guys were "guys with no power" who had "lost their war". While reality, especially in the mindset of males raised in the days of the good old boys, dictates that a man can go for years without sex, but not even one full day without a good rationalization, the hatred and the pretense at superiority of the older Veterans, realistically didn't have a whole lot to do with the war and who won what. It had to do with two-and-a-half million young men coming back into American society and threatening the feelings of entitlement that the older men had taken for granted. These young guys, with their strange taste in music, their good looks and their relaxed clothing choices, and all those young women who "Grandpa Vet" would watch and fantasize about, but never try to engage in a conversation because their wives would kill them, were now hanging all over these new Vets.

The new Vets, as soon as they got back, would let their hair grow long and grew beards and mustaches, which the older guys, because of convention, could never have done. These boom babies were annoying with their cars and their personal freedom and besides, didn't they all smoke that "grass or pot" and do drugs? So, the best way to handle this massive number of new Vets was to perpetrate a sense of disdain to hide the insecurity and jealousy felt by men who were in their forties and fifties and life had passed them by. They had shitty jobs and even shittier lives that they could try to pretend didn't exist when they were at their make-believe clubhouses and now these young guys who didn't have to "live the right way" and were able to be whatever they wanted, now wanted to invade their space. No way! The consequence of bad behavior was that those who came back from Vietnam did not need any new enemies or to be made to feel that their sacrifices weren't enough or appreciated and so what the older Vets did was, by far, more inhumane and ugly than any civilized people should behave toward their own counterparts who had just come back from the same Hell that they had endured all those years ago.

Before going into the history of the survival of the Vietnam Veterans, it is really important, from the get-go to explain that rather than emulating the bad behaviors of the Veterans who came before them, the Vietnam Combat Veterans have to be recognized and admired more than even they could ever have realized, because they taught America about how a citizen who puts their life on the line for a whole country of strangers and often for no reason other than the greed of society's upper class, is supposed to be treated while they are fighting and especially when they return home. Wide support for those who served in the Middle East not only while they were overseas, but especially upon their return is a direct result of the Vietnam Veteran community receiving their younger brothers and sisters, with arms wide open and teaching the new Veterans that they are welcome in the organizations that the veterans of Southeast Asia created to replace the original good old boys clubs. And by using the old adage of "God Bless the Child That's Got His Own", they assisted in showing and standing shoulder to shoulder with the "young'uns" to teach them how the system is supposed to work. Organizations such as Veterans For Peace grew in membership size by the joining together of Veterans from Vietnam to Afghanistan. The multitude of problems encountered with the VA by the Vietnam Veterans may not have shrunk in problematic size, but because of what the older guys went through mostly on their own, the new Vets now at least have allies and sounding boards. As lonely as the personal journey of someone who has been in combat may be, the guys who came home and were made to feel even more alone, is why they now go out of their way to ease the loneliness and often the suicidal despair being faced by their younger counterparts.

The best thing that the Vietnam Veterans fought to get and, just like all else at the time, had to create, build and staff by themselves, were and are the Vet Centers throughout the United States. While the methods and the services afforded to the Veterans who now go to the Vet Centers may have become more professional and even more clinical, the purpose and the original protocol has not changed from the days when this author was instrumental in their creation. That remains an incredible source of personal pride for this old lady, who used to be the young wife running around with a broomstick and a spaghetti pot on her head.

In 1979 when A.O.V.N.J. set up their original Vet Center we taught the spouses and significant others that when their Veteran came home from work, to give him space to unwind, and as much peace and quiet as a house, especially with small children could afford. We advised to wait to give him bad news, good news or really any news until it was obvious that he was wound down from dealing with whatever and whomever his job required him to deal with. That was the best direction that we could provide to avoid conflict or chaos. However, in today's society, the Veteran can very easily be Mommy, or both Mommy and Daddy, so what do they do now? Yes, the world has changed a whole lot, but at least now there is not the added pressure of those who served turning on those who served more recently which, this author takes pride in having had a part in changing. These niceties or broader ways of thinking do not mean that depression, combat flashbacks, thoughts of suicide and violent outbursts are no longer a part of the Veteran experience. To be quite honest, there are more suicides today than the many that we, in the Vietnam Vet community ever had to deal with back in our time. To my way of thinking this is an outcome from the same DEROS date that put war-stressed youngsters back on Main St. without any deprogramming or understanding within hours of leaving a war zone. That inhumane practice is now small potatoes when based upon the members of a volunteer military being thrown back into the war zones on a constant basis. Some are going back four or five times and it is almost as if these young patriots are so expendable that they are just being used until they are broken completely.

These words may not sound very supportive of our government's misconception of what freedom should cost, but they are simply the way that I and most of the Vietnam Veteran community see what is being done, once again to the nation's best and brightest. The number of armed troops are much lower than the draftee figures were because it is all-volunteer military and yet the number of combat scenarios are higher as a part of the government's uncaring redeployment policy and the politicians' need to appease their contractors and big business donors. Those who serve in the halls of the Congress and the Senate, regardless of what their personal financial worth was when they were first elected, are now all millionaires many times over. It is for this greed that young men and women must die to feed the coffers of those who think that they are kings.

The biggest tragedy that has never changed in the most progressive country and society on Earth is the overwhelmed system known as the Veterans Administration. Had Ronnie RayGun not convinced Chuck Hagel to take over the VA, even if it was just for one year until Chuck became too frustrated by the waste and stupidity, there never would have been the VA Vet Centers, which depending upon who is in charge on a local level, usually run more efficiently than the incredibly well-funded VA. However, when the veterans came back from Southeast Asia, the care and service wasn't there because of inept management and a total lack of concern over anything other than the problems that were considered as caused by the war. For example, if someone was injured and their legs didn't work, well, let's just try to either fix those legs or get the man a wheelchair. But, if the man's legs worked except that they were covered with a sort of fungus known as chloracne which was rapidly and painfully eating his skin from exposure to Agent Orange, well, this guy probably inherited a skin condition from his ancestors! No one bothered to think that a case of really bad chloracne could only be inherited if one's ancestor was an armadillo. That if a veteran was having trouble hearing, well, he was probably effected by the shelling and was suffering from hearing loss and even some slight "shell shock" (oops, wrong war), so let's get him hearing aids. If what he's having trouble with, though, had to do with hearing strange voices or imagining that he hears the enemy coming for him, well then pump him full of anti-psychotics, tranquilizers and pain pills and send him home to shoot himself in the head or to first shoot his family and then himself. That was the "Old VA" which had not yet heard of computers. The new VA is actually more medically concerned BUT, Still Has Yet To Hear About Computers!!!

Because of the ways of war as they are now, there are less body bags filled with young Americans, but there are far more young Americans who need medical care and services which an agency that is funded by billions of dollars should be able to provide, especially for the walking wounded who need disability and compensation funding. Yet because of the paper mountains, while the rest of the country's medical and relief services are computerized, the VA, without computerization, has hundreds of thousands of returning Vets who are receiving no help for even daily living expenses. Theodore Roosevelt said (as was posted on AOVNJ's stationery): ***"A man who is willing to shed his blood for his country, deserves a square deal afterward"*** and that makes sense, or at least it did before big business, major corporations and wealthy PAC's became more important than "a man's (or woman's) blood".

In the early 80's, the VA did not recognize the illnesses and conditions caused by dioxin poisoning at all. When there was some acceptance, it was very minor and included only conditions like chloracne, but not the cancers or any of the other medical problems. The only thing that the VA would even consider compensating was combat stress or as we had named it PTSD. Even then, their criteria to be accepted as suffering from this very broad list of symptoms, was limited to some very simple and ridiculous behaviors and situations. For example, my husband was a classic case of PTSD, from the flashbacks to the anger issues, the punching of walls and the night terrors and so many more. Yet, when we went to the VA and he was questioned by the psychiatrist who was determining the condition that is really not a psychiatric one, but psychological, they asked him just two questions. He came out of the interview and told me that the doctor had denied him having stress syndrome. The "shrink" asked him if he wet the bed, to which he said no, as most males would never admit to even if they did. And then he was asked if he ever hit his wife; his response to that was "You obviously don't know my wife!"

I was livid with Johnny and told him to go back into that room and tell the doctor that he was too embarrassed to admit that yes, he did wet the bed and yes, he did hit his wife. He was granted 40% disability compensation for PTSD and then because he had jumped out of a burning Huey and had messed up his ankle, which caused him pain all of his life, they gave him a 10% disability for that injury. What we learned from that experience became an exercise that was practiced all over the country amongst our network organizations. Knowing that if you got hurt in a firefight they would give you a whopping 10% or about $45.00 per month compensation, but if you wet the bed, that was worth over $400.00 a month, it became almost a game to get men who were sick from dioxin poisoning to be able to go to the VA hospitals and doctors because they were "service-connected" even if it was for bed-wetting., But they would treat you for your other ailments anyway if you were 40% or more. The other thing that the psychiatrists would immediately do was to prescribe anti-anxiety pills, scheduled pain pills, tranquilizers and anything else they had a lot of, in big bottles filled with a three-month supply of five-a-day pills.

An example of what actions had to be taken just to get our guys medically treated, is best described by our sojourn to Chicago. I and some of our AOVNJ members flew into O'Hare Airport and were picked up by VVAW members who took us to where we were staying and then we went to a meeting hall where there were, over two or three days, hundreds of vets who we coached and even denied some sleep to prepare for the C&P examinations at the VA. One of the most curious phenomenon was how many of the Combat Vets had the good sense to marry women who worked in the nursing field. How that proved to be very helpful was in situations where a Vet was not that comfortable in speaking to anyone at the VA or was insecure about his ability to explain his condition. One of the nurse-wives, would go with Vets, stating that they were either their wives or girlfriends; because they were licensed and registered nurses, the medical staff was happier talking to them anyway. As crazy as all this may sound forty years later, that's how insane we believed the Veterans Administration staff and protocol were at the time. There were a number of doctors working at the VA who either were Veterans of the Big War or English was a second language that they hadn't learned yet. Their attitudes were that the Vietnam Vets were lying, malingering or pretending, and for a very short time there were cases where these so called medical professionals were out and out hostile and condescending to the vets. But just like I had originally warned the vets that they would stop punching holes in their walls just as soon as one of their fists came in contact with the beam in the wall (OUCH!), these ill-suited medical workers learned very quickly that saying the wrong and insulting thing to a really stressed Vietnam veteran while he was in an agitated state could and most often would cause them great physical pain. It always concerned me that a doctor who was working with men he considered to be suffering from drug addiction, violent malingering, etc. would deliberately go into a closed door room with the guy and piss him off. Sounds pretty crazy to me. It did seem that over time, these doctors had some attitude adjustments, but it did take longer than expected. Dealing with the Veterans Administration medical workers was very similar to falling down a rabbit hole, because one never knew how long they were going to be stuck in the rabbit hole of a waiting room, or what was going to happen when their name was called.

As the non-military population became more familiar with what they perceived to be the "typical Vietnam Vet", life in the real world really had its moments. The image of the Vet was flawed because of the simple fact that the only help that they could get from the system was based upon the system thinking that they were just plain crazy. So once the media found out and did news stories about the tens of thousands of veterans who were being treated for psychological problems, or were, as the Vietnamese said "Beau Coo Dinky Dou" (lots of nuts), people began to not only give them a wide berth to avoid any confrontations. Also due to some of the ridiculous movies that were coming out, like *First Blood* and *Apocalypse Now*, rumor had it that all Vietnam Vets were Marshall Arts experts. This was silly, but the guys never corrected the misconception because they got left alone due to fear of the myth. But, all too often, those who did not serve formed a totally insane concept about the normal condition of those who experienced Vietnam.

One Christmas week, Johnny and I took the kids for a winter

vacation to visit my parents in Las Vegas. We had rented a Lincoln Town Car because we needed a large vehicle to fit everyone in and were having a wonderful vacation until Johnny moved the wrong way and pulled his back out. He was in an awful lot of pain and so we decided to take him to the Emergency Room at Desert Springs Hospital. Because of Agent Orange and the health problems that we were familiar with amongst Vets and their children, the Veterans Movement cautioned our members to always make medical professionals aware of the possibility of dioxin related illnesses when going anywhere for care other than to one's own doctors. So, I drove Johnny to the hospital and then I went inside to tell them that we needed a gurney and some assistance to get my husband out of the car and into the hospital. I then said to the receptionist to please make a note that my husband was an Agent Orange Vietnam Veteran, so that the doctors could check before giving him any medications. The attendant who had gone to get the gurney and was standing there when I told the woman behind the desk about Johnny's health, cut into our conversation and asked if since my husband was a Viet vet, should he go and get a STRAIGHT JACKET..... I was quite taken aback by that question because we, despite our political efforts, lived in a pretty boring and normal world, but then I looked at the attendant and asked him if I should be concerned about whether he (himself) needed a restraining device? I just said "Why, are you feeling psychotic?" I was hoping that he would give me some creative retort and get out of this embarrassing moment, but he just looked at me all confused. This encounter was a speaking point for me, for years to come and I can only hope that sometime, somehow, somebody explained to that attendant that he was an idiot.

There was a very large group of citizens who were unbelievably accepting, caring and helpful and who embraced the Veterans for the men that they were. In trying to show the general public just who the AOVNJ Vets were and what generous people and neighbors they could be, at a time when the government had decided, instead of providing jobs or raising the minimum wage, to issue free commodities to the needy. In New Jersey there was a problem in finding social service agencies to distribute butter and cheese without charging the state more than the free food would've been valued at. Our organization was discussing this distribution that we had read about in the newspapers and started to talk about why if the government wanted to give away commodities they had to pay tens of thousands of dollars per county, twenty-one counties in the state, every time they were to have a giveaway. It made no sense. My husband was a devout Catholic who attended a Roman Catholic Church, St. Thomas More, near our home and he was constantly involving me, the Jewish part of our marriage, into volunteering to do different charitable activities at the church. One day I brought up the distribution to a wonderful woman, Carol Puorro, who seemed to run everything that happened at the church, but especially the holiday food baskets. We started to discuss what the costs of a distribution would actually be and we both agreed that if it was all-volunteer labor and donated vehicles, etc., it really shouldn't cost any money to speak of. I offered our group to do the labor intensive work and the church ladies would hand out the commodities. We decided to contact the local social service agency that was supposed to be running the event. They had set up distribution places at other social service offices, and then we realized why it was so expensive.

Not only did all of the places giving away the free products have to stay open later, but often had to do these events on weekend days which meant that they had to pay their help overtime and expenses, whatever those expenses were going to be. The agency would also have a whole bunch of meetings where they would go over the rules and regulations that they put in place to govern who got the free food, how many they would accommodate and what transgressions would constitute being denied the free food. Then there was the paperwork that the agency came up with to make sure that every citizen who was hungry and needed free commodities had to register in advance and bring a picture identification and information about their household. The longer we sat there listening to this commodity Mein Kampf, the more annoyed Carol and I became. This was not charity, this was not feeding people. This was one agency in every county taking names and adding them to their grant requests in order to get more money for their own agency at the humiliation of the hungry and the poor.

When we got back to the church after the first meeting and told the Priest what went on, I was in total shock because the Priest just said, “that’s bullshit” and walked away shaking his head. Even though I really don’t remember spending time with or even meeting any Catholic Priests, I was pretty sure that his reaction to the rules and regs for feeding the poor was not a very religious one. What did I know and Carol, who was as devout as Mother Teresa didn’t seem fazed at all. We held another meeting, but this time it was at St. Thomas More and the only ones in attendance were the church members, and those who were lovingly called, “The Church Ladies” (before Dana Carvey on SNL), AOVNJ members, and other friends who wanted to help.

Our food distribution was scheduled for Friday and Saturday, from 9:00 a.m. to 8:00 p.m. And our rules and regulations were slightly different than those set down in social service stone. Our first rule was that there really weren’t any rules. Anyone who was willing to stand in a long line and wait for a five-pound block of American cheese and 5 lbs. of butter was given it and for any family that had more than three children, a second loaf of each was given. Any senior citizens who were willing to stand in the line were entitled too. Because even if they were not poor, they were governed by memories of the Great Depression, and although we would warn that too much cheese was not good for the system, they got that brick. Veterans, especially Vietnam veterans were entitled because it was G.I. (Government Issue). The ladies in charge of record keeping made a mark on paper every time a brick was given out and the totals were what was turned in to the "agency".

The other thing that we did which was "social services unheard of", was we had gone around to all the bakeries, bagel stores, donut shops and supermarkets. The night before the giveaway, our vets went around and collected everything that was offered because it was left over and we gave that out too. How could we give out cheese and butter, but not bread or rolls? The Monmouth County agency, Checkmate, Inc., was not very happy with our unregulated charity, but all of the recipients and townspeople who came to help were thrilled. Even some farmers came over with bushels of apples and even corn. According to Carol, the entire cost to do this giveaway was about $100.00 for water cups, napkins and such which the church paid for. The day after the giveaway, AOVNJ was invited to a special Mass and it was a beautiful ceremony based upon the service of our members, not only to their country but especially to the community. I had never seen a prouder bunch of guys than I did that day.

Approximately two months after we had been involved in that one location charity giveaway, AOVNJ was invited to a breakfast meeting for representatives of major social service agencies throughout the State to discuss future surplus food giveaways.

Governor Thomas Kean, who was our membership's Knight in Shining Armor, anyway, had heard about the job that St. Thomas More R.C. Church and our Vets had done and wanted our input and cooperation in the future. It was quite an honor, but what was really bothering me and the two Vets who had gone with me, was that this breakfast meeting was held at the fanciest hotel in Trenton, the State Capital, and the spread of food was really beyond what should have been served at a meeting to discuss which poor people were going to be allowed to get free surplus commodities. They couldn't decide whether to serve bacon, sausage or ham.

So, they had all three. There were rolls, toast, muffins, scones, bagels and anything else that someone might feel deprived of if it wasn't available. To me, it was obscene and totally unnecessary and then surprisingly, Checkmate decided to pick this time to complain about our giveaway and our "disobeying" their rules. Mr. Chris Daggart, who was Governor Kean's Chief of Staff was present and he took control of the conversation, which we then realized was what our being invited had been all about. I was given a chance to speak and the first thing that I attacked, in a very proper manner, was that I was very uncomfortable sitting in a gorgeous dining room in a five star hotel with many gourmet foods that the needy might never taste, to discuss the poor and disadvantaged. I then explained that we had welcomed the residents of four neighboring towns besides our own and provided not only what we had received from Checkmate but anything else that we could get to give to the people who stood in lines which had to be humiliating all by itself. I ended up with the cost of everything being a total of about $100.00.

Mr. Daggart then said that he hated to put us on the spot, but he would like us to take about an hour for the three of us to talk it over and then come back with an idea of how we would run the commodity distribution differently than it was being done. We went out into the Hall and I immediately got on the telephone. By the end of the hour, we were walking back into the meeting room, Me, Jim Burdge, Paul Giordano and CAROL PUORRO!! Before starting any conversation, we asked something that had been bothering the Church members and our organization, which was that we understood the dairy commodities and things like peanut butter, but we had been made aware of the fact that ships were going out to sea loaded with crates of beef, pork and other meats and dumping it all in the ocean. We wanted to know why we couldn't give those things out as well. The answer was true Governor Kean, no lying, no hemming or hawing, Chris Daggart told us that the ranchers and the meat lobby would never allow that. In other words, big business was not going to lose one dollar to give away meat to poor people and that was how that was. It made more sense to them to dump it in the ocean for the sharks to eat.

We then explained to the entire group that we believed that too much money was being spent, virtually wasted in an effort to assist the needy for two days, four times a year, and that we believed that not only could it be done better and cheaper, it could be done with much more humanity and give the people a good feeling as opposed to being humiliated and that involving the people was a good thing. To us, the key was getting people help and allowing them to keep their dignity. Our plan was to have trucks and drivers donated by either organizations, churches, veterans groups and even townships to pick up and bring the commodities to *predominantly the churches* that would distribute them. No one knew their neighbors and their neighborhoods like churches; Catholic, Christian, Muslim, Lutheran, Baptist and all the other houses of worship. And so instead of one distribution site for

5,000 people, it would be easier to have ten or more spread out in towns. Senior citizen housing did not have to have their elderly or disabled residents come to a site, the Vets would bring it to them and all of the labor would be donated and supervised by our Vietnam Veterans or their family members. We also shared what our experience had been with local businesses, farmers and even restaurants, some of which we had actively solicited, but the majority heard what we were doing and just showed up to not only donate food, but to stick around and help.

Carol talked about an idea that she had which just fell into place at the St. Thomas More distribution. Teenagers who belonged to the church were on hand and when people showed up with smaller children or handicapped people from kids to the elderly, the teens set up a section in the community room with toys and books and kept the children occupied, so that they were not just running around or hanging on their parents in the waiting lines. The one thing that Carol kept talking about, was just how pleasant an adventure the day was as opposed to a disheartening display of people waiting for a "handout". Our group always stressed that "no one needs a handout, but so many need a hand up". The true result of our distribution had been that the media coverage was all about the good work that the Vietnam Veteran community had gotten together to do for the people and we ran with that.

Our group, as previously mentioned was predominantly suburban, working, family men, but their personal feelings about themselves quite often, because of the hatchet job that had begun with President Nixon's horrendous insults and then Ronnie Ray-Gun's deliberate slighting of these brave and honorable men had taken its toll on their self-esteem, Now, for once their own neighbors, friends, co-workers, etc. would see them for the heroes that they were, not just in Vietnam, but on Main St. U.S.A., as well. The meeting ended and we came away feeling good about our involvement in the commodity distribution program, even if we also noticed that the breakfast was not comprised of any surplus commodities whatsoever and that the only thing recycled was most likely the dishes and the silverware which was far too expensive to not have been washed and used again.

The next commodity distribution was scheduled to happen right before the Thanksgiving holiday and we were anticipating that we would once again help out at the church, but around the first of October, 1982, AOVNJ members were invited to the State House to attend a press conference being held by Governor Thomas Kean though our invitation was more like a formal summons to attend. Of course there was absolutely no way that we would not have gone to anything that Governor Kean asked us to because the man was, bar none, the best political friend that the Vietnam Veterans and especially the Agent Orange families could ever have. He had ordered that if a Veteran, had civil service priority for any civil service job in the State of New Jersey, as well as all municipalities, counties or whatever. And that priority allowed an additional ten point advantage for any position requiring a test or exam for qualification. If the Veteran did not apply for a position, but his non-veteran spouse did, that preference would be transferred to the spouse. Governor Kean also had funded the New Jersey Agent Orange Commission which was the first of its kind and the only one to actually be doing scientific evaluations, testing and research and those were just the most notable accomplishments on behalf of the Vets, so anything he wanted from us was his for the asking.

His speech was mostly regarding the economy and his concern for what was a slowdown in the economy and its effects upon the middle class and the working poor. He then announced that the State of New Jersey would again be taking part in a commodities distribution right before the Thanksgiving and Christmas holidays, as well as a commitment to continue on with four distributions a year, for at least three more years. He said that some changes were being made in the orchestration of these distributions and the list of who would be the lead agencies in each of the twenty-one counties for this last distribution for 1982 was available and was the same agencies that supervised the previous giveaway, however, some changes might be announced with regard to the 1983 programs, at a later date. The Governor then took a deep breath and said, "There will however be one agency change for this November distribution with regard to Monmouth County, the second most populated county in the state; and that distribution shall be led by AGENT ORANGE VICTIMS OF NEW JERSEY, a member of the International Vietnam Veterans Network". There was a long stunned silence and then to our surprise, even more of a surprise than the announcement just made, was the length and the volume of the applause, but I think I spoke for all of us when I said the immortal words of "WHAT DID HE JUST SAY?" The shock had me, me of all people, speechless but the reporters and the television cameras wanted me to say something and I was totally in shock. I do remember thinking to myself, how the Hell are we going to pull this one off?

The following day, the front page coverages were accompanied with pictures of our members at the press conference, however, except for my ever-present hat, to match my outfit, all of our members looked like everyday people, dressed for the State House. No one was wearing camis or t-shirts, just suits and ties with very big smiles. The only way to identify who we were was by the headlines which said things like: ***Vietnam Veterans Walk Point, or, AOVNJ Leads The Way*** and another one showed our smiling faces with the ridiculous headline of "Just Say Cheese!" The only people who seemed to be less than glowing were the heads of Checkmate, Inc.

It is important to remember that the Governor had said that there might be more announcements at a later date, because, it seems that one of the problems with these Food for the Needy Programs was that the average social service lead organizations were charging the State upwards of $200,000 per distribution to cover the expenses and costs of distributing Free Commodities for each of the 21 counties and the Secretary of State wanted to see how successful AOVNJ was at organizing and running a large county distribution for one large New Jersey county and what our reimbursable costs were going to be by doing it our way; which would determine if the State of New Jersey was going to convert to Vet Power. By using churches as distribution sites with church parishioners volunteering not only their labor, but also delivering commodities to those who were housebound or transportation lacking, etc. and enlisting donations from businesses in their areas, the distributions went off without a hitch and without any bills for "services rendered" being turned in to anyone. As soon as the news had come out, the amount of assistance that was offered was unbelievable. Town governments who had not been involved with prior distributions, donated the use of trucks and drivers to pick up and drop off the government surplus to be given out. A truck rental company donated the use of their trucks, as needed for the same purposes. One fraternal organization who had a member who owned an appliance company, donated five very large standup freezers which we gave to the churches that operated food pantries, soup kitchens, or just had a larger percentage of baskets that were given to needy families.

Other social service groups were using the needy to load up their files with names and statistics regarding anyone who needed just this one time distribution, an expression which we called "padding" and were asking people questions that were invasive, personal and really no one's business. They were very upset that our county asked recipients to sign up with their name, address and contact numbers if, and only if, they felt that they would like to be considered for additional help or needed a job. Otherwise, our policy was based on the "OR ELSE" factor of "or else they are going to drop it in the ocean" and we only kept count of how much we gave out and that was only pertaining to government surplus. There seemed to be a consensus amongst the agencies that unless they ran a very tight program, the rich and privileged were going to storm the distribution lines to get a 5-lb. brick of unmarketable, un-meltable yellow cheese product or 5-lbs. of over-salted butter to take home for their families to have with their dinners. Our belief was that anyone who felt compelled to stand in a line to receive free food, in very limited quantities, for financial, emotional or whatever reasons, actually deserved to get the hand up without showing their picture identifications or telling the world about their family problems. For the entire time that we ran that program, not even once were we made aware of anyone showing up in a limousine and sending their chauffeur to stand on the line for them. Any product left over that would stay good by freezing or refrigerating was donated to those churches that gave out Thanksgiving and Christmas baskets. The biggest paperwork problem that we did run into even with our relaxed rules and information needed, was getting the church ladies to remember to keep tallies and paperwork to be turned in after the distribution. However, that problem was solved quickly when I reported back to each of them that our Veterans got into "big trouble" with Trenton because they didn't have the forms filled out in a timely fashion. The idea of the Vietnam Vets that these churches had embraced so closely, getting into big trouble was enough incentive to get them to appoint a paper pusher in each group. I can only imagine what sort of hideous fate they conjured up in their minds that would befall AOVNJ Veterans at the hands of the all-powerful OZ (Governor Kean).

The total bill reflecting costs for Monmouth County's large population distributions for a one year or all four events was approximately $60,000 for gas and travel reimbursements, as well as the few necessities that we couldn't get donated. What was worth more to us than any money could provide, was the image of the Vietnam Veteran was forever changed and the only haters that we accumulated were the leaders of the organizations who were changed from grant funding to reimbursement funding by the State of New Jersey. But, we never were able to convince anyone that steaks and pork chops don't know how to swim or that the meat lobby was not realizing that the recipients of surplus do not usually ever buy steaks, so the industry would look good and not lose a dime!!!

We were busier than could be imagined during that first distribution and as much as it would be nice to say that every distribution for Monmouth County ran without any incident, while the commodities flowed without any problems having to do our abilities, the very first time that we were on our own, running everything, a Vietnam Veteran situation made us all media heroes one more time.

Our County distribution was set up at the New Jersey State Police Academy and National Guard Headquarters in Sea Girt, N.J., and we had scheduled the entire distribution and giveaways over an entire weekend so as not to cause any of our members or volunteers to have to lose a day's wage. The three tractor trailers had arrived on that Friday and so at about 6:00a.m., we started unloading by forklift and pallet jacks, and then loading the vans, trucks and township vehicles with their individual allocations. All was running smoothly until about 1 p.m., when one of the State Police Officers came running into the loading dock and said he was looking for "The Veteran Lady". Keeping in mind that this was the mid 1980's and before anyone had any cellular phones, so when the officer told me that I had a very important phone call, everything had to stop while I followed him into one of the offices. By the time I got on the phone, I was imagining all types of scenarios, but not the one that was actually taking place.

The voice on the other end introduced himself as a member of the Toms River Police Department, which was confusing because Toms River was in Ocean County, so why were they calling me? The officer on the phone was so nervous that I wasn't sure that I understood what he was talking about because he started telling me about a local resident, a Vietnam Veteran, who lived with his daughter and his parents and that I had better get to Toms River quickly. I was about to read him the riot act because not only didn't we deliver commodities to anyone personally, and especially not in another county, when I heard the words, "hostages and shotgun".

The next words he said was that this Vet was holding his entire family hostage and the police had his house surrounded. The guy refused to talk to anyone except ***"that Veteran Lady"!*** I remember thinking, 'what the fuck does he want to talk to me about?', but, I quickly realized that if this was about cheese and butter, Toms River was going to have to send a car to pick some up across county lines!!! The cop on the phone said that he wouldn't talk to anyone but me so when could I get there? OH

MY LORD, I COULDN'T LEAVE THE ARMORY!!!!

I told the cop to give this guy the phone number that I was at and either have him call me or get me his name and phone number and I would call him. All these years later I still can't believe that I told a man with a loaded shotgun and three hostages that "I would get back to him!" The officer was either in shock or that kind of stuff happened all the time in Toms River because he quickly gave me the phone number to the house with the guy who was threatening to blow his whole family away.

Before I could start dialing the veteran's number, another phone rang and the officer at the desk told me that it was for me, it was "The Governor's Office" (and he looked impressed). Chris Daggart was on the line and had been informed of what was going on in Toms River. Chris had only one concern and that was, "Rena, is this going to have any bearing on the distribution or have you got it covered?" I swear that this is a very true and almost exact play by play of the events of our first major distribution as a lead agency. I responded in the only way that a bureaucrat wants to be handled, and just told him that everything was under control and not to worry. He said "fine, glad to hear it" and hung up on me.

Next minute I was dialing the number in Toms River and before I could even think how I was going to handle this situation, the phone was answered by a male voice, who obviously thought my name was "The Lady" because all he said was "Is this The Veteran Lady?" Since I knew that a bureaucratic response was not going to work I figured that this was obviously one of "my people", so I would deal with the situation truthfully and as if this was an everyday thing. I asked the guy's name, which was Steve and told him my first name. Instead of asking him any questions, I just bluntly said, "Listen Steve, I have a bit of a snafu situation here and need your help!" I just kept on talking and he kept on listening, as I told him that I was stuck in Sea Girt and while I understood that he wanted to see me, that I was dealing with government bullshit and he knew how wacky that was.

I still hadn't asked him any questions or inquired as to why I was told there were cops surrounding his house. He remained quiet and so I explained that whatever the problem was, I would be there and we would deal with it, but I had to handle this distribution nonsense first and so I would be calling him back every half hour or so, and if he needed to talk in between, just call me back and I gave him the number (since caller ID had not been invented yet). I knew something that all the cops both at the site and at the armory should have known but didn't, and that was that if this guy wanted to kill anybody, they would already be dead and that people who are homicidal or suicidal, don't quietly listen to some strange woman explain about surplus commodities and show concern for how she just needed him to sit down and calm down for a while until she could fit him in.

I assured him that no one was going to bust into his house, guns blazing or do anything at all, but that they had to leave some cops there to make sure that they didn't get fired or get into trouble. I asked him to put the gun that I was told he had down and to unload it, and I promised that I would be there as quickly as I could and we would get through this. This man, I had never heard of before said "Yes Ma'am, but you promise you are coming, right?" I told him that I would call him back in about a half hour and hung up, keeping my fingers crossed, hoping that my thought process and method was really working because by this time I had realized just how crazy this whole scenario actually was. I ran back to the loading dock to tell our group members what was going on and went back to getting the commodities unloaded and reloaded.

For approximately three more hours, while we waited for some other of our organization members to get to the Armory, I helped with the distribution management and made constant trips back into the office to call Steve so he wouldn't feel abandoned and reconsider the whole ordeal. Finally, we had enough people who could handle the commodities and the distribution and so the guys told me to get to Toms River, insisting that one of the A.O.V.N.J. Marines go with me. There was suddenly a State Police helicopter in front of me on the tarmac and before I could freak out in pure terror, I was pushed into a seat and we were leaving the ground.

The trip just took about fifteen minutes and we were landing in the parking lot of a strip mall, where I was ushered into the back seat of a police car that then sped toward our destination. The cops in the front seat turned and looked at me like I was crazier than a loon when I ordered them to stop at the first Burger King or McDonald's they came to, but I guess they figured they better stop because look at the fuss everyone was making over this woman with the cowboy hat on her head. I ordered a bunch of food and got back in the car and off we went.

When we got to the house, both of us took off for the front door and I made sure the cops stayed back. I knocked and an older woman opened the door looking like she was ready to pass out. I gave her a hug and whispered to her, "You're alright now, don't worry." Steve had stood up but had left the shotgun perched up against the chair behind him so I handed the bags of food to the woman I realized was Steve's mother and told her to take her husband and their grandchild into the kitchen and eat. I then walked right up to this 6'2" guy, in my 5'6" toughie magnificence and hauled off hitting him in the side of his face and saying what my father always said to us as kids, "Are You Crazy? What the fuck are you doing?"

I should mention that the guy with me had quietly placed himself between Steve and the shotgun, which he then retrieved and made sure it wasn't loaded. Steve broke down crying and I put out my arms like he was a child, holding him and getting him to sit next to me on the couch. He finally started to apologize for what he had been doing and explained that ever since he had returned from Nam, life had been a nightmare. He had gotten married and they had a baby girl; then he had so much trouble holding on to a job that he had started to feel like he was losing his mind. There were so many problems that his wife walked out one day and left their daughter with his parents over two years ago.

He moved in with his parents but he had no medical coverage and the VA told him that he didn't have any service-connected conditions but they could make him an appointment in about six months. This was nothing that we hadn't heard or dealt with before, but this guy was stuck with no friends, family or help except for his elderly parents. Steve told us that he wanted to commit suicide, but he didn't want his daughter or his parents to have to see that; and then he realized that the Christmas holidays were fast approaching and he couldn't even buy his little girl a small present. His parents were supporting the whole family and so there would be no money for a tree or anything; and he said that he just "flipped". It was his mother who had brought him the newspaper with the article about our group and our Vet Center, so when the police showed up he told them he would only talk to me.

This situation of desperation, maybe not as dramatic, but no less heartbreaking was what we had learned to expect and thankfully how to handle, in our own ways and using as much creativity as any of us could come up with. We were able to defuse the police action against Steve. We turned the shotgun over to the cops and called some of our members who lived in Toms River to come and sit with this family; setting up a schedule not just for that one day, for getting this veteran over the hump. While we were calling around, I also made arrangements for a member to drive us back to Monmouth County because there was no way I was going for another chopper ride! My name was Rena not John, and I wasn't hitting the sky in anything that was held up by a hand mixer!!!

Steve was "ordered" to allow himself to be brought to our weekly sessions and then I came up with an idea, which years later he told me not only saved his sanity, but gave him the confidence to fight for a good life again; Steve was put in charge of the "just conceived" AOVNJ TOYS FOR TOTS PROGRAM. The newspapers and television news shows were thrilled to help out in getting us donations in exchange for a chance to interview and share the story of how Steve joined our group.

This experience has been related, as have some others, in a manner which displays humor where, while it was taking place, as well as the fear and total commitment we were all feeling. It shows too the one thing that we all came to count on: that *Laughter Was The Cure.*

CHAPTER THIRTEEN

AND A CHILD SHALL LEAD THE FIGHT FOR SURVIVAL

VERY SOON AFTER THE settlement of the Agent Orange Lawsuit against the chemical companies was approved by Judge Jack Weinstein and was then deemed official, as stated, the health insurance companies started looking into all new customers records and refusing to take care of certain conditions of applicants and their dependents. Subsequently, if a man changed jobs and because back in those days, very often health insurance was part of an employment package, depending upon the size of the insured group, an illness or condition that the employee was treated for and covered by insurance might now, under the new policy, not be covered because it was, their new and much adored term: *pre-existing*. A large company employee had nothing to worry about, but for those, which was most, who worked for a small or family-owned and operated business, might find themselves or anyone in their family as uninsured for the one thing that they needed coverage for most of all. For Vietnam Combat Veterans who had health problems that were not covered by the VA, or if they had a child or children with conditions or birth defects, the problem could be astronomical. If a person, a family man or woman with children, has a job where health care is disallowed and something happens, the feeling of helplessness can be devastating. And when there is incredible tension and worry, the first thing to start to come apart is the relationship between a man and a woman. Regardless of how much they may feel for each other, stress and depression can destroy the simplest of any conversations. Without being able to face things as a unit, or for one person to blame either the other person or even themselves, nothing can be solved and anger takes over where love is supposed to be.

In 1985, my beloved Johnny was diagnosed with Diabetes II which, at first, could be controlled by diet and medication. Right after that, he was hospitalized with massive blood clots in his right leg and embolisms that were threatening to spread to his lungs and heart; either one would cause a very quick death. His osteoarthritis was also spreading and effecting his ability to walk; and if he didn't stay mobile, his blood clots would throw off embolisms. So, it was almost like a medical Catch 22 situation. We were adjusting to long hospital stays and then being confined to a hospital room that we had set up just for him in our home. It was a very hard time for us because although my older son, Eddie was trying to keep the business running, everything that Johnny had worked for was in jeopardy of slipping away. I gave up most of my activities and even counseling to be there to help him and to take care of Alex, who was only eight-years-old and still had health issues of his own. Finally, it became obvious that I was going to have to take over my husband's vending machine business, which I knew very little about and Johnny's father started coming over every day to stay with Johnny and Alex. What ended up happening turned out to be some of the wildest experiences that any family ever survived, but we did.

Since we homeschooled Alex, and because I had spent more than half of my week traveling, lobbying and doing speaking engagements, I wrote Alex's curriculum and Johnny would take him to work with him and teach along the way. So, when I was suddenly going to be a truck driving, vending machine operator, I did know how to drive the step van, but that was about it; until Alex said, "I can run Daddy's business" and instead of telling him not to talk nonsense to grownups, I decided to take him up on his offer. For months I drove the truck and said things to my little boy like, "What do I do now, Alex?" And he was even able to give me perfect driving directions on how to get to each client, as well as supervising and addressing problems with machines, encountered by the other drivers. Bless the dyslexic mind, because he had such an ability for detail and learned from seeing how something is done, that together we were able to not only save the business that his Dad had built from one machine into becoming the contracted State vendor with about two thousand machines in less than twelve years, but Alex also used his Radio Shack Tandy computer to computerize all of the locations as well.

When this was done and over, we wanted to thank our son for all he had done and that is a subject for another book, but I contacted the Junior Achievement Organization and since Alex had not started his own business but had actually saved a very large business, they got in touch with the Mattel Real American Hero Program. Alex won that National Award, which was presented to him by Mayor Ron Laurie, of Las Vegas, in 1989, after we had just moved to Nevada, leaving the snow behind.

In the midst of all that was happening with John's health and the fact that Alex and I were able to afford him time to get his strength back, we hit another major snag in life as we knew it. All private health insurance has a "cap figure" which once hit, the company does not have to provide health care which involves major medical and if they do, the co-pay figure is beyond manageable. That is what was happening to us where Johnny's condition was involved and the insurance company gave us notice that we were reaching that cap figure very rapidly. We knew what was causing Johnny's conditions and so we applied to the Veterans Administration for medical care for John. What we were told really threw us because it was absolutely insane. The VA counselor advised us that because John's illnesses may or may not have been caused by Agent Orange, our income was far too high for him to qualify for VA Hospital care, but as soon as we used up all of our savings, assets, home and whatever else, we should come back and they would take care of the indigent veteran that they had created. We couldn't believe what they had said and the fact that Alex's health and education was costing us tens upon tens of thousands of dollars each and every year, what were we supposed to do? I was busy for years, showing the VA how to treat combat stress veterans and now because of their regulations, my own incredible husband was talking about committing suicide so that Alex and I would have his life insurance and not be burdened by his problems. My world was falling apart and for the first time in so many years, I couldn't figure out a solution that would work quick enough to save my family.

Earlier, I had spoken of a veteran who worked for the VA, named Eddie Corbett, who had worked with us to start the Agent Orange Movement and who had become a good friend. We decided to call him and talk to him about what we were dealing with. He told us to come down to his office to discuss what our options were, which gave us some hope that there were "options". We went to his office at the VA in Newark, NJ and as soon as we sat down, he said that he had an idea, but we should hear him out before we commented. Ed went on to say that of all the couples he had ever met, we were probably the only one that he felt comfortable in even suggesting what he was going to say without having to worry about the end result. He was very well aware of the nature of the business that Johnny had built from just one juice vending machine, that we had overpaid on when we bought it and he also knew that everyone who worked for Johnny's company was a Combat Vet. If a Vet was on the down and out, Johnny never failed to either give him a job or insist that he really didn't have the time to paint our house or landscape our property, so the guy he was talking to would be doing a big favor for us, and of course we would pay him for his efforts, if he would help out with this or that. That was the kind of man that my husband had always been, or at least for as long as I'd known him. He helped his brother Vets, always making it sound like they were helping him, so as not to bruise their already suffering dignity and self-image.

Ed had heard all the stories and just wanted to be able to do something for my Johnny. What he suggested was that the VA would have to take care of Johnny's medical needs and whatever else he needed, related to his health, but only if he could not afford to pay for anything himself. Ed explained that the relationship between my husband and me was so strong and we were so very close, not only as husband and wife, but as business partners, best friends and intellectual equals, that the Vets had named us "The Dynamic Duo." We were actually totally devoted to each other; so that if we divorced and I took everything we had, my income and his business, as well as all property and even wanted child support, financially he would be eligible for VA medical care, and I would have the ability to provide for Alex's medical needs and educational costs. It really sounded too easy and we told Ed that we had to check with our attorney because we did not want to be breaking any laws. Our attorney said the same thing that Ed Corbett had said about our relationship, but he then said that under normal circumstances he would be very much against anything, such as we were asking him about. Although, it was not in any way illegal, for any man to turn every cent he had ever worked for and everything that he owned over to his wife, it took either an idiot or someone who had unbelievably incredible trust in the other human being. So I flew to Las Vegas to visit my parents and while I was there, I got an uncontested divorce and I took everything; I left Johnny totally penniless!!

The day that I went before the Judge in Las Vegas and walked out of the courthouse with the attorney, as a pretty wealthy woman, the lawyer asked me if I would like to have dinner with him "to celebrate" and seemed very let down that this newly-single and well-to-do lady told him that she had other plans. Those other plans were that my now ex-husband was going to be at the airport to meet my plane, back in New Jersey. While he had all the understanding in the world for *why* we had to take this step, he would have absolutely *no* understanding at all if I wasn't on that plane and home in time for dinner. He didn't have to worry because I really did deserve how much trust he had in me. We had been married for twelve years when we got our divorce and twelve years later as soon as he was granted 100% service-connected Agent Orange VA disability which was retroactive from the first day he had filed, almost twenty years earlier. We remarried and the biggest thrill was that it was our son, Alex who gave the bride to his dad. Most people only knew of our marital status for those twelve years if it was totally necessary and at first the only confusion was that our son knew that his parents had gotten a divorce.

We had explained to him that nothing whatsoever was going to change, and it didn't; however, he was a very young boy and so when, as so many couples did in the 80's, his friends' parents got divorced, Alex could not understand why their Dads didn't come home for dinner every night and go to soccer on Saturdays like his "divorced" daddy did. Fortunately, he grew up understanding that his parents had so much trust in each other that they did what they had to do to survive and take care of him, which has, to this day had something to do with his still being unmarried. He always says that he will only marry once and only when he finds a friendship and a relationship like his parents had. I guess that there really can be no greater compliment to what his dad and I had shown him about loyalty, caring and trust.

I think that one of the things that kept me humble and never losing sight of what was important to me was that everything I was doing was for my family primarily and for the other veteran families whose lives were as medically precarious as ours. Regardless of who I met or how important other people thought I was because they saw me on television or read about me in the newspapers or magazines, I always had to try to be home for dinner and definitely had to be at soccer practice on Saturdays; as well as making sure that our son Eddie knew how to dance in time for the Prom. There was also my husband's extended family, his Aunts and Uncles who were aware of some of the trials and tribulations that were our cross to bear, but took great pride in John's success in business and so, to them, what I did was not nearly as important. This was fine with me because I had always known how uncaring Johnny's mother was and the negativity he had been raised to think was somehow his fault or that he wasn't as bright as he now knew that he was.

The one event that sums it all up about just how normal our

life was to his relatives happened in 1987, when Woman's Day Magazine, in their October issue named me as one of the Fifty Most Outstanding Women in the first fifty years of their publication, and so I was the 1987 Outstanding Woman of America; and Johnny was so proud that he called his Aunt Lottie, who was more like a mother to him, than his own mother and told her about this wonderful award and title. Her response was priceless, she said to him, sounding perplexed, "*Woman's Day Magazine*, Wow, I didn't even know that Rena could cook!" I had heard him talking to her on the phone about the award, but then he told her that he had to call her back and hung up. Johnny was laughing so hard that he fell back onto the couch with tears running down his face as he told me what she said. See, definitely it kept me humble and yes, I have always been an excellent cook. But not once did I ever send a recipe to any magazine! Just when he was able to stop the tears of laughter, I said to him "Thank goodness, it wasn't a *Good Housekeeping Magazine* Award or she would have canceled her subscription" and the tears and laughing started all over again. That Christmas, Johnny and the boys bought me a full set of Farberware® with a card that said 'Outstanding Cooker Woman of America!' I have always kept at least one piece of the set in plain view in my kitchen, on both sides of the country and all these thirty-five years later, to remind me not to get too carried away with my own self-importance, and it has always worked.

Not sure if it is the pot or my own grandmother's constant warning that "self-praise stinks"; however, I am the same woman, who I was when I first started trying to make the world a better place, with the battered women's shelter and then the veterans. I was mad at myself because I was changing the world, but my apartment was a mess and Grandma said, without hesitation, *"Renala, the bed will wait to be made, but life doesn't wait for anyone"*. I never forgot that because except to me, my grandmother was just an old lady who very seldom left the house except to shop for my grandpa's dinner and when I was a little kid, if we took a family ride on a Sunday, she always baked a chicken and carried it in a shopping bag because she said that my father was always getting lost. So just in case the "kynda" got hungry (she was right, he always got lost, and we always ate the chicken); however, to me, my grandma was my best friend and my biggest supporter.

One of the few times that I used the importance that politicians thought I had, for my own personal needs was in 1978, when my grandparents who still were living in the Bronx, NY, in the project that I'd grown up in, but the element and the neighborhood had changed drastically. I would drive into the Bronx every other Saturday, stopping at the kosher butcher in Linden, New Jersey, and getting my grandmother enough meat for two weeks; and when I got to their apartment, I would take them out in my car to go shopping or whatever else they needed to take care of. I had gotten a call from my mother a couple of days after my New York trip to tell me that my grandfather had gone downstairs to sit on the bench and he was mugged and beaten, his arm was broken and my grandmother was upset because this eighty-one-year-old man, "hadn't fought back". What I did next was not something I normally would have done, but my grandpa needed me, so I called the Mayor of Freehold, New Jersey, the next town over from ours and asked him about the brand new apartment buildings that had been built just for senior citizens and told him what had happened and then I begged him for one of those apartments.

The next Saturday I called my grandma and told her I was coming to take her shopping because I had to be in the city anyway and went to pick up both of my grandparents. While we were running all over New York, "doing stuff", Johnny, our son Eddie and a couple of veterans were using my key for my grandparents' apartment, to empty out the entire apartment and kidnap all their belongings, driving it over the George Washington Bridge, over the State line and delivering it to their brand new apartment in Freehold. There wasn't anything I wouldn't do for that Mayor and kept apologizing to him for using my influence; he really must have thought I was crazy.

When it was time to take my grandparents back home, I headed for the George Washington Bridge and when Grandpa realized that we were heading in the wrong direction, I lied and told them that we were making a surprise party for my sister and decided they should spend the weekend (I was so slick!). But when we took them to their new apartment, the tears in their eyes and the look on their faces was worth using whatever influence the Mayor thought I had. Grandma only lived for about six months after that because we didn't know that she had cancer, but I got to spend every day with my best friend for those months at least and she was very happy spending time with me and my family. One of her favorite things to do was to read the articles and reports about what I was doing with regard to Agent Orange and combat stress and then discussing the subject with me.

It was my grandmother who dubbed me with the name and title that I still am worthy of today, which was, with a pencil in her hand, "The Queen of the Run On Sentence"; and is still the one thing that makes any editor I work with batty as a loon. I often think of how much she would have loved the experiences of the years directly after her death with all the demonstrations and the television cameras because she was so vibrant after moving to New Jersey that I was sorry that we didn't force them to move sooner. In those years, senior citizens were very set in their ways and didn't like change very much, but we missed out on so many good times. Right before she ended up in the hospital, this woman who had refused to use any electrical appliances other than a radio or the television in their living room, fell in love with my Cuisinart and would spend hours chopping everything she could think of. Alex, who was a two-year-old dynamo would be racing around the house and as soon as my grandma sat on the couch, there went the dynamo and became a couch potato that required snuggling. As of this writing, she is gone thirty-three years and I still remember the telephone number of her Bronx apartment and even find myself thinking to reach for the phone on a Saturday or Sunday as I did every weekend from the age of seventeen.

There was something that I found out about my grandparents that I don't think that even their four children knew, it was that they thought they were in love back when they weren't even twenty years of age, and got married very quickly so that the man who would be my wonderful grandfather would not have to serve in World War I. Their marriage lasted over sixty-two years and my grandparents were the only two people that I had ever seen who, despite everything and anything that they had to endure, were totally devoted to each other and no matter if what the day might bring, they could always find something to laugh about. My grandmother was very hard of hearing and a Type I diabetic since early childhood. She had suffered a very hard and abusive childhood which affected her very badly throughout her life and combined with the hearing disabilities, as well as the childhood humiliation of having to inject herself with insulin all of her life, she had some psychological issues which her own children were embarrassed about. However, Grandpa was protective of his wife and then as I grew up with only my grandparents to protect me from my own abusive and dysfunctional parents, I protected my grandma and made sure that her own children were never in a position to take advantage of her or, as they often discussed, put her into a "home". So, I guess that if my marriage was the best part of me, that came from emulating the way that my grandparents had shown me what loyalty and sharing was all about.

Right after Grandma's sudden death, my grandfather who I never remembered having been sick, had come to live with first Johnny and me and after just a few short months began to suffer from what, at that time was something no one ever heard of, Alzheimer's Disease, originally called the Rita Hayworth sickness of senile dementia. My parents were moving to Las Vegas and so they thought it best if they took Grandpa with them, where he died very shortly after; but I knew it was really hastened by a broken heart. I guess that I really became even more understanding of how and why he so suddenly failed and so quickly passed over after I lost my Johnny Weeble, who finally wobbled and fell down.

We didn't move to Las Vegas until late in 1988 and since my grandparents were buried in Woodbridge, New Jersey, I never missed a weekly visit to their graves, even having a little picnic with Alex on nice days. What I did learn from the loss and then the fact that once we moved, no one, none of their children or other grandchildren who lived just across the river in New York, went to visit their cemetery resting place, and so I swore never to bury anyone I loved in a plot of land. Besides my Johnny and then our beautiful grandson Giovanni, as well as my own father, resting on our mantel are the ashes of about five dogs and two cats; so wherever we go, so do they. Even though our shrine is beautifully set up and appointed, and we keep prayer candles burning 24/7 for Johnny and Giovanni, I am pretty sure that some visitors may feel a shiver when they realize what they are admiring, but just as I used to tell my kids, "My house, my rules." I am prepared to one day have to say, "Don't like it, don't look"!!!!!

Something that may be surprising about the lives of Vietnam Combat Veterans who suffered from combat stress and/or Agent Orange poisoning, but who, as our generation was supposed to do, went after the American Dream, is that although, as was common also for our generation, most first marriages ended in divorce within about five years; those who remarried or didn't marry at all until later on, beat the odds of our age group and stayed married for decades. It is very possible that even though the normal reason for that first divorce was, as my Johnny's first wife stated, "erratic behavior", by the time that Combat Veterans remarried, they had sought out some help in understanding and dealing with PTSD. If that is the case, then I guess that I have every right to be very proud of myself for establishing a simple protocol that ended up helping so many. The realistic truth is that the protocol that I created was done, not as an effort of psychological accomplishment, but in an effort to find a way to help my own husband find some peace in his own mind and to be able to enjoy the life he was entitled to. When I talk to Vets and in some cases their widows, all these years after our wild ride into flashbacks, night terrors and personality disorders, and they are still thanking me for saving their marriages and in some cases, their lives; I am still at the same loss that I was thirty or more years ago, in that it was my marriage and my husband's sanity that I was trying to save and preserve. As crazy as it may sound, I often feel like a fraud if I don't make sure that they understand that all I did was to come up with a concept and a method, but that they, as a couple and as a family did all the work. It has also always been my belief that we cannot count on strangers to solve our problems; especially with personality disorders, they can only be cured or changed for the better when the person with the disorder admits that there is a problem and decides to make the changes necessary. No therapy in the world can make someone change the way they think and react to stimuli, only the person with the problem can solve that situation.

What I did learn very early in my working with veterans and their wives, was learned by being a suburban housewife who became familiar with neighbors whose husbands normally had never served in Southeast Asia, or for the matter, the military in general. The couples who lived on our block were supposed to be living the all-American dream and according to the talk shows and the motion pictures of the time, everybody sat down to dinner as a family, never argued and spent every weekend just tooling around on a lawn tractor and playing with the kids. When we had found out that we were expecting, Johnny had insisted that I stay home because we were worried about a high risk pregnancy and so for the first time in my adult life, I wasn't working and had to figure out what to do with all the free time.

One day Johnny came home and found me sitting on our bed with tears running down my face. Not knowing if it was either hormones, something bad had happened or whatever, he asked me what was wrong and I showed him a group of neighbor women sitting outside the house next door and just talking. I told him that they never invited me to come sit with them or came to visit and I thought there was something wrong with me. He sat down next to me, put his arm around my shoulders and said, "And what is it that you would talk to them about?" I was a community organizer, a political activist and a psycho-therapist who got her education by being a first responder in the biggest city in the nation.

He was exactly right, what would I talk to them about or how long would it be before they would be looking for free counseling services? I remember feeling better and while I always knew that it wasn't my fault they didn't seek me out, it wasn't their fault either. This all had happened approximately two months before I saw that news story on television about herbicide spraying and after that I really didn't have any time for having coffee or idle gossip at all. Since most of my neighbors had children the same ages as mine, I finally did get to know my neighbors and to spend some time with them either sitting outside and watching our kids play or inside having coffee and watching our kids play, but when I started running counseling groups with Vets or their wives, I realized what the difference was between women married to Combat Vets and why Johnny had been so very right about my having nothing in common with these other women. They were nice enough and we had very similar ideas about raising children, but our interests were so far apart that I spent most of my time listening because on the few occasions that I did talk about interests, I was met with blank stares and quick departures. I was reading "A Woman's Room" by Marilyn French while my daytime friends were, if reading at all, were engrossed in romance books or movie magazines. The one thing that I began to realize almost immediately was that these women, bar none, were constantly complaining about their husbands; everything from his intellect, his job or his lack of concern for his wife's needs or feelings. It was as if they really didn't like this person they had vowed to spend their life with at all. One of the women, who later on ended up leaving her husband and kids for someone else, turned toward me and said, "You're a good listener, but you never say anything about your husband." My husband? My best friend? My soul mate and partner in everything? What did they want me to say that wouldn't make them hate me? Apparently, what I did say either really did make them feel stupid or at least realize not to ask that question again. My response was pretty simple, I said "if I am unhappy about something my husband does or doesn't do, what will it accomplish if I tell you guys? We have an agreement that we discuss everything with each other and, (then I said what I thought was pretty funny) as soon as he finds something about me that bothers him, I'm sure he'll mention it." Total silence and then everybody decided that they had to go home and make dinner, even if it was only mid-morning!

What would I have told them even if I were so inclined? Would I tell them about flashbacks or anxiety attacks? In the suburban lifestyle, or any marriage, there were situations where husbands were physically abusive to their wives while they were both wide awake and he was just a bully, but we had gotten through some crazy nights that my husband dreamed he was still in the place that scared him the most and acted out in a drastic manner that when he awoke in the morning had no recollection of. Not the same thing because this man, where I was concerned, did not raise a hand or physically hurt anyone and we had worked through Vietnam to the point that if he felt himself slipping into a flashback or a temper flare, he would say something and the boys and I knew how to react. I actually felt bad for some of the husbands after hearing about them at their wives' gab fests because they probably didn't even know how their family saw them, which is a waste of a life, in my opinion. For me, my marriage was the best place for me to be and my husband was, more important than any other feature, my closest friend and my buddy, who I could tell anything or be anyway I was and it was okay with him. Ironically, we were the only ones in our neighborhood who actually did have that make-believe dream marriage that we were taught every suburban family was supposed to have. The only major problem in our marriage was that Johnny was of

Polish descent, and if one spells the act of cleaning furniture or polishing and then spells Johnny's ancestry, that explains why he was a really organized neat freak and I took my grandma's statement about beds waiting, to include everything else as far as immobile objects in my life. How we solved that difference was a shock to my in-laws and a source of jealousy to my neighbors. My life was so busy by the time that Alex was a year old that we decided that when it came to housework and laundry, etc., what we truly needed was a housewife, so we hired one. Once we set up the AOVNJ groups, we, as wives did shared some of our experiences about being married to a Combat Vet, but not as a complaint, as either an opportunity to share how we had individually handled a situation or if we were dealing with something that we needed suggestions about how to handle. In other words, we shared, not bitched! The only similarity was that most of us were drinking coffee during our meetings. We all lived a pretty precarious daily existence because we never knew from one day to another if our husbands were going to be sick or if we were going to find out some new health or neurological problem was going to rear its ugly head. Socially, once we all found each other, we did most of our socializing with each other. If a Vet felt claustrophobic or anxious, everybody just gave him space and no one bothered him, unless he, himself sought out someone to talk to. To my mind, the stresses one has to normally face when socializing with neighbors or strangers did not exist and so having a nice time was easier to do. I do remember that one of my neighbors decided that after her baby was born, instead of inviting people to go to dinner or do something one couple at a time, she and her husband would hold a house party for all their friends and neighbors who had been there for them during her pregnancy and when the child was born, so they could be "repaid" all at once. Johnny and I lived next door to them, but we were trying to out-convince each other how one of us should stay home with Alex instead of going to the party. Our son Eddie, was fourteen-years-old at the time and he was just watching us come up with reasons for why, between the two of us, which one had a better reason. Finally, he just said, "listen, take the baby monitor with you to the house NEXT DOOR and I'll stay here and watch the kid". We were then out of arguments so we went, both secretly planning our individual retreat back to our house. What we were both expecting to happen, did happen, which was that we only knew a couple of the guests and so we just stood in a corner and since this was in the 70's when smoking cigarettes was not yet a mortal sin, yet I kept running outside to "grab a smoke "and some fresh private air. The party hostess came over to me and told me that she wanted to show me something upstairs, so I dutifully followed her, but she pushed me into a bathroom, opened the window and asked me for a cigarette, then she knelt on the commode cover so she could blow the smoke out the window. It was the most ridiculous action I had ever seen, she was a grown woman but she explained that her husband would go nuts if he found out she was still smoking. All I could say to her, in this late 70's day of the feminist, was *"I sure hope that you don't smoke Virginia Slims!"*

When I went downstairs with, what I thought was a good reason to leave because I had obviously served my purpose, I found myself in a dark room but with a movie projector showing a film on the sheet that was tacked on the wall. Oh my goodness, it was a movie of our hostess giving birth, taken by the proud Daddy, in the delivery room of the hospital and he didn't miss a step or a shot. Johnny, who had faced death in Vietnam, saved lives in Newark and fought fires in Old Bridge, saw me and looked helplessly trapped and like he was about to throw up. She was afraid to let her husband know that she still smoked but he had no trepidations over showing her, in all her glory, giving birth. What was wrong with this whole evening? The irony is that six months later, her husband left her and the baby, to move in with his secretary. I never asked who got custody of the home movies. That evening was the last time that we looked for reasons not to spend social time with our neighbors, we just said we had other plans. The entire country seemed to think that the Vietnam Combat Veterans were a threat to society, but we, in the societal threat category really not only felt comfortable only around each other, but when we did talk about our neighbors, it was usually a real laugh fest of who had the craziest stories. The main thing that it took us a very short time to realize was that, the happy family man who lived next door or down the block, was never with his kids at sports activities, taking walks or throwing a Frisbee. Meanwhile our erratic and unstable veteran husbands, stuck to their families for dear life and preferred to go on picnics or to go feed the ducks at the park more than going who knew where with who knew who.

I do believe that the difference between the Vets who had families and had finally made it far enough through the storms to have found themselves as husbands and fathers, held on to those simple feelings of doing things with their children or even just sitting down to a game of gin rummy or a television show with their wives after the kids were in bed, because it was something that they never thought they would have. That they had made it all the way home from the place that they were sure was where they were going to die and they had achieved a quiet place to hide, inside their homes with their kids and a wife who understood the nightmares and stayed up all night just holding them to ward off the terrors until they passed. They were unlike their counterparts: the men who just took the house, the wife and the kids as what was due them and so surrounding themselves with crying kids or a complaining wife was a fate worse than death. How sad for those who thought they deserved what they had and didn't have to treasure every minute of it like the men who had what they never thought would be theirs and so they tried to envelope themselves in all that belonging.

CHAPTER FOURTEEN

TAKING IT TO THE STREETS, THE STATES AND THE HIGHWAYS

VERY SOON AFTER THE In late 1985, our group found out that about 80 or more drums of 2,4D and 2,4,5T, which weren't listed by its internationally known name of Agent Orange, were being offered at public auction at the Lakehurst Military Barracks in Central New Jersey. This auction was kept secret, although when we challenged it, the Base claimed that it was advertised in spite of not being able to come up with one public notice. The only reason that we were made aware of what was happening was because we had received calls from reporters from the *Newark Star Ledger* and the *Asbury Park Press* to get a statement from us as to what we felt about the auction or, probably to make sure we knew about it. Of course, they could not print the actual words that we used, but they had their story because we were on hand the day of the auction to picket and demonstrate to try to stop the sale. We were not foolish or stupid, and knew that we were not going to be able to stop the sale completely, however we did believe that our reputation would create some apprehension for any company in the states of New Jersey, New York, Connecticut and Pennsylvania from buying this poison.

The newspapers covered our objections and were even able to find out that the entire lot of 55gallon drums was sold to a company in Austin, Texas and not only that it would be shipped by truck, but were also able to get the name of the trucking company. For some time in our fight, both the chemical companies and the government had accused the media of "instigating the Veteran Movement" but no one ever helped us, other than the media, so we usually had great respect for all that they did for our cause. This time, it became a national media event because one of our most active network organizations was The Brotherhood of Vietnam Vets, with a strong chapter in Austin, Texas. We had an organized effort keeping track of the transport trucks, with groups watching the highways and since this was before cell phones and Internet, all of our phones were ringing day and night. When the trucks made it across the Texas border, imagine the drivers' surprise when they were met by a large number of Vietnam Vets and their supporters in cars, pick-up trucks and some even on horseback, which I'm pretty sure was more for effect, but what the Hell! They were pointing shotguns at the truck cabs and brought them to an abrupt stop and then forced them to turn around and leave. We had no way of knowing where the trucks finally crossed back into Texas and we weren't fooling ourselves into thinking that we had stopped the sale and delivery, but we were able to bring attention to the continued poisoning of the American people right here in the United States.

While incidents similar to the parades and the demonstrations were few and far between, one of the things that our group did to raise money was to take advantage of town festivals and county fairs by running game booths, giving away everything from live goldfish to stuffed animals. We probably would have made more money if we refrained from giving a prize to every child that played whether they won or not, but the sight of tears in a child's eyes was not something that these big, tough Nam Vets could quite handle and so that became our trademark, "everybody wins". My sons had a tankful of goldfish and I never understood how those fish had survived being in the warm sun at the event, transported in a plastic bag and then being dumped into a tank with the fish that survived from the year before. When my family made the trip across country to move to Nevada, we took a small tank with the three remaining fish in the RV that we drove across America. No matter how many times we stopped short and the fish ended up on the floor, needing to be picked up by a ten-year-old and put back in their little water tank, they lived and they survived. And they were never even supposed to make it home from the fair that was held years before!

By the end of 1987, we had gotten all that we were going to get from the elected officials in Washington DC, and the State of New Jersey was trying to do liver biopsies on Vietnam Veterans who would volunteer, however the Commission had not taken into consideration that the cost of these medical procedures would not be covered by private insurance or by the VA and the State of New Jersey having done so much more for the vets than any other state, did not have nor could they allocate the funds necessary. As it was, by the time the Commission was disbanded in July of 1996, having become little more than a clearing house for referrals to Vet Centers and service organizations. The dedicated, intellectual and scientific genius of the Commission, Dr. Peter Kahn of Rutgers University was never paid for all of his efforts because of the miscalculations and expenses of the original staff. Betty Mekdeci of the Birth Defect Registry located in Florida, took over the job of trying to accumulate data and provide assistance when possible that AOVNJ had handled from the Commission's inception until we moved to Nevada for Johnny's health. And Agent Orange Victims of New Jersey disbanded in September of 1988. What was a frustration for the members of AOVNJ was that everyone affiliated with the Commission, that our organization had written the legislation for and worked tirelessly to assist Veterans and their children, was now being paid for the work that we all did free of charge and at costs that we all absorbed from its beginning while we had turned down paying jobs within the government structure!

When his doctors explained that he would not be able to survive many more Eastern winters, the hardest decision that Johnny and I had to make, which should have been the easiest, was made worse by knowing that the organization and all the good work we had accomplished would come to an end once we told our friends and compatriots that we had to relocate. Although, we had sold our business months earlier, we stayed in New Jersey throughout the summer months trying to convince AOVNJ members that they could keep the movement going without what was essentially just two people out of many. We had already decided that we would be moving to the dry and warm climate of Southern Nevada, since we had family living there already. I spent every moment that I was not packing to move an entire life, writing articles for homeschooling magazines, Veterans newsletters and doing speaking engagements with our dear friend Dave Cline. I would even, which I can admit now, write very forceful letters to the editors of newspapers in our four-state area and put my name with the name of one of our members in each publication area. Then I began just putting their names as the authors. My reasoning was to sort of introduce readers who cared about our plight to them in an effort to transition other AOVNJ or Agent Orange Network, into the position of spokespeople. It was our hope, Johnny's and mine, that after we moved things would not change. However, even though we said that we were only a phone call away and would always be there to assist where we could, it became obvious very quickly that most of the Veterans were still intimidated by being the "voice" in a public setting of strangers or cameras and without what the Veterans called "The Dynamic Duo" and their wives called "The Leaders of the Pack", No one was going to jump into the activist lead. Amongst the wives, who were the members that I was always trying to groom to take my place for the same reasons that I started the fight, although there were a number of them whom I had thought would be able to handle the activist part and arrange for Dave Cline's new group, Veterans For Peace, or the psychotherapists at the Vet Centers who used the method we had created; I didn't realize the biggest problem that women, even in the late 80's still had to contend with in trying to change the world. When a woman is married and especially if she has a home and children, or at least back in the last century (WOW, I've wanted to use that term for a long, long time), unless the dynamics of that marriage and the ego of the male partner were extremely healthy, it was almost impossible for her to pick up the activist's sword.

Whenever I speak of my husband, Johnny, and my activities and contributions over the years, I am always careful to explain that unless a husband is also a life partner who believes in what his wife is trying to do, it is not possible for her to have the freedom and support to do what has to be done, *when* it has to be done. In the 80's a song came out related to the movie "Beaches" with Bette Midler. The name of the song is "The Wind Beneath My Wings" and the first time I ever heard it was even before I saw the film. I was out of town and went to a concert which included the old 60's group The Platters, who sang this song and as I listened I could feel the tears running down my face because, from that day forward, when anyone asked me to talk about my relationship and my cause, I would always and still do now, even though he now really is the one with wings, I describe him as the wind beneath my wings. Nothing that I did, have done or am doing would be possible if I did not have a life partner for over forty years who let me be as much as I could be and gently pushed me ever further when I was unsure of my course. He had that much faith in me, not just as his wife and the mother of his child, but as a person, a friend and I guess that his pride in me and my always wanting to prove that I could be all that he thought I was truly made me soar. He was the wind and the atmosphere that kept me flying high. How very lucky and undeserving was I for all that he gave to me. But quite honestly, unless any married woman or man has a partner like I had in Johnny and that I can only hope he had in me, it is almost impossible to do the work that is involved without creating drama and stress upon a relationship, which is why so many women don't take on such huge endeavors.

Once we relocated in Nevada and for the next few years, while Johnny was still very active with different Veteran groups and did quite a few radio interviews with radio talk shows from all around the world. I was very busy with working, homeschooling, getting our beautiful new house in order and establishing our new business and existence both socially and professionally in an entirely different environment. Our home here was everything that we had worked so hard to attain, it was only missing a swimming pool. In landlocked Las Vegas, where it was warm enough for swimming at least ten months of the year, a pool was essential for a private home, so we contracted a pool company to put in an in-ground pool and spa. The commissioning of this pool provided us with a culture shock when the "architect" came over so the pool could be *"designed"*. That was an experience in itself since for people like us, a swimming pool was for swimming, for Johnny's aquatic exercise, our sons' recreation and practice for competition as well as entertaining. There were a couple of requirements that we were adamant about having to be installed just for safety reasons and that was when the initial shock of the difference between the East and West Coast lifestyles hit. Our older son was 6'9" tall, Johnny was 6'2" tall, Alex at eleven years of age was already about 5'9", so we knew that his height was going to be somewhere between his Dad and his brother. We explained to the gentleman that we wanted a diving board on the deep end and that the deep end had to be no less than 11', but preferably 12' feet deep. We knew we were in trouble when Mr. Frye, the architect asked, "What deep end?" Apparently, all the new people moving to Las Vegas and those residents who had lived here forever and had pools, were quite content with four feet of water throughout, which was ridiculous to us. After all, the house already had two deep bathtubs, so why bother? Mr. Frye explained that in Nevada there was something called "a caliche problem". He knew he was in trouble when I said "what does an Italian person have to do with our pool?" We had never known much about the land formation of our properties other than what had to be mowed and what was not a good place to plant vegetables, fruit, or even some flowers. The New Jersey underground formation was none of our business. However, the ground under the desert is composed of many different forms of shale, rock and a soil that is *very expensive to remove or cut through* and that is a type of rock known as "caliche" which is a very hard type of subsoil encrusted with calcium-carbonate in arid or semiarid regions; the only part that I totally understood was the *very expensive* part of the explanation. I was, in a sense relieved to learn this, only because of the stories and myths that people kept telling us about the desert of Southern Nevada and that did involve “Italian guys” or Mafioso that disappeared and were later found, or never found buried under the topsoil of the desert! The next questions on Mr. Frye’s checklist involved matters related to “decor”. He asked us how we wanted the pool shaped; and our response of “like a swimming pool” just didn’t cut it. He drew some rough drafts for us, none of which looked like a swimming pool, but more like works of art with a number of death traps for swimmers. Our pool in New Jersey was a rectangle 20’x40’ which was about 3 feet deep on the shallow end, gradually deepening to 12 feet by the diving and slide area. Simple! If you will recall, earlier I mentioned that I had sons, and my sons had friends, all of whom were into competitive swimming and now we had moved to a climate where not only could Johnny exercise by swimming laps, but our sons could make new friends who swam. Still with me? It took many hours of arguing with Mr. Frye to make him understand that his concept of high style was not what we required. That placing concrete stools in the shallow end was rather a frightening concept of someone diving into the pool and swimming only to be knocked unconscious by going headfirst into piles of concrete! When we told him that the thing that we were required were full handrails down both sides of the steps leading down into the shallow end and into the spa, with yet a third type of holding or handrail attached to the wall next to the ladder on the deep end; all of which should be covered with a heat resistant wrapping, because of the sometimes 115 degree temperatures in Vegas, we were, just for a moment, sure that the man was going to have a massive coronary from the shock of this last demand. He finally stopped with his recommendations and suggestions, turned to us and quite seriously said, *“Just what kind of statement are you trying to make?”*

Okay, now we understood his dilemma, and as Johnny and I had been able to do for years because it felt very often as if we shared brain waves and thought so much alike; we both said, simultaneously, "We know *who we are.* We know that *we're not swimming*". By the time we were finished, the work order had, in big black letters, **TFP**, which I was sure meant "Two Fucking Psychos". But when I asked, the architect said "totally functional pool" and was waiting for us to straighten him out somehow. We were in shock now because he understood, he really understood, and we were so happy at the progress we were making in learning to speak Nevadan. The swimming pool that was supposed to take six weeks to construct, took six months because we learned another lesson about Nevada, which was the work ethic that we knew from the East Coast, had not made the trip West.

To be fair, when we moved to Las Vegas, the entire population in 1988 was 264,500 residents in all of Clark County, and well under one million in the entire state where now, in the second decade of 2000, it is over two and half million people in Clark County alone. The most memorable experience of our trip into backyard construction was when one of the construction workers knocked on my back door, with a small child at his side. When I opened the door to see what he needed, he pushed the child into my kitchen and told me, not asked, not inquired, just told me that his wife had a headache so I was "going to have to watch" his child! Let's keep in mind everything anyone who has either read this far or who knew anything about my entire life to that date already is laughing at the mental picture. It took me a minute or two to wrap my mind around what was happening since other than offering to entertain a child to play or swim with Alex under my supervision or a friend's need for someone to care for their child due to some emergency or event, nothing in my many, many experiences fit this profile. The man obviously mistook me for someone else. And so when I explained that he needed to either call his boss and have him babysit, tell his wife to take two aspirins or just take a sick day, I handed the child a cookie as I escorted him and his father right back out the door. Actually I had experienced quite a bit of male mental misconceptions regarding women in general, but this was the first true misogynist I had personally encountered.

The most influencing change in our lives was that after we sold Johnny's business and had time to take trips to Nevada to look for a home and do some investigating with regard to demographics and the possibilities available for opening a new business, as well as traveling to cities like Boston for professional reasons and because we always loved Boston and Cambridge. Alex especially loved going to the museums and the sites. What we realized was that for the past ten or twelve years, we were basically living our separate lives together, which was not our original intention. I had been extremely involved with the Veterans and the Agent Orange Movement and even though Johnny was a part of that, but most of his life and time was spent running and building his business. Because we now had the time to just sit and talk, that was what we talked about and why we believed that things really had to change. When Johnny was so ill and could have lost all that he had worked hard for, I realized that solving people's problems or helping them to solve their own problems involved hanging a shingle which was portable and would always be there, but my husband had started with just one simple vending machine and regardless of hired help and whatever assistance I could provide, he had created a major business with government contracts that supported his family and his employees' lives very comfortably by working like a mad man. And he could have lost everything if he hadn't taught a little boy of nine-years-old to understand his lessons by understanding Daddy's business. I saw that Alex's math was easier to learn from a business aspect than a textbook. One thing that we never discussed and maybe we should have, was to basically take the money made by selling the business and our home in New Jersey and just retire. We were in our early 40's and both of us were over-achievers and workaholics, so even if we had known anyone, any friends, who were in our financial position and had just decided to stop working, we probably would not have taken that road to retirement. Here we were in Las Vegas, Nevada, but we weren't drinkers and we had made a conscious pact not to gamble, which was easy because neither of us were gamblers at any time in our lives except on ourselves. We loved the buffets and the restaurants, which were always situated at the end of a long row of slot or poker machines, which were also the long lines one had to stand in to wait for entry; so when we came out on vacation, Johnny would sit down at a poker machine with a $10 roll of quarters and play poker. He would quit as soon as he was either out of quarters or if he hit four of a kind. Once in a while he would hit that winning combination as soon as he sat down and at first I would ask him why he just stopped until I realized that this was his practice and wasn't I a lucky woman to have a husband who maintained the courage of his convictions? I would sit next to him, for lack of anything better to do and play one quarter at a time, if I won money, great; if I lost my roll, I was done and I was pissed at myself. Even though the amount was very insignificant, I knew that no one built those magnificent casinos so that I could win their money, which I had worked hard for when it was my money! But that was when we *vacationed* in Vegas, our pact was made when we decided to move to Vegas. At one point, during the Agent Orange lawsuit I had come to Vegas to assist in explaining the lawsuit to the Nevada Vietnam Vets and to help set up a Las Vegas Vet Center, so when

I had mentioned that we were thinking of moving to Southern Nevada, one of the members of a local service organization was very serious when he told me that, he knew me and he knew that I was 'a straight arrow', but if my husband had any personality failings or problems, such as alcohol, gambling, women or drugs then Vegas was not where I wanted to live. I took his advice and thanked him because it just annoyed the Hell out of men and women when I would try to explain that I had a husband that other women would kill for!

Little did we know that while we had no such problems, our eldest son had most of them and a couple of others which would nearly destroy us, in trying to help him or get him to change, as it did him; but that is a story for another book in itself. Our youngest son, Alex, as a grown-up, became an entertainer on the Las Vegas Strip and blessedly inherited his parents' disinterest in donating money to big buildings and rich casino owners. Of the three of us, not even one has ever experienced winning a royal flush on any machine, in all these years, but Alex recently explained to me that it is very similar to winning a lottery, first you have to buy a lottery ticket! What a concept!

The business that we opened was also a unique concept, ice cream in the desert, delivered to your neighborhood. In other words, we brought state of the art Good Humor Street Vending trucks from the company in Boston that made them and loaded them with all of the ice cream novelties from the Good Humor Ice Cream Co. Our drivers were all people who had been thoroughly vetted, background checked and totally above reproach, each of whom we had well-trained in dealing with the public. It was unbelievable to us that the only ice cream street trucks in the entire Clark County area, where the bulk of the entire state's population could be found, were individually owned and makeshift built vans who used dry ice to keep their products cold. This was unlike anything we had ever encountered in our entire lives with no safety features, no insurance and no cleanliness or rules for how their products were stored or for that matter, no restrictions on what they sold or how the products were handled. Even though we were aware that this environment and the population was much smaller than any of the cities or even towns on the East Coast, we were amazed at the reception that we received from the business and the residential communities. Once we had our grand opening, covered by the media in great detail, business took off like we were not even prepared for or had anticipated. Upscale gated housing developments and apartment complexes that were normally off the grid to the independently owned trucks were calling our office to request that we provide service for their residents and were thrilled when we offered to set up an actual time schedule for when we would normally be on their property. The television news shows would send everyone from anchors to weathermen to do a ride along, on the air which not only helped with their own needed community involvement, but our credibility as the "accepted vendor" for residents to allow their children to buy from. The Metropolitan Police Department worked with our company to give away free treats to entire neighborhoods whenever they wanted to show that they were community and clean neighborhood aware. The list of involvements was endless and Johnny was like a kid in a candy store because of all his endeavors, being an "ice cream man" had always been his favorite.

Before we had met, and then again after our son Eddie became a teenager, Johnny had bought walk-around Good Humor trucks, in the first instance, for extra income and when Eddie got his driver's license, Johnny thought he should own his own business instead of working for strangers in order to put away money for college. I always suspected that like Willy Wonka,

Johnny Kopy was inhabited by a type of Peter Pan character who was only happy when he was the Good Humor Man. So, in Vegas, his favorite part of this large business was actually setting up new routes and with the precision of what is now a GPS, he would write every route, street-by-street and even made notations so that the driver would know where the speed bumps were so that nothing unexpected would dislodge any of the candy from the shelves.

Johnny came up with ideas, based upon his love of seeing happy children and being a positive part of the community that went from everything from a free ice cream for A's on report cards to another freebee on birthdays. He would also encourage drivers to carry dog biscuits on their trucks and if a child came up to the window to buy an ice cream, if they had their dog on a leash, a free biscuit was on hand. It had to be free because dogs had no pockets, ergo, no money! It was great to see how happy he was with the new business considering how sick he had been just a year before and how hard he had worked especially in the severe weather of New Jersey. In Las Vegas, the only weather adjustments we had to make as far as business was concerned, was to the incredible heat of Nevada Summers which really did take some getting used to.

Right before we had left New Jersey, Johnny was unable to walk for any distances due to his acute arthritis and the massive blood clots in his right leg. We had a manual wheelchair that we took everywhere we went so that if there was walking or he became tired, he could use the chair, but, my Johnny had always been such a strong and vital man that being confined to the chair was embarrassing to him, so, we decided that as a less humiliating alternative we would purchase a handicap scooter that could be dismantled and carried in the trunk of a car and which Johnny felt was not only more comfortable, but also provided him with more personal mobility. It was about three months before we were scheduled to move across country and we weren't sure if the VA, which was now providing for his medical needs and costs, was going to provide him with the scooter or reimburse us the $6 thousand that a scooter designed for John's height and weight would cost, but we bought it anyway. Yes, we had gotten a divorce because of the hundreds of thousands of dollars that Johnny's illness cost every year, but there was no way that he was going to go without something that he not only needed, but which would allow him the dignity that a wheelchair seemed to take away from him. So, we paid for the top of the line mobility machine and gave it no more thought about who would pay for it, *we* did.

Now Johnny was tooling around wherever he wanted to go on his state of the art "big man's scooter" and his inability to walk was no longer as embarrassing a problem for him. In fact, if we were in a store and I mentioned that we needed something from the other end of the store, he would take off careening at the racing speed of about 5 mph. to get what we needed and put it in his little basket. I would never say anything to him but I would smile inside at how "cute" my grown husband looked on his big man hot cycle!!!! About six weeks after we had arrived in Nevada with its dry climate, and had begun to set up our new business which involved having to climb on and off of street trucks just to set them up and check them out, Johnny began to notice that the dryness of the climate must be responsible for the fact that he was able to stand, walk and even climb the steps into our offices or onto the trucks without the incredible pain and discomfort that he had become so accustomed to dealing with. It was only about a month later that Johnny declared that he no longer needed the use of the scooter. I found myself torn as a devoted wife who was so happy that her husband was doing so much better medically and physically, while another part of my psyche was screaming "Six thousand dollars for a scooter we only needed for a few months!!" For Alex's 11th birthday, he was very happy with his almost brand new big seated, double battery scooter birthday present. Fortunately, it was some while before anyone told him that no matter how many decals and flags we had put on it, it was still a handicap three-wheel scooter!

My goal was to make our company self-sufficient through popularity as I possibly could by the use of media and acceptance. I joined every group and organization that had anything to do with being in business in Southern Nevada. I became a founding member of (NAWBO) the National Association of Women Business Owners; a Board member of D.A.R.E.; a member of the Special Education Ad Hoc Committee of the Board of Education; Vice-President of NEW Nevada Executive Women; a Board member of Friends of Channel 10 (PBS television station); and about ten other high profile organizations, as well as a member of the Southern Nevada Gang Task Force because of our affiliation with Metro and I suspect, more importantly, because I came from THE BRONX, NEW YORK. The only groups I did not join were Veteran-related since in the Las Vegas area, all service organizations had only one interest in the wives of Veterans and I didn't bake if I could avoid it.

Johnny got the chance to do the one thing that he couldn't enjoy while he was killing himself back East; he sponsored sports teams and worked at soccer, football and baseball games for youth sports, running the concessions and giving back a percentage to each team. We got to work together most of the day and again after the trucks came in at night, as well as to both have interests that we liked being involved with, and it was all much less taxing than our lives and problems before we relocated. We were working hard and tired, but happier with our lives than we had been in a long time; and we were the three musketeers. Alex would come down to the warehouse with us every evening, when the trucks came in and was probably the youngest forklift operator in the United States.

For a short time we were able to practically forget the health nightmares that we had lived through for so long. The move across the United States in an RV had been a major horror for Alex, because by the second day of this six day journey, which was supposed to be a sightseeing vacation of sorts, Alex developed a viral infection and massive oral canker sores that didn't allow him to eat at all or to even drink nutrition without enormous pain. Regardless of how we tried to make him comfortable, it just wasn't happening and there was no reason to turn back because none of the doctors who tended to him for so long could explain what was happening before anyway. And so we shortened our sightseeing plans to straight driving in order to make it to Vegas in four days but our hearts were breaking for our very sick little boy. Once we arrived in our new home, we were able to take him to a local doctor and had elected not to give him a long dissertation about Agent Orange, but to just have him treat the viral infection and the canker sores as opposed to him ordering Alex to be hospitalized for a zillion tests while the doctor went shopping for a new boat or car that we would be paying for. Besides, by not mentioning his "pre-existing condition", his care would be very thorough and paid for by our health insurance. We had due to insane costs learned how to play the insurance game when we could. We also were well aware of what symptoms meant what problem and how serious our actions had to be when it came to Alex's health. We had made an enormous amount of effort in trying to find the best pediatricians and specialists in Clark County, Nevada while we were still back East but we couldn't even find any doctors in New York or New Jersey who could recommend anyone in the entire State of Nevada, so we knew that we had a job on our hands once we were settled.

It is virtually impossible to find world class medical help in a state that does not have a major University or medical facility within its borders. More importantly is the fact that the Las Vegas we were moving to was not the major city that it is now in the twenty-first century, Nevada was a sparsely populated state with its most populated county being Clark County where the only major city, by their standards, was Las Vegas and its population was less than a quarter of a million residents, as previously mentioned. The second problem that we seemed to constantly run into when speaking to medical professionals, was either that they had never heard of dioxin poisoning, Agent Orange and amazingly, the condition of Luekopenia. Those who had some idea of the existence of Agent Orange, probably because of our federal lawsuit, were sure that we were looking to involve them in litigation and wanted no part of it. All we wanted was a doctor of some intelligence and ability in his or her field, to keep our son alive and functioning. My way of doing things, which was much harder before there was an Internet, was to go through the telephone book and look at physicians' names and ads and then call and ask where they went to school and when they graduated. There were of course quite a few who refused to give me any information and were actually leery of my reasons, but hopefully I was able to do some personal good for those people who obviously didn't think that a mere human, non-medical professional did not have the right to make such inquiry in order to make an informed decision.

Having come from a position of dealing with everyone from

the President of the United States on down, trying to play the "who is capable of being snootier" game with me really was an effort in masochism on their part. I, in my most nasal snobbery explained, and I always loved this one: "Excuse me, same or better education, but different door!" Then I went on to explain that I was making inquiry as to whom I could trust to care for my most prized possession, my child and his health. The majority of those who allowed themselves to be intimidated into believing that another human being is superior to them, usually gets embarrassed and hangs up or allows the person on the other end of the phone control their interaction. While it has always been my belief that if someone says no, when they should say yes, they obviously did not understand what I was asking for, so I explain it again, just slower. The only problem that wasn't fixable was if we needed a specialist who was up-to-date on science there didn't seem to be anyone medical who knew what I was even talking about anywhere in Vegas.

We were finally blessed to find Dr. Robert Gordon, quite by accident, and I do mean accident; since we had allowed one of our employees Donna, a girl of twenty-one, to take Alex and his friend Carl, with her own eleven-year-old sister to the drive-in movie one evening. I mistakenly trusted this girl's maturity and judgment since it was usually NEVER that Alex was allowed to go anywhere without one of us or his tutor or nanny, but we let him go, what possibly could go wrong? Right??? Johnny and I took in the trucks for the evening and were getting ready to go somewhere for a late supper when the police showed up at our office and told us that they had stopped a car with a woman driving for speeding and they heard a young boy screaming in the backseat that she had to stop and get the police or an ambulance. When they looked at the child, he was covered in blood and all cut up. The police put our precious eleven-year-old son, our only reason to keep going every day, into their car instead of waiting for an ambulance and raced to the hospital. The officers told two other officers to take a report from Donna and talk to her sister and Carl to find out what the Hell had happened, while they drove to our office after another car had gone to our home and found it empty. We followed the police car to the hospital, their lights flashing, but if truth had been known, as fast as they were driving, had we gone without the police escort, we would have been there in half the time. Alex was on an Emergency Room table, the clothes and the skin on the entire right side of his torso was torn from his body and he had been sedated, but only after the police radioed the hospital from our office and told the nurses that we had given permission. He was crying and begging for his parents when we walked up to his side. We still had no idea of what had happened because it couldn't have been a car accident since, when we came running into the hospital, we saw Donna, her boyfriend and the other two children were fine. What we were told by the police who had interviewed Donna, as the driver, was that Alex got ran over by another car and she didn't really know what had happened and that she wouldn't let the police talk to the other two eleven-year-olds. The officers told us something we already knew, her explanation made no sense so as soon as we got Alex calmed down and promised we would be right outside. The first thing I did was call our son's best friend Carl over to us. I didn't even have to ask what happened, before he blurted out that when they had gotten to the drive-in movie, which was one thing that Alex had never been to in his life. Donna told the kids to sit on the hood of the car so that they could see better while she and her boyfriend watched from the car (????). Alex had never sat on the hood, the roof or in the trunk of any car before and must have thought it was a cool teenage thing or maybe he was just obedient as good boys always try to be. Carl said that the car that had been parked in front of them, closer to the screen, moved from that spot and that Donna yelled out the window that they should stay where they were and she was "just going to move the car forward". Carl said that he and Donna's sister were sitting on the hood on either side of Alex and that before they could all jump off, not only did she put the car in gear and move forward, she didn't unhook the speaker from the car window so that when the speaker pole broke, Donna stopped the car short and both kids fell off the sides, but Alex was thrown off the front of the car and then Donna *drove right over him*. He was screaming and so instead of looking under the car or yelling for help, she put the car in reverse and backed over him, running over him a second time. All of the skin on Alex's right torso, his arm, his thigh and part of his face was burned off by the heat of the muffler and whatever other hot parts were able to touch his body.

By the time the police, my husband and I went to talk to Donna, the officer was holding my arm, supposedly to support me; but Nevada is a gun state and I worked with money, so my side-arm was in plain sight. I don't think that the police originally thought it necessary to disarm Johnny and me but they did by this time.

When Alex was released from the hospital and sent home, his bandages had to be changed no less than once every two hours and he had to take medicated Jacuzzi type baths every four hours. The hardest part was that the loose skin had to be removed from his burns, the skin treated and medicated and then bandaged again. From the night of his accident, just like when he was born and needed us, one of us was always with him at the hospital. Once he was sent home, I took an indefinite leave from work and all obligations, so I could be with him all the time. Johnny and

Alex's much loved Nanny Grace were the only other people that he saw or who took care of him. The doctor at the hospital had released Alex with the instruction that if there was any problem we should either bring him back to the Emergency Room or take him to his pediatrician. When I explained what I had been going through trying to find a good doctor for Alex, and that what had us really frightened was his Luekopenia and what these injuries would do to effect his health and immunity ability, the doctor gave me a name and told me that the doctor he was giving me was who he trusted with his own children, Dr. Robert Gordon.

We shall herein refer to him as Dr. G. He was the answer to a prayer and considering not even the health problems that our son had always had to live with, but this new trial for him to come through, we needed and Alex deserved a wonderful doctor. One week after Alex got out of the hospital, I made an appointment for us to go to see Dr. G. and when I explained to the receptionist what was going on and my even greater concern regarding his white cell count, she spoke to the doctor and then made an appointment for Johnny and I to bring Alex to his office at the end of the day so that there would be no sick children in the waiting room. Just from that understanding I felt that we had found exactly what we needed in a doctor. Dr. G. spent a lot of time with us and it turned out that not only was he very aware of the problems caused by Agent Orange, but he had served when Johnny did, where Johnny did, as an Army doctor, so his joke was that it was ironic that just like in Vietnam, Johnny brought in the wounded and he fixed them up. There wasn't much laughter though because this time the wounded was our young son. But the comradeship between Dr. G. and my husband began from that first visit and since we had brought Alex's medical records since birth with us to show him, he took them and told us that when we came in the following week for another check-up of

Alex's injuries he would have some opinions with regard to our son's health situation. I can speak for both my husband and myself when I say that this was like the end of a nightmare when it came to our son and we felt that, just like with Dr. Bennett Shaywitz of Yale, those years before, we had found another pathway to get through the terrifying paths of our lives.

The following week when we returned, the doctor explained exactly what Luekopenia was, which, although we had heard the term and looked it up with minimal results; none of our doctors back in New Jersey seemed able to actually explain what the diagnosis was to any understanding that wasn't frightening. What we learned was that Alex's condition was almost the exact opposite of Leukemia, but not as deadly, as long as it was monitored consistently and treated. The concept of there being any treatment was also alien to us as none of the doctors tending to Alex had ever mentioned what was happening, why it was happening and more importantly, what could be done about it. Dr. G. told us that he had made an appointment for Alex to be seen by a hematologist/oncologist for white cell count and testing and that he wanted the specialist to determine the right dosage of gamma globulin to build up and maintain a suitable level to enhance and build Alex's immune system.

The shock of not having to argue with our son over not being able to take part in normal social events was tremendously exciting. He was not out of the woods, but at least there was hope and a control in sight. I still had to borrow the sky box owned by some friends of ours at the Thomas & Mack if Alex wanted to attend a concert or sports event, but at least he could go without being sick for a week after. The best time for me, as noisy as it was, was when he was about thirteen and I took him to a New Kids on The Block Concert and we were able to sit in the general guest area. We acknowledged that Alex's white count would have to be monitored for the rest of his life and that he would eventually be able to consider getting off the gamma globulin, but that was just fine as long as he remained healthy. The only adjustment that we had to make was when he was about fifteen and started to deal with bouts of dehydration that would end up with a long hospitalization, for which we had no warning and no reason; nor would all the Gatorade in the world rehydrate him. Dr. G. figured that out as well. Alex's health was about as normal as it could be until he was in his early twenties, when a whole new Agent Orange nightmare took hold of him and is still a case of constant concern and anticipation.

About two years after Dr. G. began treating Alex, Johnny, who had been seeing private doctors since we moved to Nevada because there was really no Veterans Administration Medical Center in the Las Vegas area, had taken Alex for his shots and surprised me when they came home and my husband, this man of forty three, was elated to tell me that Dr. G., a pediatrician, had agreed to be Johnny's primary physician as well. I wasn't sure how my husband, nicknamed Tank, was going to fit into those little seats and baby scales, but he seemed like the weight of the world was removed from his shoulders. The thing he thought was funny about this whole scenario was that because Johnny suffered from Agent Orange Diabetes II, something that Dr. G. said the VA still wasn't recognizing that was caused by the spraying, so Johnny could not get a lollipop after being given a shot! He did however, pay closer attention to the blood clots and embolisms that were constantly threatening my Johnny's very existence, than any other doctor that Johnny had ever seen before.

The greatest heartbreak of our lives, was sometime in 2003, when we called Dr. G.'s office to have copies of Johnny's medical records sent to the new VA Medical Center specialists office, to be told that Dr. Robert Gordon, our friend and our medical savior, had passed away from complications of Agent Orange poisoning. That night Johnny and I just sat down and cried for the man who had saved our son's life, but couldn't save his own. Nor, as it turned out could anyone else since the longevity of those who served in Vietnam is anywhere from fifty to sixty-five-years-old, if they are lucky. Robert Gordon, this wonderful doctor was fifty-seven-years-old when he passed, a young and very brilliant man. As I retrace my life, with my son still in a constant battle to stay alive, I would be so grateful to be able to once again find a doctor as dedicated and knowledgeable as this man who had saved my son before.

CHAPTER FIFTEEN

LEAVING IT ALL BEHIND, OR SO WE THOUGHT

AS MENTIONED EARLIER, the entire reason for us to leave home, family, friends as well as everything we had ever known from our life in the Northeast part of America, was not because we had any desire for the glitz and glitter of Las Vegas, Nevada. As we had also checked out Scottsdale, Arizona and toyed with the concept of Southern California; the reason, the only reason for our relocation was based on Johnny's serious need for a warmer and dryer climate. Arizona felt more like being trapped in an oven with no off switch. California was not possible either. My husband who had jumped into firefights to save the wounded and then came home to run into burning buildings, had no way to adequately express his fear of earthquakes. He swore they could only be survived if people could flap their arms rapidly enough to take flight, soaring above the crashing buildings and opening earth. Subsequently, the lesser of all evils became Nevada, which in 1988 was actually a much less expensive place to live than any other state in the country.

The greatest part of our life in Vegas, for almost ten years, was very pleasant and we really did spend most, if not all of our time together. While we did have to make some concessions because of Johnny's medical conditions, they were minor ones. For example, any trip that we wanted to take was best being done by car, rather than plane so that he could stretch his legs and avoid any clots. We had to watch his diet too, because even though he was a diabetic, he was diet controlled and didn't need insulin, at that time. One thing we had to monitor constantly wherever we lived, was that because of his propensity toward clots and embolisms, he had to live on blood thinners which made him similar to a hemophiliac in that if he got a cut or an injury his bleeding would either take a very long time to clot, if it wasn't too large or deep. But if it was major, he had to be rushed to a hospital immediately. Whenever we would have company at our home and especially anywhere in the backyard where Johnny would often go barefoot, if anyone brought anything outside that was glass or breakable, one would think they had killed someone by the way we all reacted. Just one experience was enough to make our entire family hawk-like in our paranoia.

For the most part, John's life was much easier and his health was not a constant worry, and although, we lived in Las Vegas, Nevada, my husband, as I mentioned before, was actually almost totally vice free. He never drank alcohol, gambled or even looked at another woman, but his self-control was almost non-existent when it came to his diet and all the things that a diabetic is supposed to avoid. I would beg, argue and yell, but this was his Waterloo and so I bought every cookbook for diabetic cooking I could find and even invented some safe desserts that he could enjoy, like homemade sugar-free cheesecakes before they were available commercially. My grandmother, suffered from Juvenile Diabetes all her life and was forced to take insulin shots daily, but what I thought back to was the fact that she was very careful about her diet and what I had learned were "exchanges" which covered everything from fruits and vegetables to breads and starches. There was no way to watch Johnny every minute and we did own what was basically a junk food company. Johnny admitted that his love of food was something that he just didn't seem to have the willpower to control and used the excuse that *it wasn't that bad* because he wasn't on insulin; until he was.

In 1996, we had decided to sell our distribution business since it was getting to be too much and consumed too many hours, but probably more importantly because we not only saw the economy changing, but anyone and everyone who had a van was constructing a makeshift ice cream truck and selling not only ice cream and candy, but cigarettes, drugs and anything else they could think of from trucks with no permits, licenses, safety features, insurance or even health certificates. Were not only rules in Nevada and maintaining all were very expensive costs for maintenance, insurance and proper product handling as well as salaries. We finally decided it was time to retire or so we thought. It was then that, Alex at nineteen, who had always worked in our family businesses took the opportunity to tell us that he wanted to follow his dream of working in the music industry. We knew that he loved music, danced and wrote lyrics, but we had never thought that this "shy" young man wanted to be a performer.

Alex had not had a medical crisis of any high degree since he was hospitalized when he was sixteen for his last bout with extreme dehydration, but we also knew that he was very conservative about his social encounters, to the point that if he had plans to go out with anyone, male or female, and that person had a head cold or any even minor condition that was transmittable, he would immediately put off those plans. Once he had even stopped seeing a young girl because when he went to pick her up for a movie, she was coughing and sneezing. He turned around and walked away. We knew how he hated the extents that we had to put him through as a child, but in a sense, we were gratified to see that when he was too old for his parents to interfere, he was taking very good and preventive measures to avoid anything that could challenge his immune system. By the time he was 18, he was no longer in need of gamma globulin shots or medications and he really did try to avoid crowds or unknown situations. That was the first thing that we thought of when we were discussing the choices that Alex had pretty obviously set as his future goals, but his argument was already prepared with the actual facts of what was happening in the entertainment industry.

We did not know about other cities, but Las Vegas which has long been known for its extravagant shows and nightclubs, had recently angered the musicians unions by cutting back and even eliminating live music, orchestras and bands wherever they possibly could and replacing accompaniment with canned music or a new phenomenon that was becoming almost a performance art in its own right. It was called deejaying. A disc jockey was who our generation listened to on radio as if it were a religious experience; but those were disc jockeys, guys like Uncle Brucie, Wolfman Jack and Murray The K, who played the latest records and talked to their teenage listeners about matters of teenage interest. However, with the advent of a new form of music, known as Rap or Hip-Hop, while the performers recited a form of rhyming or poetry, there would be the "DJ" who played the all-important background music on turntables with big speakers and the DJ would make moves known as "scratching" which would often get him more applause than the "Rappers" got. This is what our son, the child we had poured so much love, effort and education into, wanted to do with his grown years. He wanted to be a "Hip-Hop DJ" and he just expected us to jump up and down in anticipation of his stardom. Didn't he grow up with Johnny and me as his parents?

Did anything about us give him an inkling that keeping him alive, healthy and highly educated was never because we wanted him to play records for a living? If he had said, he wanted to be an actor, a professional dancer, singer or a film director, maybe we could have found some way to clap our hands on the way into the kitchen to stick our heads in the oven, but he wanted to be *the guy who played the records*. When we were teenagers and went to parties, the guy who played the records was either the owner of the hi-fi who didn't want anyone else to touch it, or he was the guy that we remembered who couldn't get a date or anyone to dance with him so he monitored the 45's on the record player. But this was our six foot, four inch incredibly handsome and popular son and he didn't even own a portable hi-fi! I even blamed myself because when he was two and a half he coated my stereo with Play Dough and I let him stay alive!!

We did, however, have a great argument to try to dissuade him from this choice, because we pointed out that the job he wanted to do involved going into crowded clubs, stadiums, etc., where people with all kinds of "airborne and contagious germs" just floated around looking for someone with a sensitive immune system. I really was proud of that point, until we realized that he had already either weighed out the possibility of what we were going to try to stump him with, or he was a really quick thinker in a debate situation. He countered our objections by telling us that we knew how he loved music and how he loved going to parties, clubs or events, but he didn't really enjoy being in the middle of a crowd. Besides the health threat, but also because he was very claustrophobic ever since that car accident, he told us that when he did go to these events, he always became friendly with the DJ's and would hang out above the crowd and on the stage, so he was in the midst of the excitement without being right in the crowd: and because he was with the DJ, who was the celebrity in the room, girls figured he was a DJ and so it was "GRRReat".

Johnny made a deal with our son to insure that while he was learning and practicing his trade, Johnny would come out of his short-lived retirement and they would open a pizza place together that would be Alex's but his dad would work when Alex had a "gig", because we convinced him that every entertainer knows that when he first starts out, "it's always necessary to have a day job". Where we ran into a really big problem was that the pizza place was such a success that it turned into a couple of larger restaurants and then a supper club at the same time that all those infrequent DJ gigs brought Alex to the attention of the owner of Club Vivid, which was the nightclub inside The Venetian Hotel & Casino. He was offered the position of Resident DJ at the major nightclub at one of the Five Star resorts on the infamous Las Vegas Strip. This was a job and an honor that usually requires years of small clubs and most never get that far, but Alex did have the talent. The restaurant business didn't stand a chance and Alex at age twenty-five, became DJ Lexo!

Around the time Alex was about twenty-years-old, he started to develop a skin condition which was very different from anything that he had suffered when he was very young and which went from a type of pimply rash into painful open sores on his arms and legs. Then they began to spread drastically all over his body. His doctor sent him to a dermatologist whose diagnosis for the condition was psoriasis and prescribed topical medications which seemed to help for a very short while with the itching and some pain, but did not stop the spreading. For someone who was trying to run a restaurant and appear on stage which means that he was constantly in the public eye, this situation was not only incredibly painful, but very depressing and embarrassing. Alex tried asking his doctors if this could be a related consequence of his father's exposure to dioxin poisoning in Vietnam. But again, even after so many years and so much publicity, none of the doctors knew anything about the subject and were immediately almost hostile to the imaginary reasoning that this question was somehow going to involve them in some kind of civil suit or tort action. Realistically all Alex wanted was answers, treatment and to make the pain and disfiguring sores stop. This situation remained the same for two or three years, during which time, our son who, especially in the incredibly hot weather in Las Vegas, suffered even greater discomfort by wearing long sleeves and long pants that of his public image. He began covering the visible areas of his skin with tattoos, colorful and elaborately designed pictures and statements commemorating events and family members, as well as religious symbols of all of the religions that he admired.

When his son Giovanni was about two-years-old, Alex had gone out of town, on tour, and when he got to his hotel room and started unpacking, he realized that he had forgotten to pack the pictures of Gio that he always set up when he traveled. When he got back to Vegas, he went straight to his tattoo artist with a portrait of his son sitting on the floor with a toy truck and had the entire portrait copied onto the inside of his forearm, from the elbow to the wrist, with the inscription "My Reason" on a banner under the portrait. His motivation, as he told anyone who saw this beautiful picture of his beautiful son, was "this way he is with me all the time".

When his beloved father passed away in 2008, Alex had his full facial likeness copied from a picture that took up his whole upper arm and inscribed with banners on both the top and bottom stating "My Teacher" and "My King" and the very first tattoo he had done originally was my first name "Rena" over his heart, for which he explained that unless he had a daughter, his Mother's name was the only female name he would ever have inked into his skin, which I took as a great honor, although I would have been happy to share space on my human billboard with a granddaughter or two.

In about 2002, Alex began having major problems with pain in his back and his legs that he thought was related to either having to move the heavy DJ equipment and then thought that he had somehow suffered a strain or incident to his spine. He went to a chiropractor but that ended up causing even greater pain and so did exercise and working out so his doctor gave him pain medication and sent him to a sports pain specialist thinking that he had pulled something while playing arena football. He underwent treatment and testing to try to figure out what exactly was his problem. It turned out to be disc problems which required laser surgery, however, it was also found that he, still in his 20's was suffering from arthritic spurs, which Johnny and I recognized as what Johnny had developed in his mid-30's. While we quietly watched and worried, we did not want to alarm Alex or even believe that this condition, which by this time had again confined Johnny to a wheelchair that he would never be getting out of again, was taking a toll on our son, who had already been through so much.

In early 2003, we were given a surprise that we never saw coming. Johnny and I were in the process of leaving Vegas and retiring to beautiful Rosarito, Mexico with great climate and weather and conveniently only about thirty-five miles from the VA Hospital in San Diego, California. Our original retirement dream, started with the first time we drove past an RV sales lot while on a date very early in our relationship and we both said simultaneously, “Someday I’m going to own one of those”. With Johnny confined to a wheelchair, the idea of traveling the country in a sort of hotel on wheels, had to be forgotten, so we researched many different destinations until we fell in love with Rosarito. One of the biggest reasons that Johnny, an American hero, was anxious to leave the United States, was President George W. Bush, because he considered this man, not a President but an embarrassment and a coward because of his behavior during the Vietnam War and ever since then.

The surprise that ended up changing our plans completely was that our son Alex, who had always said that unless he could find a relationship like Johnny and I had, would stay single, had stated to us that although he wasn’t ready to marry anytime soon, he at twenty-five, was ready to be a father and was actually thinking about that prospect. We had taken that conversation as just something that grownup children say to see how many hairs will turn gray automatically. About three months later, we were advised that a young woman that he had known for a number of years was pregnant and that he did believe that he was to be a father. Since, as an entertainer and very popular with the opposite sex, we had been confronted with this claim previously. As soon as Alex demanded a paternity test before he would acknowledge any responsibility, the subject was dropped and he never received another call about a baby again. This time was very different in that, first of all this was early in a pregnancy, and when we suggested that we all wait for the birth and a paternity test, our son told us that it wasn't necessary as Maria had been a close friend of his since their teenage years and he was sure that it was his child.

The real surprise was that since she was already a single parent and our son would not consider marriage under these circumstances, the girl did not want the child. Alex told her that he would take custody and all responsibility for the child and would go through the entire pregnancy and childbirth at her side. He was going to be a sole custodial father and raise this child by himself, which put a very quick and final end to our plans for retirement in Mexico or anywhere other than Vegas. We were going to be *grandparents*, full-time grandparents who were going to help our son and take care of the baby when he was working. Even more surprisingly, Johnny and I were pretty happy at the task ahead. We didn't even think about Agent Orange or the prospect that anything could happen to yet another generation. Boy, were we naive!

Johnny and I returned to Vegas two weeks before Maria was to have the baby by C-section and moved into Alex's guest quarters until we could figure out what plans we would all be making. We set up a new crib in our room since it was downstairs and easier than climbing up and down with a baby and then we waited. Giovanni was born on August 19th, 2003, the same day as the Hundred Year Flood or Monsoon hit Southern Nevada with such force that it made news all over the world because it destroyed homes, roads, cars, businesses etc., and first responders were saving people for most of the day and evening. Years later, that storm would become almost a catalyst for déjà vu.

We were very surprised that Alex was not only right there in the operating delivery room, but never left his son's side until it was time to take him home. Giovanni, was born with such a beautiful face that nurses and hospital personnel were coming from all the wards and floors to see "the baby with that face". His Grandpa Johnny lost all of his skepticism when he looked at that child and said, "No paternity tests needed, look at that Kopy Unibrow!" There was a bonding between that little bundle and his grandfather from that first day, even before the baby had sight and the only bond that was stronger was between Giovanni and his proud daddy. Although the doctors had assured us that our grandson was perfect, from the day Alex brought him home, I noticed that Johnny was reaching down and running his enormous hands over Gio's stomach and I knew that the nightmare of Alex's infancy was on his mind.

What was really funnier than anything I had seen in quite some time was that my husband and my son, both very large and muscular men with the ability to reason and think better than most, were terrified of this little miniature person. They weren't trying to shirk the changing or the bathing, they were actually afraid that this little bruiser would break, and it was very funny. It was also quite obvious that Giovanni was going to be one very spoiled little boy because before he could even lift his head or turn over, his father was buying him everything he saw whether it was age-appropriate or not.

He was a very good baby and we took him with us everywhere we went during the day so that Alex could come home from work in the mornings and sleep until early afternoon. Our Gio was very alert and incredibly bright with none of the health problems that we were constantly checking and watching for. Such a happy child who was always smiling and laughing so we anticipated that Gio would start to speak early, just as his father had. What he did do earlier than we expected was to *climb* out of everything and onto everything. Gio never really learned to walk, he went from crawling to standing to RUNNING and boy was he fast! He figured out how to climb up the staircase in our home and when we put a gate across the stairway, he figured how to climb over that easily. He could climb out of his highchair in record time too. His pediatrician was informed of our fears about the inheritance of Agent Orange poisoning, but although she told us that we didn't know what the future would bring, she was very satisfied with Gio's growth and his health.

An incident that alarmed her and us was when Giovanni was about a year old and quite unexpectedly, his birth mother, who had less than no interest in this child except on special birthdays, etc., asked to take him to her friend's house party on a Sunday afternoon. Johnny and I dropped him off at her house and told her that we would be back in the early evening. When we came back to pick him up, Maria came running out of the house and unceremoniously dumped a screaming child into his car seat and then told Johnny, with real annoyance that Gio had been running around the backyard of her friend's house and then jumped right into the swimming pool "on the deep end" and went to the bottom. What she was angry about wasn't that she hadn't been watching him as she should have been, but that she was wearing a brand new outfit and had to "jump into the pool and get him out". Johnny looked as if he was going to grab her throat, but through clenched teeth asked how long he was under the water. Her response was "oh less than a minute". We took off and Gio cried all the way home and finally fell asleep in my arms which was where he stayed all night long.

Alex called Dr. Henderson and told her what had happened as related by Maria, to which the doctor advised him to give Gio some baby Tylenol and bring him into her office in the morning instead of taking him to the hospital as Alex wanted to do. The next morning, Alex, Johnny and I got to the doctor's office when it opened and we went right in. This was the first time I ever heard any doctor, especially a young female doctor, when she looked at Gio's ears, yell out "Bullshit, less than a minute!" Then realizing that we looked shocked and really scared, she quietly told us that he had to have been underwater longer than what we were told because both of his eardrums were shattered! She gave us some medications and advised us how to take care of our precious baby's ears and what to look for as far as any problems. She told us that unless something happened to come back in a week and hopefully if all went well that he wouldn't need surgery and his ears would heal by themselves. That was going to be the last time that Alex would allow Gio to spend any time with his bio mother without strict supervision. Besides Alex's decision, the doctor had strongly suggested this as well.

For Johnny and me, the nightmare of this entire situation was that we weren't Gio's parents, we were his grandparents and even though we were Gio's legal guardians when Alex was working or on tour, we could suggest, but we were not in a position *to demand* any specific actions where our grandson was concerned. Luckily, this was never really a problem because Alex was a wonderful father and even though his schedule was insane, he never missed spending as much time as he could with Gio and insisted upon knowing everything that his son did or said. In mid-2004, as if Gio was responsible for miracles, right around the time of his first birthday, the VA claims for 100% Agent Orange related service connection that Johnny had first filed in 1981, but were constantly stalled and put off for years, were granted 100% retroactive to 1981!

Gio started to talk when he was about a year-and-a-half and knew the names of all his friends on Sesame Street and on the DVD's that were bought for him as soon as a wholesome show or Disney/Pixar movie came out. Grandpa spent hours watching those movies with him and his grandpa was as Gio got older, his constant companion and favorite toy, but especially his talking buddy. Johnny was also the first person to realize that Gio wasn't just an active kid, he was *an athlete* with what Johnny called "perfect balance".

At first people thought that he was just being a proud Gramps, but after spending time around this child, our friends, relatives and everyone would be in awe of the things that Gio could do. He had a Fisher Price playground that usually sat in the backyard of a house, but one evening I came home to find it in the middle of our family room, just sitting there with Gio sitting in the swing and watching one of his movies with his grandpa. As soon as he saw me, he jumped up and pointed to the television and then said "stop" to his faithful remote control grandfather!!! Gio climbed up onto the top of the playground and there was a balance type bar across the top about 4 feet long, which this tiny person climbed onto and then stood up. I watched with terror in my heart as he started to walk across the beam as if it was a sidewalk. I was afraid to yell out at Johnny for letting him do this, for fear Gio would lose his footing, but when he got to the end he just climbed down, sat back in the swing and motioned for the television to resume. I was in a state of shock and disbelief and Johnny just looked at me and said "I told you, perfect balance!" Whenever the weather was nice, we would have to go to the park with the most climbing activities and sometimes instead of climbing on the parts meant to climb on, Gio would climb up the outside awnings, with one of us in attendance, under him with our arms outstretched at all times.

It was late in 2004, when Alex began to suffer from very debilitating back pain and started to see specialists because we were terrified that he was suffering from the same Agent Orange related arthritic deterioration that had taken away Johnny's ability to walk when he was about thirty-six years old. The first surgery that Alex was told he needed with a minor laser adjustment done by the orthopedic pain surgeon as an outpatient, but the outcome was not what he had been told to expect and instead of pretending that the Agent Orange connection was a myth, as doctors had done for years after the Vets started getting sick, and seeking medical help wherever they could, since the VA was not complying with their mandate to take care of those who had borne the battle. This new phenomenon that most of us were faced with when it came to our grown children developing the same problems that had overtaken their fathers, was now being blamed on the herbicide poisoning that the VA wasn't recognizing.

About one year after the expensive and ineffectual laser surgery, Alex underwent invasive back surgery which was blamed on two herniated discs and not osteoarthritis after all. He spent about a month recuperating and then life went back to being our own kind of normal, until Gio was two-and-a-half-years-old. By this time Johnny and I had moved into a nice small house with a swimming pool and a large backyard as well as a room for our grandson. Alex had gotten engaged to a lovely young woman named Kenya McQueen and the two of them had moved into a beautiful new house with plenty of room for Gio to have his own room, a playroom and a tree house in the backyard.

Both Alex and Kenya were working one day in March of 2006 and Gio was due to go the pediatrician for his booster shots, which when he was just a few weeks old, and was being given his necessary vaccinations, we related that although the common practice was to double and sometimes triple up on different preventive medications, that since "Grandma is old school," we did not want him to be given more than one serum or vaccination per visit. Multiple inoculations was very often given due to parents who had to work or for some other reasons and were relieved to not have to make six trips for six shots, as parents of my our generation normally had to do. However, to our way of thinking, it wasn't necessary and we were all concerned about possible side effects from not only our own health worries, but from things we had heard. The day that I was supposed to take Gio for his first booster shot, Johnny went into a medical crisis and had to be taken to Nellis Air Force Base Hospital by ambulance. I called Alex and asked him if I should postpone the doctor's appointment and take our grandson to the Base Hospital with us, or if he wanted to call one of his friends to come and stay with Gio. He told me that he would call me right back and about five minutes later he told me that he called Maria and she was going to drive "their son" to the doctor and he would try to meet her there. When I came home from the hospital, I called Alex on his cell to find out where he and Gio were and that's when I heard that Gio had been admitted to Sunrise Children's Hospital due to a very high fever and constant vomiting.

I called Nellis and asked the nurses to tell Johnny not to call me because I had to run out somewhere. He had enough to deal with and I really had no information to give him and so I was deliberately vague to the nurse, who wouldn't have kept the truth from my husband if she knew what it was. I drove so fast that I'm surprised that my tires weren't leaving the ground and only stopped long enough to pick up a special stuffed animal for Gio to hold onto. By the time I got to the room he was in, he was calm and sleeping but still very feverish and both Alex and Maria were lying on either side of him, also sound asleep. I sat in the chair by the side of the bed and watched them all sleep. I realized that I was monitoring every breath that Gio took, just like my husband and I took turns doing for the first two years of our own son's life. Now here I was, not letting myself fall asleep or even close my eyes except to blink, watching my grandson and my grown son as they slept with the same fear and concern of so long ago right back in the front of my mind.

By the time he woke up, Giovanni was much cooler to the touch and did not seem to be in any physical distress, but he did seem rather lethargic and very quiet, which we thought was from his attack since he was *not* a quiet child. The doctor at the hospital checked him out and told Alex to take him home and whatever had caused the problem seemed to have passed, but give him Children's Tylenol and keep him on liquids and bed rest for at least a day. If he still seemed ill then, Alex was to take Gio to his pediatrician.

Two days of trying to keep Gio resting and quiet was no easy task; but Johnny was home from the hospital and he kept his grandson in bed next to him. When it became "monkey" jumping time, either Johnny or one of us would whisper, "watch your movie Gee, Grandpa's sick"; and the sweetheart would lie down and put his hand on his grandpa's arm or belly or whatever he could reach. By day three there was no keeping him down and we gave up trying, so Gio was running and jumping and doing all his Gio stuff. We were all so relieved that it took us about two or three days to realize that Giovanni had not said not one recognizable word since we brought him home from the hospital. It was a Friday when we made the discovery, and no matter how we tried we could not get him to say any of the words he always said or sing the songs that he always sang along to on his favorite shows and DVD's. On Monday morning Alex called and made an appointment with Dr. Henderson to bring Gio in for a follow-up visit for the next day. I met Alex and Kenya at the doctor's office so I could take Gio with me and they could go to work that evening.

Dr. Henderson checked Giovanni's vitals and looked him over and attempted to get him to verbally respond. She looked concerned and told us that she suspected that our little boy was showing signs of "Autism". This had never been a word or a condition in our vocabulary other than that my sister Andrea was a special education teacher in the Clark County School System and she worked with Autistic children. We had seen her class and Gio was nothing like those children, he had no tics or jerky movements, no tantrums or violent behaviors. But we agreed to have him tested. When we were leaving her office, we asked when he was scheduled for his next booster shot and it was then that we learned that when Maria had brought him to the doctor and took him in before Alex got there, the nurse asked if she still wanted, as the notations said on Giovanni's chart, to give him just one shot per visit instead of a cluster of five vaccines. Even though Maria had never taken this child to the doctor and the nurse did not know the custody situation, when Maria told her that she "wasn't going to make a bunch of trips" and to just give him the shots, the nurse did as she thought she was being told by someone who was a parent. We were in shock but tried not to react because there was nothing that we could do except upset each other and Gio on the drive back home.

Although we never found out why the symptoms of autism took effect when they did and we did research as to whether the vaccines he had been given had any such side effects, which we learned that none of them individually had any neurological side effects, I had a always suspected that the vaccinations of five different medications did create a reaction of the high fever and nausea that put our little boy in the hospital, perhaps it was the effect of the fever that brought the autism to the surface.

What seems to happen in most people's lives, is that things can be happening to a large part of the human population but we are, somehow oblivious to whatever it is that does not affect us personally. Johnny and I did not have any knowledge about learning disabilities or special education until we had Alex tested when he was four and a half you will remember because we could not teach him to read. We were originally very worried because there were no private schools that we knew of equipped to help us then. Ironically, the subject of special educational needs for children was in the late 70's and early 80's just becoming a topic of conversation which, while it was covered in newspapers and on television talk shows more and more, because it was not something that we had been facing in our own lives, we didn't even notice, until, we were forced to face it and then we did pay attention to what we had been oblivious to. So it was, not for Johnny and me where our little boy was concerned, but for that little boy who was now a man; a father with his own child who had just been diagnosed with a condition that none of us had been paying any attention to. Autism, was, to our surprise, not only very much a real problem but it was at epidemic proportions in 2005.

Just as Johnny and I had, when we were faced with what our son needed, Alex who normally hated scholastic research and studying, began to learn all that he could about the condition known as Autism Spectrum. The actress Jenny McCarthy had just written a book about her own son and her successful efforts to "pull him through the Autism Window"; and even though she admitted to be as lost about the causes and effects as we realized that we were, she had found some success and so her efforts became our game plan for Gio.

Gio started the Autism-developed K.I.D.S. Program at one of the schools in our district when he had just turned three-years-old. It was a twelve-month school and a full-day program, which our immediate concerns about whether it was simply a sort of babysitting service, as opposed to an educational experience were soon waylaid by a wonderful teacher and trained aides, who prepared almost a full time one-on-one daily program. Gio loved going to school and his teacher fell in love with him, as most people did as soon as they met him. He was just that kind of a warm little kid, who couldn't speak, but had a wonderful sense of humor and a most addictive laugh.

Alex never missed a teacher's meeting and took the same interest in Gio's I.E.P. (Individualized Educational Program) that we had taken in his education. Alex's attention and devotion to his son was incredibly surprising in that even though as many children with autism are, Gio was a runner who had to be corralled and kept a constant eye on especially when he was first diagnosed. But Alex dad took Gio everywhere with him and enjoyed every aspect of being with his son. If he went to California to ride ATV's on the desert dunes, Gio, with his own smaller helmet and pads went with him and whenever Alex had someplace to go that was a long drive, his little guy was right there in the car, listening to music and singing in his own language.

The most surprising part of our son's life that he changed without notice or even regret, was, as Johnny became sicker, Alex stopped touring or doing any out of town work, so he could concentrate on being Gio's dad and his father's strength. I don't think anyone could be prouder of their son than we were or of the deep love that Alex had for his own dad.

What we did learn was that in 2005, autism which twenty years earlier been about 1 out of every 2500 children in the United States, with much less professional or concentrated study of a problem that was not as prevalent at that time, was now about 1 out of every *190* children. At the time of this writing, in 2013, the numbers are basically pandemic. In the general population 1 out of every *88 girls* and 1 out of every *55 boys*. This is the average except where the offspring and grandchildren of people, such as Vietnam Combat Veterans, Koreans who resided near the DMZ or served in Vietnam, Australian Veterans' families, and of course, the citizens of Vietnam and Vietnamese Americans who left Vietnam after 1974. Due to the exposure to the chemical by-product known as dioxin poisoning from the spraying of Agent Orange; the numbers for our groups in connection with autism are now *1 out of every 34* children born to these groups. To be candid, although in 2005, through our involvement and research with Autism Speaks, we knew of the rapidly growing problem in the United States, but it was not until I testified before the International Conference in Paris, France in May of 2009, that I learned of the pandemic that was covering the globe's effected inhabitants, nor was I planning to pick up the activist sword once again.

It really wasn't until after we lost our wonderful Gio in August of 2009, that because of that loss and the near loss of Alex's life as well, that the anger from the late 70's consumed me again, but with a greater fervor than ever before because I had been fighting to keep my loved ones alive and now they had almost all been taken from me. Gio's accident never would have happened if we had broken through the Autism Window and freed our boy from being trapped inside himself. And so, after the accident, as Alex fought for his own life and we both became devoted to stay alive for each other, I became a totally involved part of the Epigenetic Autism Fight and the effort to get the research, the recognition and the treatment that the government still did not recognize where Agent Orange offspring were concerned.

CHAPTER SIXTEEN

THE GIFT OF GIOVANNI, THE SMALLEST VIETNAM VET

BY LATE 2006, JOHNNY'S MEDICAL problems were becoming so incredibly severe that we moved closer to Nellis Air Force Base Hospital and also nearer to his VA doctors. His Agent Orange Diabetes II was out of control and he developed a sore on the bottom of his foot that would not heal and in fact, kept expanding and deepening. His doctors tried everything that they could and eventually had a nurse coming to our home twice a day, every day, to use a medical vacuum to clean out the wound and also inserted a tube, called at pic-line, into his body to give him intravenous antibiotics. He spent so much time in the hospital that we finally got the VA to provide him with all the hospital equipment and furniture he needed right in our home. The new house that we had moved into had a very large backyard and a cement patio the length of the house, with gardens in the front that had a cement walk running through them so

Johnny could go outside in his electric wheelchair and water his flowers, something he really loved to do. He had always loved to swim, day or night, anytime it was more than seventy degrees outside and I hated to see how he would look with longing at the big pool in our backyard, but even though we had bought an airtight rubber sleeve to go over his bad leg, it was too hard for him to maneuver in-and-out of the chair and the pool. After that horrible experience with his bio-mom when he was a year old, we made sure that Gio could not only swim exceptionally well, but that he knew how to control any situation involving himself and deep water. Johnny's pleasure would come from watching his grandson, who was a real fish. Alex would throw Gio from over his 6'4" head as far as he could into the other end of the pool like he was a football. That kid would come up laughing and swimming right back to his daddy! Their water act, like Gio's climbing always made me cringe in fear!

Gio had learned how to dive and he could go from one end of the pool to the other, underwater, as if he were trying out for the Olympics. It was about that time that I began to introduce him as "and this is my Grandson Giovanni, he is going to be an Olympic Something". People would look at me as if I were a totally insane human being until, like his teachers, they saw him in action, climbing to the top of not the playground climber, but the chain link fence that went around the school, or once they saw him swim. But his grandpa was always his best buddy, his biggest fan and his favorite toy. The VA had supplied Johnny with a large handicap accessible Chevy Conversion Van that he could drive with hand controls and after he was forced to have to allow his diseased leg to be amputated to the knee, his van was his freedom, his pride and joy; and it was Gio's favorite of all the cars. Even though there was a school bus that would come to pick Gio up every morning and bring him home after school,

Johnny had decided that at three-years of age, he wanted to drive him to school every morning and so Gio just came home by bus. The best part of Gio's morning was when they got to the school. He would stand on the motorized floor rack that was supposed to lower Johnny in his wheelchair to the ground, but Johnny would stay in the driver seat and Gio would let himself out of his car seat, step onto the moving floor rack and Grandpa would use the controls to open the doors like a stage; the rack would come out and then be lowered. What was happening during this daily theatrical event was, Gio standing with his arms out to his sides, like Siegfried or Roy and making his entrance while his teacher, Mrs. Hyka, was waiting there and laughing like she didn't see this every day.

Considering the pain and the illness that was consuming my husband and how I wished there was some way that I could take some of his hurt from him, I believe that our grandson came into our lives because Johnny needed something to hang on to and to bring some reason to laugh and feel joy, especially since Gio left us so soon after his grandpa passed over. It has always been my belief that, regardless of the pain and how ill he was, that Johnny stayed with us for at least three years longer than he comfortably should have because his grandson needed him so. Even when Johnny would be in his hospital bed, I gave up on trying to chase Gio off of the trapeze at the head of the bed that Johnny was supposed to use to lift himself up. Our Olympian would be sitting in it and swinging over his grandpa's head. At first I thought he was going to fall on Johnny or kick him with his long legs, but then I looked in when they didn't know I was outside the door and saw that every time Gio swung across, Johnny would tickle either his feet or his bottom as Gio went giggling over him as if they were getting ready to do a show at the Mirage Hotel.

The last time that Johnny was in the Base Hospital, before the amputation, which was done in University Medical Center, there was a problem with MERSA, a bacterial infection so severe that it caused death and was almost impossible to cure. We did not know that Johnny had contracted this infection because the military were closed mouth about things. I never would have even known about it at all if I hadn't overheard some nurses whispering in the hospital cafeteria. That was when Johnny and I decided that the Base Hospital was a place to avoid and were able to find an excellent doctor at UMC, which was not only a teaching hospital, it was an excellent facility. It was at UMC that we found out that Johnny had also contracted Sepsis, an infection from which he never recovered and which was one of the causes of the horrific symptoms that also shortened his life. For about five years before he passed away, Johnny was diligent in collecting every single piece of paper of his medical records from the VA, any private doctors and all hospitals because he desperately wanted to sue the VA and the hospitals for worsening his conditions and hastening his demise. He was always talking to lawyers on the phone or sending out copies of his records to the point of compulsion and when I complained about how much effort he was putting into this, he finally explained to me that his illnesses and new health_conditions had used up much of what we had saved toward our retirement. He said that he had to be sure that I was going to be okay. I really should have realized at that time that my loving husband knew that he did not have much longer to live, but, I wouldn't accept or even acknowledge what he knew was inevitable. I don't know if my inability to see what was happening and that my Johnny was trying to tell me caused any harm to anyone but myself. Nor do I know if Johnny had wanted to have any kind of conversations about what I refused to accept; and I shall always feel unsure about whether I did somehow let him down. Alex often would tell me that I was the only one in the family who could never see what the situation really was.

I do remember that the weekend that we lost Johnny, we had called the paramedics to take him to the hospital because he fell and was feverish. The EMT told me that it was time for me to start thinking about putting Johnny into a Hospice and while Johnny also must have sensed something because he did not want to go to the hospital, just to be put back in his bed. The paramedics did not feel it was the right decision to move Johnny. I became very angry with the EMT and let him know that his job was to tend to my husband, not to tell me what I should do with my husband and so they took Johnny to the hospital, where he died twenty-four hours later. I often think that he knew that he was dying and wanted to die at home with the people that he loved and who loved him more than anyone could ever imagine and that somehow I denied him the right to do that, which even all this time later, still brings me to tears. I'd never known that anyone could love another person the way I loved him.

How ironic was it that it was a known fact that Johnny had been 100% related. But how was a civilian doctor supposed to know any of that? As devastated as we were, Alex and I had to go to the VA Clinic and see, Dr. Maria Diaz, Johnny's doctor to get the cause of death rectified. I remember how angry she was when we showed her the letter from the VA. She was not being flippant, just really angry when she made the changes necessary and then wrote a stinging notification to the VA office that "be more concerned about what caused the heart to fail, because when it does, there is no longer life". Johnny, even after crossing over the Rainbow Bridge, was striking a blow for veterans' rights.

We chose a small funeral parlor and a very simple ceremony because neither Johnny nor I ever wanted a dog and pony show type of send-off. We were quiet and not involved with the many people and business associates that we had been in the years before. Our only close friends, Marvin and Roberta Price who I had grown up with back in the Bronx and then got together again when they moved to Las Vegas, had both passed on quite suddenly about five years earlier and so except for our sons, and those that we had adopted through the years, so there really wasn't anyone that needed an invite. Funerals had become a very overdone sort of fashion show and a massive display of feelings that no one really felt, yet thought it necessary to pretend deep and unbridled sorrow for others to witness, over someone that they very often didn't even have any real connection with.

As stated before, there was no way that I would allow my beloved Johnny to be buried in the barren and foreign soil, and no matter how many years we had lived in Southern Nevada, it was never actually our home. The decision was made to have his remains cremated so it was not going to be possible to have a full military salute, however, the funeral parlor was able to arrange for a military chaplain to officiate and speak of the hero, the man we had told him all about, ***JOHN VINCENT KOPYSTENSKI,*** a man who was so very much loved. The Base Guard sent two officers to honor Johnny and present the flag in his honor. It was a beautiful ceremony but all I wanted was to die!

The day before the funeral, Alex, Giovanni, David and I, as well as some other family members went to a viewing at the funeral parlor so we could spend some time with Johnny's remains, hoping that his soul was above watching over us. Gio was with us, but because he was non-verbal, we did not know how to explain to him that the Grandpa that he so adored, was not coming home again and we had no one to leave him in the care of, so we just told him that his grandpa was sleeping. He sat quietly for a while and watched as one-by-one we all went up to say a prayer or tell Johnny something private, when suddenly he bolted up and climbed onto his grandpa's body. Gio put each of his little palms on his grandpa's cheeks and clear as a bell said, "Poppa, wake up, watch Shrek!" There wasn't a dry eye in the entire room and finally Alex stood up and went over to Gio, telling him that Grandpa was very tired and to let him nap. He had his arms wrapped around his little boy so tightly that I thought the child would break in half as his daddy hid his face in Gio's neck and I could see that my son was trying to hide the fact that he was crying.

I guess that all things do happen for a reason because the weeks after the funeral were and remain a blur in my mind but I remember that I couldn't seem to get out of bed; and yet, I recall that I didn't sleep either. About two weeks after we lost Johnny, our world was torn apart even further. When we realized after Giovanni was born, that we had to stay in Southern Nevada, Johnny and I thought that we should buy a new house which we could leave to Alex and his son when the time came. However, every house that we looked at in late 2005 and early 2006, that we liked seemed to come with its own set of financial problems. It wasn't that we couldn't afford the payments or even a down payment, it was that the realtors, every single one of them, when we sat down to make an offer and apply for a thirty-year fixed mortgage, explained to us that "that's not how we do it anymore!" Even when Johnny said that we had a very large VA mortgage allowance, they tried to talk us out of going VA. Apparently they were all pushing, what we all later knew to be the "sub-prime mortgage" which was a two-year A.R.M. financing that required that we only pay the interest for two years and then there was a balloon due! The promise was that when the two years was up, the realtor would find us a fixed long-term mortgage at a low interest rate. To Johnny, who was a pretty shrewd man with numbers, and could recognize nonsense faster than most, this made no sense at all because we had the VA, which was about as low interest as one could get and incredibly secure.

We were in the car leaving the last house that we liked but weren't going to buy unless we could get the same kind of mortgage that we had had with every house we ever owned, on both sides of the country; when Johnny said something that later came back to remind me of how smart he was. He said that if this kind of financing was allowed to continue, people who couldn't afford expensive homes but were being lulled into buying them with what he called the "two-year bullshit scam", the bottom is going to fall out of the economy within about two years.

How ironic that we had, at that time, decided to just find a nice house on a long-term lease and just rent until we saw what happened, and what happened was that two years later, *THE BOTTOM FELL OUT ON THE REAL ESTATE MARKETS!* How did that affect us since we were renters? Well, the beautiful home that I last described, with the gardens and the pool, etc., the home that Gio's teacher, Judy Hyka, called "GioVille"; which we were renting for $2,000.00 per month, never missing a payment, was owned by a couple who had bought the house during the "sub-prime" period and didn't even wait for the balloon to come due. It seems that while we were paying them not only what their mortgage payment would be, but an income profit as well, they weren't making the mortgage payments at all and no one bothered to tell us. At that time, the laws in Nevada did not protect renters, at all, regardless of any situation. So, one morning, two weeks after Johnny's funeral, there was a knock on my door and there were armed Constables at the door to advise me that my house had been foreclosed on and we had thirty minutes to evacuate the premises! I don't remember if I screamed, yelled, or called out to Alex, nor do I remember passing out, but apparently that's what happened. I recall sitting on a chair in my bathroom with an oxygen mask over my face with paramedics trying to convince me to let them take me to the hospital, the same hospital where just weeks earlier my husband had lost his battle to stay alive.

Almost three weeks later, after being forced to stay in a weekly apartment, having put all of our belongings into storage, we were able to find a new house in a guard gated community and I am sure that the rental agent thought I was crazy because of how many demands I had to be assured that the owner of the property was reputable and that the home was securely financed. The agent was terrific in understanding what we had just been through and not only did she provide us with a five-year lease with three options to renew, but provided proof that the owner, who lived in Japan, owned the house outright. She even went so far as to write into the lease, that should the homeowner decide to sell the house, we would have right of first refusal to purchase. Even though the house did not have a swimming pool in the backyard and the backyard itself was very much smaller than the one at GioVille, it was its own kind of paradise for Giovanni. It was not only guard gated, there were roaming guard patrols day and night with not only a very large golf course across the road, which supplied Gio with a never-ending supply of stray golf balls in the backyard, but the onsite country club not only had playgrounds and swimming pools, but it was also the location of the only private Water Park in Southern Nevada, including the Mega Resorts. The gigantic house had a winding staircase, twice the height of regular staircases, with a polished wood railing all the way from the top landing to the living room which was Gio's only method of descent. It was quite obvious that he really loved his new home._When he came home from school, before he went upstairs to change his clothes, he would jump into Grandpa's big electric recliner in the living room, push the buttons on the controls so that he was sitting sprawled out where he used to sit on Grandpa's lap for hours, and he would have a quiet conversation, in his own language, with what I can only assume was Poppa's Spirit, a voice that only Gio could hear.

Word of Johnny's passing had spread through the international veterans' communities and I received condolences and letters from hundreds of veterans and even some old friends of Johnny's from before I had met him. I found that communicating with Veterans and activists from days gone by, via the Internet was a comfort to me because I could talk about Johnny and old times without feeling like I was sounding like a widow to be pitied. I began to realize that the old feelings of anger that had given me purpose in the 70's and 80's were coming over me once again, but this time they were fueled by my loss and of all the plans that Johnny and I would make and fantasize over for so many years regarding what our life together would be like once we were done working and free to be what we really had never had a chance to be – just the two of us.

When we were young, we used to lie in bed and talk about how we were going to go and lie on the beach at "Pango Pango" even though neither of us had ever heard of or knew even if it existed, but we were going to go there together. He had always wanted to take me to Hong Kong, which is where he had gone during the War for R&R and had great memories of. I didn't know how to explain that the great time was because he was out of firing range; but he wanted me to see it before the Chinese took control of that city. I would laugh and remind him that when he was there, he had met and shacked up with a prostitute for the week to save hotel money; not only would he not be able to find her again--and that she had probably aged--but even more concern had to be that why would she want to have "you and your wife" stay with her just to save us some money? And how we would laugh. The Vets were the only ones I could relate these memories to and get some pretty funny feedback because they understood and probably had the same crazy daydreams with their wives over the years. Even guys who had never met Johnny, knew him because in a sense, they *were* him.

The greatest gift that I believe Johnny sent me from wherever he was watching, was a friend. I received an email from a veteran named Charles (Chuck) Palazzo, a Marine who had served in Vietnam years after Johnny's tour of duty. He was a member of some of the groups that Johnny and I belonged to and he had heard about us over the years. He actually lived in DaNang, Vietnam, having gone back there to live a few years earlier, as a number of Veterans have done, becoming disillusioned with the United States. These Veterans were still patriotic and loyal Americans, who just wanted a less corrupt and politically confused way of life; which ironically was in a Communist Nation. Despite a number of invitations to return to Vietnam on a Veterans' group tour, Johnny had never had any desire to return to where he had seen so much pain and dysfunction; however, he did speak of going to visit with the Hmong, a tribe of Vietnamese who were different than any others and who, when Johnny's chopper went down and he was injured, had found him and taken him back to their village, hiding him and nursing him with great care and then getting him back to An Khe, his Base Camp. His love of those people and for the children in orphanages never wavered over the years.

Chuck Palazzo grew up in my old neighborhood in The Bronx, and even though he was about eight years younger than I was, we had the same kind of upbringing and many memories of places and things from our childhood. Chuck had originally contacted me to pay his respects and also to tell me of the severity of Agent Orange still evident and actively poisoning the people of Vietnam. He became a real lifeline for me and we would talk on Skype for hours, sometimes every evening. I would talk about Johnny and as time went on it was as if he had known my husband and could even discuss things that he believed that my husband would have felt about things going on in my life. He had never been an_activist and would ask me a zillion questions or my opinion on different matters that he also cared about. Chuck Palazzo became not only my closest friend, but I can honestly say, without reservation, that this man, this friend, not only kept me strong, but probably saved my very life a number of times with no motive or alternative purposes in mind. He cared, not only about me, but about Alex and really loved Gio, and I could not have made it through without his strength and his friendship. The only commitment that we made to each other was that on his end, he would always be my friend and do whatever he could for me; and on my end, my promise was the same to him and that if, for any reason he needed or wanted to return to the United States, regardless of what his personal situation was, that as long as we had a roof, he had a roof, no strings attached.

I would like to believe that how Chuck profited from our friendship was that since late 2008, he has become one of the strongest and involved activists I have ever seen. His intellect and his writing ability has become a source for numerous newspapers, blogs and periodicals in the United States and all over the world and I can only hope that I have somehow been a catalyst and an asset to what and who he has become. But I also believe that he just needed someone like me to kick him in the butt and realize what Johnny had taught me about myself because when Chuck was intimidated by some idea or task, I found myself saying "Why can't you?" just as my Weeble always said to me. I really believe that we both met at a time when we needed the one thing that people don't normally understand the importance of unless they have been in any situation where one's life is one the line, a real friendship in which each person is as concerned with the welfare and happiness of the other just as much or even more than about themselves. It is often the unfortunate truth that when people are in such a vulnerable state, they are easy pickings for others with either less than altruistic personalities or fooled into relationships that are based on things other than real and lasting comradeship. So I believe that while Chuck and I did find that kind of friendship and_intellectual equality, we were and are indeed very lucky to have met when we did.

What, if one thinks about it carefully and honestly, for people like me, who many praise and credit for effecting the lives of millions, our reality, or at least my own, is that in my more than six decades of life, the real friends who have been incredibly important to me as a human being; some of whom I have never even been in a position to shake hands with, but they have changed and empowered my life. They can be counted using both hands and actually having fingers left over. I am not speaking of political allies, media allies or even cause-based friendships and followers. I am referring to those people, who when the world was a very cold place, stood by me like a warm fire. Friends who asked nothing of me, expected nothing from me, yet were there to listen, advise, help and care in any and every way that they could. Johnny and I gave so very much to so many people, but when all we needed was others to care, it was amazing how many disappeared like a magic trick. However, Roberta and Marvin Price who passed due to insane circumstances which while I would love to shout their story from the rooftops, it is their story and their children's and grandchildren's story to tell. This couple had nothing to do with Agent Orange, Vietnam or any of our other concerns, but when things went rather crazy, which is the story for another book, Marvin and Roberta Price, were our biggest supporters and most generous friends who only asked that we go out to dinner with them regularly and spend the time laughing and remembering our childhoods in The Bronx and not say one word about reality at the present time. I feel unworthy because I don't think that either of them ever realized what they meant to us. Frank Delaney and Dave Cline, who despite the fact that we were comrades in so many ways, they both were a constant intellectual oasis in a desert of despair, which for someone like me, is a commodity not easily found without having to put up with inflated egos and boring dialogues.

Even though there were some others throughout my life that were there when I needed a friend I could_trust, for the past forty years of my life, I never even realized that I knew thousands of people from all over the globe, but I didn't give much thought to "needing a friend" because I was one of the most fortunate people on Earth who was married to a man who was capable of, where I was concerned, filling every human need. It was no wonder that when I lost Johnny, my loss was so great and crippling because I lost not just a husband, but a partner in everything, a best friend who could bring light into any room just by entering it, a savior and protector and every other position necessary for a good life. What was truly amazing was to find out that everyone who knew the two of us always considered me to be the strong one, the smarter of the two of us and the driving force in all we accomplished. How could so many people have been so wrong? Eventually I realized that even those mistaken images were orchestrated by my husband because he was happiest when staying in the background and never needed any recognition for who he was and what he had created because his ego never needed stroking.

But I always knew the truth, so when Johnny wasn't there with me, while condolences were by the thousands, not one person asked me, "So what are you going to do now and how are you going to accomplish anything?" Then, suddenly, it was as if Johnny had scoured the Earth from on high, found and sent Chuck Palazzo to cover the "best friend and confidante" slot. Within a very short time, our son Alex, who had also lost his best friend and wisest life-guide, started talking to Chuck and seeking counsel with an open mind, often repeating Chuck's words and advice with obvious gratitude. I used to tease Chuck because both Johnny and Alex were physically such large men and Chuck, although an insane Marine (since one learns quickly that all Marines were insane) was all of about 5'9" and under 200 lbs. easy but capable of such "tall wisdom" so I began calling him "vacuum packed". The uniqueness of our relationship was that sometimes I would realize that I had been talking to a complete stranger about my husband for hours and so I would apologize. Chuck would tell me that he was so sorry that he_didn't ever meet Johnny because mutual friends within the Veteran Movement had told him some and now he felt like he knew Johnny better than anyone and it was his privilege. Wow!!!

Chuck also told me that wherever on this planet that Dave Cline stood up to speak about Agent Orange, he would start every speech with the story of John and Rena Kopystenski, which I did not know he had done; so I googled and found Dave's speech in about ten different languages, all starting with that one introduction, so Chuck said that now he understood why Dave was telling the world about my husband. In September of 2008, right after what would have been Johnny's sixty-fourth birthday, I received a call from a woman named Merle Ratner, from New York City who told me that she took over the lead of Dave Cline's organization Veterans For Peace, and that although she wasn't a Veteran or a spouse, she had been working with Dave for years and had heard so much about John and Rena Kopystenski that she felt like she knew us well. She apologized for not contacting me when Johnny passed but didn't want to bother me. Her purpose for calling was because before Dave passed away he told her that once he was gone because he was so very ill, that if a powerful speaker was ever needed to take his place, that she should contact Johnny and me. He gave her our private phone number and swore her to secrecy since he wanted Johnny's serious health problems and our privacy to be respected.

Merle then told me that in May of 2009, there was going to be a hearing before the International Tribunal of Conscience on Agent Orange in Vietnam, in ***PARIS, FRANCE*** and Dave Cline had instructed her to tell me that I "had to testify". Because I was in a bit of shock at this, I asked her to email the information to me and I would get back to her. The purpose of my stall was that I was sure this was some sort of a prank or a scam of some sort. I immediately called the head office of Vietnam Veterans Against War, which was all of our original starting place in the struggle to confirm that this woman was who she claimed to be, which they did confirm. By this time I received the email I requested and not only was it a formal request, it said that all of my expenses would be paid and I would be afforded a monetary figure to cover any additional expenses while in Paris.

I immediately contacted Chuck because I was at a loss for what I should do, although I knew that Johnny was in Heaven, laughing at this tough old lady's confusion and yelling "**GO TO PARIS!**" Chuck's excitement was enormous and he couldn't understand why I was having such a hard time deciding because he told me over and over again that I had to make the trip, as there was no one who had the words that I did. I remember begging him to meet me in Paris, but there was no way he could arrange to do that. He finally convinced me by telling me that the verdict of the Tribunal would determine so much internationally and that I "*owed it to Johnny to let the world know how he was murdered by our own government".* That was it, those were the words I had needed to hear and so I agreed to go. All those plans that Johnny and I had made, late at night, lying in bed and talking about the future; plans that we would never see happen, and now I was flying to Europe all by myself, all alone and knowing no one involved. However, the closer we got to the day I was supposed to leave, the more my anger at my loss and the damage done to so many millions of people, grew and empowered me with the words to author an eleven-page testimonial speech, so strong that it made headlines in newspapers throughout the entire world, except for the United States, the country that sprayed the poison that murdered John Kopystenski and poisoned our only son and his only son. The verdict of the Tribunal which I am told was strongly influenced by my speech, was that the spraying of Agent Orange in Vietnam was A WAR CRIME and their findings were forwarded to the World Court, which is where it has stayed and has gone no further.

Just a few days before I was to leave on this monumental trip, I found out that even though I was told that I could stay and visit Paris for anywhere from one to two weeks, I would be staying with a member of the French – Vietnamese Friendship Organization at her home as opposed to in a hotel. I_don't know if that was the reason that I informed Merle that my intention was to fly into Paris, take a day, give my testimony and then take another day before returning to the United States because I didn't want to be away from Alex and Giovanni any longer than that. However, after meeting and spending time with my hostess, whom I shall call MH, I was really sorry that I had decided to cut my stay so short. One of the things that I didn't even think about until I was already on the airplane, was that although I was fluent in Spanish and Italian, I did not speak or understand more than three words of French.

Now, in 2013, I possess an iPhone that has a translation App which allows me to speak English into my phone and whatever I say is translated to whatever language I set the App for, but in May of 2009, I was on my own and pretty sure that I wouldn't even be able to get out of the airport if it involved my having to speak to anyone. Fortunately Merle had thought of everything in this regard because there was a private car service waiting for me and a driver holding up a placard with my name on it; just like in the movies, to take me to where I would be staying. Paris was beautiful and I felt so importantly welcome; it really was a very nice experience. Merle, who did speak French was also going to be staying at MH's "Flat" (apartment) with me so I felt somewhat less vulnerable when I found that out. The entire arrival was like something in a Charles Boyer movie from the 40's and 50's, and the building did have a "lift" (elevator) except that I had two large suitcases and an overnight bag that, by themselves, were all that would fit in the tiny elevator and that was only if I took the staircase. Those caged lifts looked so cute in the old movies but in real life it was more of "you must be joking" type of experience. I finally figured out that I would have to trust that if I took one suitcase up at a time, there would be no marauding suitcase thieves who would storm the front of the building that resembled the Bastille and run off with my packed outfits and underwear before I could go back down and grab the second bag. I had put on quite a bit of poundage after Johnny's death and now I understood why the French were all so thin, it was the size of the elevators.

Keeping in mind from the beginnings of my ascent into activism, I have known many very famous and powerful female role models and have even been described as one myself, but from the moment I met MH, I knew that I was in the presence of someone who was larger than life. This lady had an obvious sense of who she was and what her convictions were. Her apartment was floor to ceiling books, with her name on quite a few of them and she, very much like me, did not waste words on banal conversation. She also obviously knew more about me than I about her, quite honestly, I knew nothing about her until after I returned home and was able to study all I could find about this most accomplished woman. She, immediately stated that she was a Communist, as if she wanted to get that out of the way in case I fit the mold of what the common belief about American politics dictated; but we knew equally as quickly that we were going to be just fine when my response was just as sure, "I am a Socialist" and we both broke out in laughter.

MH's English was much better than she realized and 1000% better than my French would ever be, but sometimes she had to ask me to repeat something or talk slower which was not really such a foreign request since I have a very heavy New York accent and tend to speak very fast anyway. And for the next few days, we talked about so many things that it was a good thing that Merle had her own social agenda to follow or she would have thought she was invisible. There was so much that we wanted to learn from and about each other's life and so little time since we also had an itinerary that was based upon my real reason for being in Paris. Besides finding, in keeping with my words about "friends", the best friend that Alex and I could ever have, in the years since, is in MH.

I fell madly in love with Paris, France, even though I got to see very little of the City. Just as in my childhood and young adult life in New York City, mass transit of buses, trains and tax-is were the best ways to get around, other than walking; and in Paris, this was a most pleasant experience. The thing that had the most profound effect on me was that in the subway train system known as The Metro, I was hopelessly lost and the signage, including the paper with the address where I was going, were all in French. People, other commuters, were stopping and asking me, in French, if they could be of some help (or that is what I figured they were asking) so when I showed a pleasant young man my handwritten destination paper, he pointedly showed me without even speaking, what train to take and where to get off, etc. In case that culture shock wasn't enough, when I did get on the train, there were young men in their 20's sitting down on the train, who, all in my vicinity, stood up when I entered the car to allow me to take their seat, whichever one I wanted. It has been many, many years since I took anything other than a car or a plane anywhere but I would love to believe that young people in major cities in the United States also had such terrific manners, but I doubt it very strongly, which is really quite sad. As a child, a Jewish child, if we were on a bus or a train and any elder and especially a Nun, regardless of age, got on and was standing close to me, if I did not stand up and offer my seat, I probably would not have been comfortably able to sit down again for quite some time, but that was then and now I do think that Paris is a much more polite place to live. Now, I have a dream for the future which is to move to Paris and spend hours upon hours talking to my dear friend and wandering around the entire city.

CHAPTER SEVENTEEN

GOING TO PARIS WITHOUT MY BELOVED TO TELL THE WORLD OF HIS MURDER

MAY 14TH, 2009 WAS THE DAY before I was scheduled to testify before the International Tribunal and MH had scheduled the entire day for her and I to take part in first, a celebration of a Vietnamese holiday and an art show which was very interesting except that I once again was thinking of Hollywood's version of Paris, because it was drizzling a light rain all day, until we got out of the art gallery and headed for the area of the grounds to observe the ceremonial event. Then it was no longer drizzling, it was pouring, a downpour that had to be a personal affront because the minute we got back into the car, the pouring rain turned back into a slight drizzle!

We went to a meeting of Vietnamese members of the French – Vietnamese Friendship Group, which was a powerful influence upon the large Vietnamese communities in France. I was introduced to someone who had been a friend of MH's for over thirty years; a very regal looking older Vietnamese woman, whose name was Madame Nguyen Thi Binh, she had been instrumental as the foreign minister, in the Paris Peace Agreement and was then Vice President of Vietnam. The thing that I also learned about her was that, very early on, she was a major force for feminism in a country that was not known for promoting women into positions of power. For someone who had actually known such power, her manner seemed so understated. After I testified before the Tribunal, she shocked everyone by coming up to me and hugging me very tightly, with tears running down her face, which touched me deeply. All of us were there to try to do something to save the children of every nationality who had inherited the horrors and the conditions of that terrible War.

I remember wondering what Johnny's feelings would have been if he had still been alive and well enough to make this journey with me. But, I also realized that could not have happened, as there would be little to no chance that I would be sitting at a meeting hall in Paris, France, with people I just had read about in books. Yet, I am also very aware that if Johnny were still alive, I would have had no reason to make the trip and he certainly couldn't have. His health had started to fail in very early 2002, and by 2005 there was no way he could endure even a long car ride, much less a nineteen-hour airplane trip, and keeping him alive and comfortable was all that I cared about, other than the grandson who was our son's gift to his Dad and I. Besides which, as far back as the early 70's, while Johnny thought nothing of writing large checks to support orphanages and the thousands of "Dust Children" (children of American veterans and Vietnamese women) who were left behind in Southeast Asia; he had no desire, whatsoever, to return to the country where he was frightened all the time. As a door gunner on a Medivac Huey, in

1965 and 1966, those gun turrets were not protected by the Dutch half door that came later, so the fact that the normal lifespan of a door gunner was figured at thirty seconds from take-off, the last thing he would have wanted was to relive those memories he'd worked so hard to overcome.

The following day, May 15th, 2009, was the first day of testimony and when we arrived at the Hall, it was standing room only and just like the United Nations, in New York City, which I am embarrassed to admit I had never been to in all the years I lived in New York, every person had a set of headphones covering their ears so that the people in the back glass structure, could translate whatever language the speakers were using into the many languages spoken by the attendees. It was really awesome and even though I normally never gave any fearful thought to speaking to one person or a thousand people, I was a bit overwhelmed and even shaky when I stood up to speak about the unbelievable accomplishments and the horrendous nightmares that had been the past forty years of my life and the lives of so many of the other victims of what could only be described as the poisoning and murder of hundreds of thousands of innocent victims from all over the world. I had brought the photo of my husband Johnny that I had blown up for his funeral and held the picture up for all to see as I introduced the entire crowd to ***"my reason for wanting to hold those who murdered my husband of forty years, accountable!"*** And then I waited for the applause to subside before reading and reciting the eleven-page testimony that I had composed and offered to my Veteran counterparts in the United States to make sure it represented their feelings as well. There wasn't a sound, a cough or even a paper rustling for the entire time that I spoke and a few times it was so quiet that I had to take a breath long enough to make sure that everyone hadn't silently escaped the Lecture Hall. When I was done and looked up at the Tribunal members to thank them, everyone on that panel was standing in honor of my words with tears on their faces and no one was more shocked than I was.

But then the entire Hall, including the translators in the back booth were on their feet and clapping wildly. I guess I was pleased that they hadn't run out to avoid all those words, but I was equally as consumed with sadness and anger, at that moment and then again when others from other countries spoke after me. Angry because my beloved Johnny was no more, my son still could only get the help that we could afford and my beautiful and adored grandson could not speak, read, write or all the things that a normal five-year-old had every right to do. So, in all these years, what had we accomplished, what answers did we get and what was going to happen to this world if 1 out of every 34 children effected by what effected their parents suffered from autism or missing limbs or epileptic seizures and the list goes on. I was grateful to this room for liking me, my family and appreciating our life of pain, but to what end; what exactly had I changed?

The break for lunch was a delightful time at a Bistro in Paris, France with the entire Tribunal Panel, myself, MH and some of the translators, however, to add to my confusion was that the Bistro they had chosen served Indian food! The only actual French cuisine that I enjoyed the whole time I was in Paris, was what MH so graciously prepared for breakfast and a late night supper. I absolutely_fell in love with the breads and the butter as well as the delicate omelets that she prepared, however, I am quite sure that had I not cut my trip shorter than I was invited for, I would have been privileged to other delicacies. At the end of the day on the 16th of May, there was a reception at the Vietnamese Meeting Hall and it was a joyous time, with a full array of Vietnamese dishes and I was given a beautiful invitation in our honor at the

Vietnamese Embassy in Paris, which I treasure. But I had already booked my flight for the very next day because I couldn't stand to be away from what was left of my little family. The greatest gift that I received from my journey, was the friendship of MH, who became closer to me than any sister could be and more dear than any friend, other than my beloved Johnny, Chuck, and Marvin and Roberta.

On the flight home and the six-hour layover in Atlanta, the entire twenty hours, I found myself setting up a plan of attack to bring what I had learned about the fact that the Korean allies were not only sprayed and betrayed in Vietnam, but had been exposed to dioxin poisoning at the DMZ before they were sent to Nam and then again when they returned to South Korea. It was no wonder that the mortality rate of not only the vets, but their children who were exposed, as were the Vietnamese, to the poisoned soil in Korea, but the mutated DNA of their fathers and grandfathers. The rate of autism in Korea was as high as in the United States, however, it had made that benchmark while America was still one in every ninety-seven, while in Korea, one in thirty-four was estimated in 2010. I spoke with Chuck as soon as I returned and told him that I needed victim numbers and breakdowns of medical problems, etc., which was no easy task considering the poverty, the many children who did not attend schools, the lack of shared statistics amongst districts and the scarcity of information able to be collected in Vietnam.

Because of Gio's autism, the need to do something was incredible, especially after speaking to and hearing from the Korean representatives in Paris. I contacted Betty Medici from the Children with Birth Defects that had taken over with the Agent Orange Commission, after I moved West all those years ago, and found out that the Department of Health and Human Services, under President Obama and Secretary Kathleen Sibelius was funding the N.I.H. Or National Institute of Health, which George W. Bush thought was "a waste of time" and that there were going to be grants available for research and studies. Trying to stay within the Veteran Community, she told me that a woman named Mokie Porter from Vietnam Veterans of America, that group that I poured my heart out to in 1978 and got a request for money in return; was working with the CBD on getting grant monies and she suggested that I call Mokie and speak with her.

What I learned was that VVA National had not only not changed much in the past thirty years, and were going to request a grant in order to open "prenatal counseling centers" at a time when Vietnam Combat Veterans were dying in their early 60's and there was no protocol for genetic testing or research involving grandchildren, since most of the offspring of Vets, who were effected, were well over the age of majority, so who were they going to test and how? Ms. Porter was at a major advantage because she knew exactly who I was and the work I had done, while I knew nothing about her other than that her organization, over the past nearly thirty years had lobbied to have the legislation that I had written for Congress to be passed, as did all of the other military service organizations and Veteran activists.

It would be months later that my own son, because of an unfathomable tragedy, would prove causation to the satisfaction of inherited DNA mutations, but at this time, I contacted Dr. Alycia Halliday, who was the Research Director for the National Office of Autism Speaks and who I had been corresponding with about Giovanni and the possibility of Agent Orange caused Neurological Autism. Alycia told me that there was going to be a conference call with members of the N.I.H. and the Secretary of H.H.S., and she invited me to take part in the call. It was an incredibly informative conversation and I learned that they were looking, especially in the area of epidemic Autism Spectrum, for ideas or concepts to examine the possible causes for this rising victimization and to fund research to ascertain the causes and any demographics regarding what was a frightening increase in cases of a number of maladies that didn't even fit the original Spectrum. The grant proposals would not be due for at least eight months to a year, however, any groups or professionals wishing to file should send "Visionary Ideas" to the N.I.H., as early as January, 2010, which was six months from the conference call. I assured Dr. Halliday that I would begin compiling information within the Veteran community and try to get figures and information to create a questionnaire to be sent out to effected families.

On July 20th, 2009, our entire world came crashing down in the greatest and most tragic nightmare anyone could ever have to live through or, more accurately, have to spend the rest of their lives dealing with. Our beautiful Giovanni was killed in a horrific gun accident, just one month before his sixth birthday. One week earlier, on July 11th, his biological mother had begged Alex to let her take him to swim, without supervision, with her other son, at her apartment complex. Alex felt that since his dad was gone and all that Gio had was his dad and his grandma, that maybe Maria, who was now married and had two other children, would bond with Gio, so that if anything happened to us, he would not be alone and voiceless in the world. Alex agreed, although reminding Maria that, if there were any children in the pool playing with water guns, Super-soakers, etc., she was to take him back to her apartment and call Alex to come pick Gio up immediately. He provided a snack bag for his gluten-free, sugar-free son's dietary needs and instructions regarding sugar or soda drinks. Maria agreed with all of Alex's demands and was well aware that in Alex's profession, it was often necessary for Alex to carry a weapon due to the experience that many entertainers had gotten used to in having to sometimes deal with drunks and other crazies. All of his weapons collection was kept under lock and key at home, just as had always been the practice in our family, and he had a lock drawer in his car where he would keep his personal firearm.

Maria took Gio to her apartment pool and Alex drove to her address about three hours later to pick up his son. When he walked over to the pool area, he saw Gio and his half-brother Tyrell, two years his junior, both brandishing toy water-guns, pointed at their own faces and shooting themselves in their own faces with the water. Alex was horrified, because while we knew that Gio knew that guns, just like Grandma's crystal collection, at home, were all ***"NO TOUCH".*** No matter how brilliant we believed this little boy to be, he was non-verbal and because of this, we had no way of knowing what instructions or how detailed information was received and understood by him. He grabbed Gio up and headed for his car with the totally wet little boy while Maria screamed after him that, he was "too strict" and didn't he see "how cute the boys looked and how much fun they were having?"

When Alex got home, he and I tried to explain to Gio why daddy was upset and he understood that he didn't do anything wrong, but we didn't know whether he understood what we were telling him about what he had been shown how to do, especially since in a mountain full of toys, this little boy had never ever had a toy gun or been allowed to watch any movies or shows other than children's features that were always totally non-violent and age-appropriate.

The Monday after the following weekend, Alex and a friend

of his were leaving the house to run some errands and Giovanni, as he often did if he saw Daddy getting ready to go anywhere, flew down the bannister and out to the car so he could go with his dad. He sat in the front passenger seat and buckled his tot seat while the other guy sat in the back seat. Alex's gun was in the drawer and the drawer was latched, or so he thought. Apparently, while they were riding, his friend unlocked the drawer and not only took out the weapon to look at it, unbeknownst to Alex, but also placed a bullet in the chamber and then when they stopped at the pharmacy drive through, put the gun back in the drawer but didn't close the hatch lock. As described earlier, Gio was a climber, and as soon as his dad stopped the car and put it in "park", he undid his car seat and went flying over the back two seats of the GMC Suburban.

While Alex was speaking to the pharmacist and our little Olympian was seat jumping, he must have seen that there was a drawer that he didn't even know existed and that it was slightly open. When Alex ordered him to return to his seat, he had no idea that Gio had grabbed the gun from the drawer. As Alex started the car and glanced over to check the rear view mirror, he saw Giovanni with the gun pointed right at his face, as if he thought that Daddy had a water gun like the one Maria had taught him was a game. Alex tried to throw himself between the gun and his son but before he could make it, the gun went off, shooting our little Angel in the head.

I could go through the horrors of that night over and over but, for what reason? We lost our baby that night and couldn't even reach Maria until late the next day, although we tried. My son, who loved his little boy even more than himself, has had to live with the nightmare of that night and the loss he can never get over; but just in case the horror of what happened wasn't enough,

Alex felt that he lost his boy on his watch, his responsibility and his gun, and he was drowning in the sense of responsibility. We didn't even realize that when Maria finally was able to be contacted by my contacting someone else to get hold of her, she told the authorities that *she* was the custodial parent, regardless of Alex's court order naming him sole custodial parent and that Alex killed her little boy. The only involvement that she wanted with regard to Gio's death was that she, who had never spent a nickel on this child, was entitled to 50% of the college fund insurance policy taken out when Gio was born!

There were over 350 people at our baby's funeral, most of who knew both Alex and Giovanni, Daddy's little co-pilot. If I sound as if I have hatred for the woman who gave birth to my grandson and then walked away, I guess everything that happened after this, the worst event of our lives, was even worse than losing Johnny because I had forty years to love him, but only a real parent, even a Grand-Mommy can truly understand the pain of losing a sweet child. To have been to Hell and back to keep my own son alive and to watch him accept the trials and tribulations of having a special needs child of his own, as if he invented great parenting and then to see the pain he has lived with all this time, without any hope of the pain subsiding makes me very angry that a woman could birth a child, ignore that child and deny that child the safety of warned precaution; then do everything in her power to blame the loving father to hide her own guilt. Yes, I guess that hate and disgust are good enough descriptions for what I shall always feel.

Right after the funeral, Alex stayed in his room, like John Lennon's song "Watching the Wheels Go Round", he laid in his bed staring at the ceiling fan for hours and then days. He wasn't coming down for meals and wouldn't eat anything that his girlfriend or I brought up to him. After a few days, I began to realize that he was trying to commit suicide without committing a mortal sin by neglecting his health, not getting any exercise, eating or taking his required medications. When I tried to talk to him about what was going on, he first told me that he just needed some private time, but, when I became insistent, he admitted to me that if he got sick, it was not suicide, it was medical and when I tried pleading with him that what it was, was crazy, he got mad at me; but I couldn't bear anything happening to my son.

After about a month and a half of this, his legs were swollen to more than twice their size and the pigment was darkening; but the pain he was in was so unbearable that I convinced him to let me get him to a doctor. He agreed to go to a doctor, but refused the Emergency Room, so we went to see a concierge doctor we had spoken to a long time earlier about Alex's health. Dr. Webb examined Alex, heard what was going on and rushed him to a lab for an ultrasound of his legs. When the lab tech was done with the ultrasound, she told us to wait and called Dr. Webb, who had Alex rushed to St. Rose Dominican Hospital and called ahead to advise the doctors to see him immediately. But, when we arrived at the hospital, it was so crowded that the doctors arranged for Alex to be rushed, by ambulance to St. Rose San Martin Campus, which was actually just down the street from our home.

By the time I got to the hospital, Alex had not only been admitted, but was in a room and nurses were hurrying around like nothing I had ever seen; and we still hadn't been told what was happening. I could tell that Alex realized that there was something very wrong and I was a virtual basket case, which for me is very unusual in a crisis. There was something that was freaking me out but couldn't figure out what, except being scared about losing my son, seemed eerily déjà vu about this experience. By the time a doctor came to talk to us and check that all the monitors and IV's had been attached to Alex, I was practically in tears and petrified for lack of knowledge. It turned out that Alex's entire left leg, from ankle to hip was one massive blood-clot and it had thrown off embolisms which were on the edges of all four valves to his heart. He was being given very strong doses of blood thinners to try to dissipate the embolisms before they got to his heart and took his life immediately and to try to reduce the mass in his leg. The doctor told him that it was a blessing that we went to Dr. Webb and that he was such a good doctor because had we waited or had there been any other response to what Dr. Webb thought was happening, Alex would not have survived another twenty-four hours. Then I realized what I was reliving and my legs went out from under me. My son, his father's pride and joy, was suffering from the exact conditions that had plagued his father and taken away his ability to walk so many times and then cost him his leg. It was happening to Alex except as a mirror image, since Johnny suffered from embolisms and clots on his right side. I was just grateful that with all the horrors that took place in some other medical and hospital facilities, somehow we remembered Dr. Webb's office and St. Rose had just been deemed one of the best medical centers in the entire nation.

I stayed right by Alex's side, for the whole ten days that he was in the hospital and I would be lying if I didn't admit that it was pretty scary for the first five or six days until they were able to get him stabilized. His attending physician called in a Hematologist, Dr. Holdridge, was very thorough and she ordered a complete DNA profile to be done on Alex. We had told her about our family's history with Agent Orange poisoning and of not only Alex's medical history but his dad's as well. Unbeknownst to us at the time, his attending physician, after hearing about the Agent Orange cost to our family, also ordered a separate DNA profile and when it came back, I had brought Johnny's VA and UMC medical records in to St. Rose for comparison of his DNA scan. We were told that 50% of Alex's DNA came from each of his parents and that the results of the workups that had been done, showed that half of his DNA, which came from me, was fine but that Johnny's DNA was completely mutated and that half of Alex's was a complete match to that of his father.

Back in 1984, the Agent Orange Lawsuit against the chemical companies had been settled without any admittance of guilt by the defendant companies because the veterans *COULD NOT PROVE CAUSATION.* Now, in 2009, after all that my family had done and given for the Agent Orange movement and the veterans, it was, once again, somehow our fate to finally be able to *PROVE CAUSATION OF AGENT ORANGE POISONING AND INHERITED DNA MUTATIONS!* But to what end? The VA still refused to recognize Agent Orange Children other than those very few women Veterans who gave birth to children with spina bifida.

Yes, we had it in writing, but what were we supposed to do now? I had no strength left to take on the VA without the man who had been my source of strength and I had a son who had just lost his own little boy who was a new generation of affliction, with Agent Orange or Epigenetic Autism. I had already testified and did all I could with regard to the International Tribunal in Paris and they had declared the spraying to be a War Crime, but the World Court in The Hague had done nothing, so where do we go from here? Now we had all kinds of written statements from some very impressive medical professionals that stated that Alex suffered from "inherited DNA mutations, due to his father's exposure in Vietnam", but all I could think of was if our son was going to suffer the same horrendous pain and suffering that my beloved Johnny had endured for so many years, how could I manage to live for however long Alex needed me to do for him as I had for his Dad? Both of us were so emotionally drained from the loss of Johnny and Gio, and so alone now except for each other, that sometimes it is so hard to even want to keep going.

After the hospital stay and two other times requiring admittance. Alex had to take a year to recuperate and should have been able to concentrate on grieving for his son and coming to terms with the guilt of what had been almost a perfect storm starting with the insane water gun incident and ending on July 21st, 2009. But first because of activities that happened that fateful night and then the total lack of any investigation, intelligence and negligence on the part of the legal agencies and actually the entire State system, the nightmare had just begun. When the accident happened, rather than wait in a parking lot for an ambulance, Alex drove like a madman, one hand on the steering wheel and the other on his son's bleeding skull, to the closest hospital that he knew was about three miles away. He carried his baby into the Emergency Room screaming for help and when the attendants took Giovanni into the examining they told Alex to wait outside the door to the room. Because memory of that night in 1978, when his own father was so frightened about him, when he was three-months-old, I can totally understand a loving father's actions. The police came running into the Emergency Room and had Alex go into a room with them, where they started questioning him about what happened and talking to him like he was some sort of gang banger or an animal who had tried to eat his young!

All Alex could say to them was, "I need to be with my son, I have to be with my son", and their arrogance gave full view to their stupidity when they told him that, "your son IS FINE, and being taken care of, HE DOESN'T NEED YOU." Alex tried to explain that this child who never spoke had been crying and saying "DADDY, DADDY, DADDY" over and over during the ride that took about three minutes, but felt like a lifetime and he wanted to tell them that his son always needed him and he was always there. They started to actually bully him, call him names and even push him physically. The insanity that took place, even now, four years later, as I am putting this to paper, is taking much longer than normal writing because I have to constantly stop, wipe my own tears and take breaks to breathe again.

Alex was out of control in trying to get out the door to go to Gio's side and the cops kept pushing him back. I don't know if their behavior and complete lack of understanding was because they had no children, were devoid of human compassion, or as owners of firearms weren't always concerned about how many police officer's children died from gunshot wounds from Daddy's police weapon. Ironically, within a two week period, before and after Gio's accident, there were three such policeman's weapon deaths of their own children, but nothing was ever done about those, not a damn thing except that one of the gun owner policemen had to do about 75 hours of community service!!!!!

However, what happened that night was that when Alex tried to push the cops out of his way to get to Gio, the cops tried to take him down, but while they knew that he was a Hip-Hop DJ, I can only guess that they didn't know that the guy that they thought was just a celebrity who was probably, even at six feet, four inches and over 250 lbs., a spoiled celebrity coward, had, in reality trained for Golden Gloves and had played pro arena football for two years. Those were not exactly any kind of wimpy wimpy efforts; so when they tried to physically attack, he hit back and knocked both of the cops on their asses. I had just arrived at the Emergency Room and was told that my five-year-old grand-baby, who couldn't communicate had being sent to UMC Children's Trauma Center and that my son had *BEEN ARRESTED FOR BEATING UP A POLICE OFFICER AND WAS TAKEN TO JAIL!!!!!*

My daughter-in-law drove me to UMC as quickly as she could and all I could think of was that our little boy was all alone with strangers because they wouldn't let me ride in the ambulance even though I was his legal guardian in Alex's absence. I suddenly realized that the light rain that had been falling when we left the first hospital had turned into a monsoon just like the one that had made news on the day that Giovanni was born, I can still feel the chill that ran through me right then and there, as I just started to relate it all over again. During the ride I tried over and over again to call Maria on her cell and her home phone, but I first got no answer on either and then I got her stupid and provocative voicemail messages until I had left so many messages that I stopped because the voice said that the mailbox was full. Not only did I never get a call back, but had to call her father the next morning and tell him what happened, and even then it took five hours for her to get back to me.

By the time we got to UMC, I was told that, without parental authority, the emergency doctors put this little five year old boy in a medically induced coma before they tried to stop the bleeding in my beautiful boy's head. *"YOU GAVE A VERY YOUNG CHILD, PROPHENOL, WITHOUT PERMISSION, ARE YOU PEOPLE INSANE?"* Years later, if you will recall, that was the exact same medicine that the doctor, who ended up in prison gave to Michael Jackson, a grown man and drug addict, causing his death.

I went into the room that they brought my Giovanni to and before I could even give him a kiss, a man came in and asked if he could speak with me outside the room. Thinking he was a doctor or something, I followed, my eyes never leaving my baby. The man explained that he was not a doctor, a nurse or anyone of any importance, he was a volunteer who was assigned to stay with family members in such "sad" cases. He looked totally confused when I pushed him aside, saying "get the fuck away from me", and I went back to my Giovanni's side. His small body was breathing on his own, but it was so labored and then I realized that the more I told him to fight and hang on, even in this coma, he would try to breathe harder, but it was so labored and I knew that they hadn't stopped the bleeding because there was more and more blood on the top of the bed. I took a leap of faith, thinking to myself that if he was going to survive, it was not because I told him to; so I put my mouth close to his ear and whispered to him "Gio-Mio, if Grandpa is there and calling for you, if you want to, you can go". I stood back up and watched as he took one last breath and then he was still and my heart died as I touched him, kissed him and talked to his soul and to my beloved Johnny, who had sent for him.

Just in case all of this wasn't enough, the craziness was going to continue. I felt so alone and overwhelmed with what was happening, my husband was gone, my youngest son was arrested for trying to get to his baby, my older son was in prison (a story for another manuscript) and my only grandson was on his way to Heaven. Suddenly I realized that besides myself and my daughter-in-law, there was a young policeman just standing there and trying not to yawn. As I sat down to wait for the attendants from the mortuary to come pick up Giovanni, I told the kiddy cop that I wanted to be alone with my grandson's remains and he told me that he was not supposed to leave me in the room by myself.

What did he think was going to happen? I started to debate it and then I told him again to get out of the room and again he told me that wasn't possible. I looked up at him and said "Okay, let's see", with which my daughter-in-law, April, stepped back, knowing me, but not knowing what to expect. I raised my hands in front of me as if to ward off an assailant and at the top of my lungs, and I have a really deep voice for a woman anyway, I screamed "HELP, RAPE, HELP ME!!". What a surprise, by the time I lowered my protective arms, April and I were alone with Giovanni and our tears. The topper of the whole nightmare, that night, was that on the way back to our house, April's car broke down; just as I mentioned that the rain was stopping, so stopped the car. While we waited for the tow truck to tow the car and give us a ride to the house, I couldn't help but think that if I hadn't mentioned the rain, would the car have gotten us home?

I don't remember sleeping at all that night, but April insisted that I try to get some rest. Instead I was on the phone with the Detention Center to try to find out if my son was all right. I had no way of knowing that they had stripped him naked and put him in a suicide watch area where he laid there, freezing from the chill and looking at the wall, where all his mind could comprehend were some pictures that Gio had drawn and we had framed and hung at the house and he cried. He never got to say good-bye, in fact he didn't even know what had happened until a guard told him, without any compassion at all. He was finally able to call me the next morning and I told him that the bail was $3 thousand and I had called a friend of his who owned a bail bond company. I told him that the bail was already posted and now he just had to wait until they let him out, which, Lord knows why, always takes anywhere from twelve to twenty-four hours.

Then I called Metro Police and told them that I had to get my phone and day planner out of the car and they took my name and number and told me that a detective would call me. I had to call four more times before a very nasty female "homicide detective" called me and very quickly and strictly told me that I could not get anything for at least a week! I tried to nicely explain to her that I had a funeral to plan and needed those things, which were mine, in my name, as was the car so she had to return them. I even tried to tell her of my background to get what has always been, everywhere, considered professional courtesy, but she was going to emulate a sphincter muscle and straighten me out about how it was up to her and she said "NO". I hung up and did my activist thing!!! About twenty minutes later the bitchy cop called me back and abruptly asked me if I had called the Under-sheriff, to which I said "No, I called the Sheriff, but he wasn't in so they had me speak to the Under-sheriff". She told me that the CSI (not anything like the television show of that name) Officer would call me and before we even hung up, my other phone started to ring and the CSI told me to "by all means, come right down or do you want us to deliver the things to you? And we all are so sorry for your loss!" Even as a sweet little grandma, it is still impossible to out-bitch me!!!!

By this time, I had lost so much and had so many things to take care of, in more emotional pain than I had ever thought I would have to handle, so the last thing that I was going to put up with was some female who was younger than some of my shoes, trying to exercise her feelings of superiority, where no such feelings should ever have existed. I also was told by the very solicitous CSI officer that while I could pick up the car, I might want to send a tow truck or someone else to pick it up because of the "conditions" which I understood to mean blood, my almost six-year-old grandson's blood. I was so grateful for his concern and kindness that I started to cry and he just waited quietly while I composed myself as best I could. An hour later, a friend of Alex's, who owned a car customizing shop sent a driver to pick me up and a tow truck to take the car to his shop and his workers would not allow me anywhere near the Suburban. The driver took me to the Budget Car Rental Agency, where Alex's friend, Joel, had also arranged for me to have a rental car while he had the entire insides of our car replaced and ready for either driving or to sell. Of anything that anyone could have done for us at such a time as this, the collaborated effort of Joel's friends in his industry, some who didn't even know Alex, to have the car redone so beautifully that one could not tell of the horror that had taken place involving the car that Johnny had left to Alex and I, but which had then been the source of so much loss and pain; was one of the nicest things that total strangers could have done for us because there just weren't monies necessary to buy a new car.

CHAPTER EIGHTEEN

WHAT DOESN'T KILL US, MAKES US STRONGER, BUT WHEN IS IT ENOUGH?

LOSING GIOVANNI WAS NOT SOMETHING hat I thought that Alex was going to be able to get through, especially when I first had to fight the system to allow him to be released from a solitary jail cell that not only didn't he belong in, but which seemed to be the system's way of involving their influence in a matter that was a private tragedy of insurmountable proportions. The fact that the newspapers were filled with the death of a policeman's two-and-a-half-year-old child who was shot by a service gun left on a living room table and the small son of another cop who was put to bed in his parents' bedroom with a loaded automatic, sitting in an open night table drawer, while the parents entertained friends in another room, didn't seem to create any outrage on the part of the authorities, however, the Las Vegas Metropolitan Police Department, who also employed both of the fathers who had allowed their sons to play unattended with loaded guns, decided that Alex had somehow willed his son to cause his own death. No investigation was made, not even asking questions as to the reason that Gio thought he found a water gun, but they listened to the raving of a mother who had spent all of forty-five days out of the 2,190 days in his six-years of life. They took what she thought and gave it merit. The local news media also jumped on the fact that a white hip-hop DJ, with a bi-racial son was involved (as in guilty!) in his little boy's death; They also spoke only with Maria, who was like a moth to a flame where talking to anyone with a microphone and a camera was concerned, the amount of dramatic license was Hollywood-worthy, but the real pain was, as far as we were concerned, our business to deal with.

From the minute Alex came home from jail, through the funeral and for over a month after, I can now equate how I dealt with making sure that Alex got some sleep was very much like the way that Johnny was able to get over the horrendous effects of Vietnam, so many years earlier. I stayed in my son's room all night long, just watching television quietly or reading while he slept and climbing up onto his bed to rub his head or his back when he would wake up abruptly, or speak out in his sleep. But after the funeral it became very apparent that, as I mentioned earlier, Alex was deliberately not coming out of his room for any reason. He wouldn't come downstairs to eat and if we brought food up to his room, it remained untouched. I finally enlisted some of his friends to come over and try to talk to him, but he would get mad if they tried to elicit any conversations or coax him in any way; so most of his friends would just sit in his room in case he wanted to talk, but mostly to keep an eye on him.

It was then that he told a friend, who broke down and told me that Alex was fooling himself with thinking that allowing a sick body to waste away was a way of dying without committing suicide. Arguing with him was a waste of time, until, I guess that the pain and the swelling became so intense, that he thought that it would prove too late for a doctor to save him and that maybe there was something that could dull the pain. That is how and why we were fortunate enough to find Dr. Gary Webb and the Angels of Mercy at St. Rose Hospitals. This was in mid-September 2009 and he was not free of long hospital stays until early November but was restricted to home and bed rest until early 2011.

In August, 2010, right after what would have been Giovanni's seventh birthday, we were made aware of the insane reality that charges for Child Endangerment with Severe Bodily Harm were going to be pressed against Alex in the loss of his son. After the shock and disbelief wore off, we knew that regardless of how insane this was in view of all we had lost, we had to find an attorney and that attorney had to be one of the best available; which in Clark County, Nevada is no easy task. One of Alex's friends recommended an attorney, Stephen Stein, who was one of the best criminal attorneys in the entire country and whose office was shared by Oscar Goodman, who was the infamous Mob Lawyer who was even in the film "Casino" playing himself and was, at this time, Mayor of the City of Las Vegas. We went to see Mr. Stein and he listened to what Alex was telling him and sized Alex up the entire time. He then hit us with the biggest bombshell possible. He told us that his retainer was $75 thousand from the beginning and then more when needed. Needless to say, that when we left his office, Lawyer Stein seemed way off our grid and we were beyond depressed. In the car, Alex called his friend Rob, who had recommended Steve Stein to tell him what we were told. Rob told us that we should reschedule an appointment with the attorney and give him between $7 thousand to $10 thousand or more if we had it, and explain Alex's health with him; he was sure that the lawyer would deal. We went home to figure out how much we could afford. After Johnny's death, it had taken over a year to get the VA to allocate my monthly survivor's benefits, known as DIC for Dependent's Income Compensation, which was about 50% of what my husband's 100%-Agent Orange Service Connected monthly income was. This was still a good income, but Alex had been out of work due to his condition for over a year and his illness co-pays were astronomical.

My strength and courage was dwindling from all we'd been through, and I had to keep my insecurities hidden from my son. I called Chuck Palazzo that night and I was beyond despondent. We talked for about two hours and I felt somewhat better afterward. He told me that he would reach out to Veterans groups and Veterans that he knew and even some that knew me, but not him, to see what they could all do to help. I really didn't expect that anyone would be concerned or want to help with my son's legal costs, but it was sort of reassuring to not feel so hopelessly alone and I couldn't show my son that I was as scared as I was when he needed me. Living in the Southwest, away from friends and not having a close or even functional family, I really didn't know what we were going to do. We had decided to make another appointment with the attorney to see what could be done and to give him all the money that we had left after two funerals and a long horrendous medical battle.

Within about four days' time, checks started arriving in our mail from all over the country and even from MH in France and Chuck Palazzo in Vietnam, through PayPal, totaling thousands of dollars. I couldn't believe it and neither could Alex, especially since the Vietnam Veteran Movement was something he experienced during his early childhood, but since we had moved to Nevada, it was really not a part of his life. Even Johnny's passing had been announced and articles written about him in newsletters and media outside of Vegas. Most of the condolence and Mass Cards that we received were from people that our son really didn't know. By the time we met with Steve Stein again, we had almost $10 thousand in an envelope and this time we told him the entire story of Johnny's forty-year fight to stay alive because of Agent Orange and how Alex had inherited the same mutations of DNA; and that Gio had suffered from a whole new strain of autism, caused by his grandfather's exposure as well. We were both very surprised when Steve told us that he too had served in Vietnam and was well aware of what Agent Orange had done to his brother Veterans. Whoever would have thought it? Making a long story short, he was very touched by the kind of man that Alex was and especially the fact that he had embraced being a sole custodial father to a very special needs child and how he had given up his career and most of his life to raise his child and help care for his dad. Amazingly, Alex now had one of the best attorneys in the United States who assured us that it would be okay and we could pay him whatever we could, when we could.

In the wake of the loss of Giovanni, Alex started a foundation in his son's name: Giovanni's Legacy Foundation, the mission of which was two-fold. The first to tell the story of Giovanni's accidental shooting, the cause and the effect, as well as to try to have parents with special needs kids, either give up owning firearms or practicing even safer standards than normal. The second phase of the mission was to teach parents to celebrate their autistic children's strengths, as we had with Gio's athletic abilities and his love of trains. We became active in setting up and running special events, with the help of other organizations and County Commissioners to provide families with special needs children with a full day of fun and activities for the entire family, since that was one of the things that families could not do without feeling that their children were being ostracized or having to explain. Too many people did not have the self-confidence in themselves to simply ignore others and just take pride in their children. Children, Autistic or not, learn to feel about themselves as their parents feel about them and so that became the mission for Alex.

Both Alex and I became faithful members of Compassionate Friends, which is an organization that holds impromptu meetings, at least once each month for people who have lost a child and not only was it helpful for each of us separately, but together in being able to talk about our Giovanni without only having each other to talk to and if necessary, there was a telephone list of members to reach out to. These were all people who, be it a baby to a grown person, a parent is a parent and we could talk about our departed and even find humor in some of our memories, with an entire room of people who not only understood our grief but could laugh with us at our memories. One evening, we were all talking about different experiences that we each had involving what some of us believed to be a sort of an epiphany experience or even a visit from our loved ones and everyone had a tale to tell.

The meeting room had a divider in the center and the portable wall was closed when we arrived so I don't think anyone gave much thought to the size of the room. We were all engrossed in what we had been reliving for the group and suddenly the dividing structure slowly moved with a sort of a creaking sound. The entire group screamed and looked like one of the ghosts we had been discussing, had come into the room. Which, if anyone ever asks what you would do if a departed loved one just walked up to you, and you do not admit that fear would be your first response, then truth is a problem. The person most frightened and whose facial color became ashen white, was the custodian who had come into the other door of the room and went to open the dividing wall!!

The biggest insanity that we could definitely relate to was at one of the last meetings we attended which was also attended by a man about Alex's age, whose daughter, a twin with a brother, both Giovanni's age when we lost him, who had gone to a firing range with their dad and were sitting on a bench behind him while he shot his rifle out in the opposite direction, at the targets, when his little boy suddenly screamed and the girl, that poor little girl was on the ground, having been shot and killed. The father was arrested, just as Alex had been even though he was shooting his rifle completely away from his children; and yet there was to be no doubt on the part of the authorities of his guilt, because he, just as Alex, was not a police officer who left a loaded gun for a child to play with.

As important as the malfunctions of authority are, the topic shall have to be the subject of another book, because it was and is the health problems suffered, that are the motivation to document the crimes against so many Veterans and then their children that created the necessity of telling the story of what was done to a family; to many families as opposed to an intellectual narrative or a historical text regarding Agent Orange veterans and then not only their children, but their entire future progeny.

Approximately two weeks before Alex was hospitalized, President Obama had just signed the Affordable Care Act (ObamaCare) into law, which was not something that we had been too concerned with before Alex became so ill. Because the inherited illnesses that my son suffered from had not been a problem for a few years, we were able to get him a very good health insurance plan from United Healthcare. However, when he was admitted into St. Rose Hospital and the results of his DNA panels proved that there truly was causation between his dad's exposure and our son's health; I didn't say a word to Alex, but I was becoming increasingly concerned that the insurance company would decide to disallow the hundreds of thousands of dollars in medical care as being the dreaded "pre-existing condition". I had already decided that just like with my husband, so many years earlier, first we would get things fixed and then we would worry about how to pay for it. Alex's Hematologist, Dr. Holdridge was, ironically, the first person to address the insurance situation that I had been so concerned. She took me on the side during one of her visits to Alex, in the hospital and told me that she was not submitting the DNA comparable analysis to the insurance company, because it had nothing to do with Alex's treatment or medical needs at the time. I was so grateful that if she had a fan club, I would have been the leader. The hospital staff also told me that they were billing the insurance company and since the President had signed the ACA into law, they were going under the assumption that Alex's problems were new and not pre-existing, which is what they told the insurance company. Considering that Alex's medications cost approximately $16 thousand each and every month, plus the constant lab work he had to submit to; and that of the exorbitant medication costs, two of them comprised $12 thousand for which we had to pay a $137 dollar co-pay. However, after about a year and a half, Alex's medical bills had capped out his insurance at between $2 million dollars and $3 million dollars so that we either had to come up with another plan or plan another funeral.

When we received the first warning that United Healthcare

was going to have to drop his insurance because of the Cap being reached, I filed a claim with the VA for Children of Certain Veterans Affected By Agent Orange and included all the information with regard to the comparison of Johnny's and Alex's mutated DNA including letters from Alex's doctors. The information when I had called the VA for guidance, was that unlike my experiences before, when the regulation was only the children of women who served in Vietnam (all forty or so of them) and only for spina bifida and the VA representative told me to file the claim.

It took over three months to receive a letter from the Veterans Administration stating that while they had proven that Alex's father had served in Vietnam, they had not confirmed that I, his mother had, and so he was denied. Johnny had always said that he spent fifteen months in Vietnam, but that even though I had never left American shores, I had spent nearly forty years in Nam. As frustrating as it was to see, once again, that the VA and the entire government could not have cared less about what they had done to so many lives; I could not waste any more time on fighting a losing battle when I was trying to save my son's life.

Even though our son, Alex, was a fully grown and intelligent man, when it came to paperwork and studying the actual laws and codes of things; these things had always been left to me by both father and son, which was okay since Johnny and I had based our strengths on that he would handle the stuff he was good at, for both of us and the same went for what I excelled at. Words and wording came much easier to me than to most people, but there were so many talents that I did not have. So, our success was in sharing and planning. I used to get a really big kick out of the fact, when we were younger, that people would credit me with being able to do "everything so well", but the truth had always been that whenever I wasn't good at something or even mediocre, I made sure never to attempt such things where anyone could notice. It worked for me and my image!!

As I mentioned before, the Foundation that Alex and I had set up, worked hand in hand with Autism Speaks and I had written the "Visionary Ideas" that won a grant from the NIH in the amount of $13.7 million which was used to fund the Johns Hopkins Research Study on Epigenetic Autism and during a conference call with a representative of H.H.S., and Dr. Alycia Halliday, I mentioned what had happened with Alex's medical insurance and then with the VA, to which the NIH representative gave me a phone number for Social Security and told me what I needed to do to get him medical based on his inability to earn a living for over a year before or afford his medical costs at the present time. In the interim, I had contacted the manufacturers of Humira and Lovenox, both of which arranged for Alex to get these $12 thousand monthly dosages free of charge while we waited for one of the programs run by one of the government agencies to come through. If neither did, then Alex would be able to, at least, get these medicines for as long as he needed them. When Social Security required an entire battery of tests and evaluations to be done by their own medical experts, we went to the first of what was going to be about four or five different examinations, but when the physician took Alex into his office and examined him, as well as reading the medical records that Alex carried with him to all appointments, he ended the exam by telling Alex that he did not have to go to any other evaluations or testing appointments because he was certifying him as disabled and eligible for assistance with medical coverage. When I had filed for this help, I had told the questioning officer that Alex did not require any kind of financial stipend because if he needed it, I could easily afford to aide him while he recovered, but there was no way that

I could cover his medical costs. Unfortunately, I was told that the Social Security Administration had to give him some monies, regardless of my help in order for him to be issued Medicaid since there were no Medicaid programs for him as a man without a dependent child or children, until the ACA went into effect in January of 2014. The doctor put his report in with an expedite status and for nearly a full year, all of Alex's medical costs were covered. What happened next was and is an insult to all citizens who find themselves at the mercy of the justice system.

When the judicial system decided that Giovanni's accident was a criminal situation caused by a father who was totally devoted to his little boy, as opposed to those police officers whose children had similar outcomes but the causes were obviously just "accidents" caused by children who should be held responsible for picking up a gun left out in the open, Alex had decided to accept responsibility as opposed to going to a trial and having to relive that night over and over again in public view. So he was put on "probation" which was and is a constant source of wasted money in cases such as this. His probation officer realized early on, that Alex was the most boring person she ever met and she found herself liking and wanting to be supportive of this man who really, because of the workings of the system and the courts, had never even had the chance to grieve or mourn. However, after about six or seven months into his probation term, his original officer was given a promotion and Alex was assigned to another probation officer who obviously had taken his GED and entered one of the "buy a certification" eight week wonder criminal justice schools. Our first introduction to this man was when Alex had a court date for a "status check" but was hospitalized at St. Rose, the day before court because of the blood clots and swelling in his leg again. The P.O., instead of just allowing the court to set a new date, chose to claim that Alex was violating his probation, which the probation department could do without cause or sufficient reason; causing us to have to hire a new attorney to handle the violation. The meeting between us and Roy Nelson, Esq., took place in Alex's hospital room with Alex lying flat on his back with his gigantically swollen leg uplifted and in full view. None of us could figure out what or why this civil servant had on his mind to bring him to the realization that he knew my son, whom he had never even met and that he knew more than the doctors at this major hospital; but we did know that we had to pay Mr. Nelson, $3 thousand cash to get his lawyer clock running. We never understood why, but the next six months were a nightmare caused by this P.O., for the stupidest and most petty imaginations of a pretty sick mind.

It did finally become clear that just in case our family had not lost enough and were having such a hard time just getting from one day to the next, this man, whose name I am purposely deleting because I desire to give him no notoriety or anything more than the image of a faceless and worthless excuse for humanity, turned out to have developed an obsession when it came to Alex for reasons that defy any intelligence. He was the same age of Alex, but very short, pudgy and had a very swarthy complexion and look about him; with a job that gave him an enormous Napoleonic complex, but as I always said, in this legal brothel state, "He couldn't get laid in a Cat House with a fist full of C-notes!" Now here comes this guy who is an award winning entertainer on the Las Vegas Strip, who despite his medical problems and inability to work his trade on a full time basis because of his health, he was always surrounded by very good looking women, and so our Napoleonic civil servant is consumed with jealousy and feelings of his true inferiority. Now add to this equation that Alex lives in a golf course guard gated community, in a very large and beautiful home as well as drives a Cadillac Escalade, which makes him suspect; regardless of the fact that this is how his family has always lived and these are familial possessions, owned to be shared. The constant harassment and misinformation with regard to Alex's life and the inability to learn anything about my son's health and the conditions surrounding his life and emotional state cost more pain and suffering than this poor excuse of humanity would ever be worth. His last act of depraved indifference was in contacting Social Security and accusing Alex of fraud, which, if it were true would not only be so totally out of character but could have sent him to prison. Of course, the investigation into what was the reality of the medical coverage and all the other matters found nothing but in the interim, Alex had to sit in jail and I had to force the system to provide him with the expensive medication and treatment that he needed.

Needless to say, by the time it was found that the allegations were all lies and fabrications and the man was removed from the position he was in which he could do so much damage. Alex refused to accept any other government services, medical or otherwise and so, we could not get a good healthcare plan because the ObamaCare was yet not in place, and Alex would not let me contact anyone in Washington D.C., or anywhere else. We were able to purchase a very limited and inferior type of insurance to at least provide a very small amount of financial relief, at three times the amount of money we had paid for United Healthcare and once again the manufacturers came to the rescue while Alex waited until his new ObamaCare insurance to begin on January 1, 2014.

Throughout all the trials and tribulations of what the system, local, state and federal were putting Alex through, we were constantly busy with Giovanni's Legacy Foundation and trying to collect names and conditions to see if we could get some figures with regard to Agent Orange Autism from all over the world. Chuck Palazzo was working so hard to try to help as many Vietnamese children as he possibly could, but getting any sort of numbers with regard to Autism was an impossible task because of the poverty, the lack of incorporated school protocols and how many victims of Agent Orange related malformations there were. But he kept trying and other than writing blogs and articles for newspapers and websites all over the world, he was also trying to make a living and deal with his own health problems.

The other very big problem in South Vietnam was the number of live mines and bombs still throughout the jungles and even places like DaNang Airport. Children were surviving Agent Orange and Dioxin related birth defects only to be blown up by tripping over a Claymore or some other explosives. I found a sphere that was originally created by a young man in Australia and was being used in the Middle East to roll out into a field, finding and detonating land mines and unexploded bombs, but although these were very durable and inexpensive, after some study it was agreed that the land in Vietnam was neither dry and barren or feasible for such a device.

To me, there is something so cruel and devoid of any type of caring when so much damage was done to what is for the most part, become even more of a third world country because of the war against the people of Vietnam, regardless of whether they had picked a side or were just trying to survive. For a family to have a child who has all of his limbs, eyes and physique intact go out to play with his friends and be blown to kingdom come, or lose his legs or sight, is barbaric to say the least. To know that the farmers are trying to grow rice or feed livestock in soil that is dioxin-laced and watered with contaminated water is so hard to understand because it has been over forty years since the last spraying and yet the poison is as strong as ever, perhaps even stronger.

During the last days of the Clinton Administration, there was a promise made that thirty million dollars would be afforded to the Nation of Vietnam, for the sole purpose of cleaning up the soil, the water and whatever else needed to be made dioxin free. The exact amount of what was spent during the beginning of the George W. Bush Administration, not because they wanted to, but because of the allocation promised right before Bush took over, was $3 million and not a penny more. What is even worse is that no one can say for sure where that money went and to whom, but more importantly, there is no evidence that any toxins were eliminated.

Right before I attended the International Tribunal in Paris, 2009, the lawsuit filed by the Vietnamese organization VAVA, against the chemical companies, had been, as all those since the 1984 settlement, dismissed by Federal Judge Jack Weinstein, who once again, stated that the reason for dismissal was the lack of causation. While in France, I spoke at length with their primary attorney in New York City, John Moore Esq., regarding the theory that it made no sense to sue the contractors for a product that had been ordered by specifications and then misused by the contracting agencies, namely the U.S. Department of Defense. Even if the chemical companies had, as we discussed earlier, used additives or ingredients that were not in the original specs, then the lawsuit against the chemical industry had to be brought by the DOD, not by the victims who were poisoned. He really seemed to be interested in what I was saying, however, that was the last that I had heard of anything related to our conversation.

Meanwhile, the nightmare of dioxin poisoning on the residents of South Vietnam does not subside because the chemicals are not evaporating and the eventual dissipation of the negative compounds does not seem close at hand. The twenty-five year half-life seems to be, in actuality, a fifty-year half-life, or it is even possible that the harmful effects in the soil, the water, the trees and even the livestock may be undergoing a transformation that may make it even more harmful in other ways. To see Vietnam on a news broadcast or even a magazine, the topography looks very modernized and commercially advanced, however, that is the cities, Ho Chi Ming City, Hanoi, DaNang, etc., not the outlying areas where the real citizens live, where the huts of forty or fifty years ago are still the same and where old Vietnamese couples are trying to carry their fully grown children, twice their size, but without the ability to walk, to see, to move or with whatever birth defect they have had to live with all their lives. Go to the orphanages or a place like Freedom Village, started and run by RoseMarie Mizo to honor her American Vietnam veteran husband who died from Agent Orange poisoning. At these places are the birth defected Vietnamese nationals who were orphaned or abandoned by families that could not care for them and hidden away in a back room are shelves on top of shelves filled with the birth defected embryos that couldn't survive, sitting in jars and filling every shelf. How was this allowed to happen?

The children of Vietnam Agent Orange Vets, here in America, regardless of the birth defects and illnesses are in much better shape than the majority of their counterparts in Southeast Asia, because even though they were conceived in a mating of mutated DNA with unmutilated DNA, the soon-to-be parents were not living amongst the contamination which probably meant that there was a mutual mutation or the consumption of dioxin in the food and water. The medical facilities and prenatal care in America were not, nor are they yet available to most of the people in Vietnam, and so the birth defect rate and inherited illnesses are far more severe and money for services really does not exist for most of the general population.

In the United States, the implementation of ObamaCare on January 1, 2014, means that for the original children of Vietnam Agent Orange Veterans, like my son, most of whom are in their 30's or early 40's, with pre-existing conditions, will be afforded the ability to receive medical care and medications without having to either lie or simply hope that no one asks them any questions before allowing them to buy health insurance. Even though, the care and treatment of the children of Vietnam Veterans and the grandchildren, as well, should be borne by the Veterans Administration, just as the children of these Veterans should be able to sue the DOD and the VA, because they, unlike their fathers who were precluded because of the Feros Doctrine, are victims of a government action and are being discriminated against since female Veterans have been afforded VA privilege for their children as if only female DNA was susceptible to mutation.

It was not until 2013, that a very brave politician, Congresswoman Barbara Lee (Democrat-California) brought forward a bill H.R. 2519 requiring the care, treatment and compensation of not only the children of American Vietnam Agent Orange Veterans, but the children effected in Vietnam. However, the reality in 2013 and for most of 2014, is that nothing, and especially not any spending bill that doesn't favor the rich or corporations that might require any financial assistance or health care will ever pass a vote in the Republican majority Congress. Realistically, no such bill will even make it to the floor of Congress in this "Do Nothing" body of government.

The pandemic of Autism Spectrum which in large part is environmentally or genetically becoming, in the United States, a glimpse into the future of our civilization that is, not even looking at the one out of every thirty-four children born to Agent Orange families, but the one out of every fifty-five births in the general population, an entire population of special needs citizens and yet, still no one is listening to our children and grandchildren screaming out against the wind. It is as I said in 1984: that the future that has been our lives since our men returned from Vietnam to claim their American dream, shall become all of America's nightmare.

CHAPTER NINETEEN

THE DESTRUCTION OF OUR NATION, THE FINAL CHAPTER

OVER THE YEARS SINCE WE first began our fight to try to save our own lives, we have suffered so many losses of incredible veterans, friends and family members. What was and is even worse is that now, into another century, we are learning of how many other veterans, who either served on the waters surrounding the Southeast Asia coasts, the incinerators at Osiago, Japan; the DMZ between North and South Korea and Guam, amongst other locations were also affected and mutilated by the spraying of 2,4,D and 2,4,5T or even just the storing of those chemical poisons. What has been other forms of America's dirty little secrets, is the use of other chemicals and the exposure of our own troops to those chemicals in just about every war zone; since mustard gas in World War I, to Dapsone and Malaria pills in World War II and Korea. Which, all in their own way, destroyed the health and lives of so many who have borne the battle that it is almost like the military machine should become known as the Enola Gay Armed Forces.

When Daddy Bush sent troops to Desert Storm, upon their return it became known within the Veteran communities, but kept as quiet as only this country can keep a secret, that children being born to parents who, at least one of, had been exposed to depleted uranium in the Middle East Arena, were coming into this world with birth defects, incurable maladies, organ and brain deformities that were comparable to the children of Vietnam; not even the Agent Orange children of the Vietnam Vets, but much, much worse and once again there has been no recognition or treatment by the government. One of the biggest ways to keep these truths from the American people was that after Vietnam, which was a war brought into every home daily on the evening news, the lesson was learned that if the government, big business and the political machines were going to maintain business as usual, there simply had to be a way to protect the money-making business of WAR. So, smaller efforts, such as Granada and our weapons of mass destruction to occupy a medical school, to save students who didn't know why they were being "rescued" or from what, were not covered by the national television industry.

By the time that the Middle East debacles were instituted by the Bush Family Dynasty, the all-volunteer military and the horrors that were happening to them were hidden in plain sight because there was such a lack of daily TV news. No one could complain, because there was no longer a draft forcing youngsters to put their lives on the line against their wishes; for the majority of Americans, what was going on was of no real interest to them. The watchers and the critics were, for the most part, Veterans who knew the reality of a war zone and the fallacy of what and why our children were involved. We all know the crimes and the incredible profits enjoyed by Halliburton and Black Water, after the fact, but the head injuries, the missing body parts and the trauma of combat stress, in addition to the rotating re-deployments were ignored by the government, the public and especially big business. War is money and blue collar, working class, poor and Veterans' kids are simply cannon fodder while we all sing "God Bless America."

One more sorry fact is that, of PTSD, Agent Orange, Traumatic Head Injuries and all the other residuals of war upon the warrior, after Vietnam, at least 40% of Vets ended up incarcerated for crimes caused not by criminal minds, but by situations created by what they had endured; and since Vietnam, at least 33% of all homeless have served in one war or another. The only citizens who seem to know who these people are just by looking at them and are then moved to assist them, in any way that they can, are other Combat Veterans from either their war or one before. When Johnny was younger and we were in business, if he drove down the street and saw someone standing on a traffic median with a sign that said "Vietnam Vet" or even just "Veteran", he would actually stop his vehicle and talk to the man, asking when and where he served. If the panhandler gave some made up place or unit, Johnny would reach out of his car window and take the sign, cursing the guy out for lying, as only an Army 1st Air Cav. vet could. But, if this was truly a vet he would tell the guy to get into the car or truck he was driving and offer to take the man to get something to eat or offer a job.

My husband was a really nice and caring man, who loved people, and veterans always came right up there with his family. We very often had some guy that Johnny simply said needed help, sleeping in one of our guest rooms. However, my Johnny was no different than the Chuck Palazzo's, Willie Hager's, Ward

Reilly's, Dave Cline's, and thousands of others I have met over the years. Guy's like Chuck Searcy, who didn't just go visit Vietnam, he moved to Hanoi, with the exacting purpose of trying to help and repair what had been broken during the war.

These men are not ex-patriots or anti-American, they lived in the United States, raised families and had good jobs, however, as some of us, the boomers, who are still in good health, have retired or stopped working, being able to try or do something new for whatever is left of their lives often has to do with "giving back". Losing my husband to Agent Orange made me find new strength in trying to do something about these criminal acts. Strength that I had lost in the hard job of having an Agent Orange husband, a son and then a grandson, all effected by this horrendous poison that no one wanted to take responsibility for mean that I now want vindication from their murderers. Finding out that every Vietnam veteran family I spoke with had at least one, but usually more, Autistic children in their lives did not make me feel good because our little Giovanni wasn't the only one. It made me so very angry that my words in 1984 to that uninterested Judge Weinstein, that "by poisoning their best and their brightest, America had broken its own back", obviously have come to fruition over and over, decade by decade.

In the earliest days of our fight, the majority of veterans who passed away, did so by either some insane form of cancer that could not be stopped, or by suicide because their night terrors and feelings could not be stopped; but, as we age, it is stated that Vietnam Veterans are dying at a rate of 285 each day but no longer from the suicide of bad dreams. While the majority of our senior population is living longer and staying more vital as they age, the men who answered their country's call to arms, are dying at sixty of diseases and conditions that are supposed to be at life's end, of much older men; yet, still no one, no government or medical organization is willing to take the responsibility of admitting what has been done wrong to so many. Moreover, no government official from that time, so many years ago, has yet to say they are so sorry or to use their influence to help Agent Orange children and grandchildren to understand and be treated for the afflictions that have been handed down from generations now.

The Agent Orange Bill H.R.2519, by Congresswoman Lee and all of her democratic co-signers, should be passed and signed by the President because although for us here in the United States, the new ACA Healthcare programs will stop the nightmare of not being able to get or afford healthcare, unless the Veterans Administration is called to responsibility, doctors in the private sector are flying blind when it comes to inherited mutated DNA caused by dioxin poisoning. Without the information and research that has already been done and distributed amongst the VA facilities only, treating illnesses like my son's are for most, who do not walk around with forty years of information and medical records, etc., like I do, elusive and not believed.

I took this fight on because I wanted to save my husband and my own family which doesn't make me anybody special or more able. I took this fight on because my entire life including childhood, had been an uphill climb and the only person that I could ever really count on was me, until I met Johnny Kopystenski. So, for a man like that, I would fight lions and I was tough and strong enough to take them on. But, Americans are not supposed to have to think of their own government agencies as lions who must be tamed or beaten, those agencies are supposed to do their jobs, their work and be committed to their supposed purpose.

In this 21st century, men of sixty are not supposed to be crippled by osteoarthritis so severe, for so many years, like my husband who at 31 was in perfect health and physical condition (or so we thought) but at 35 was diagnosed with 75% of his spine involved in acute arthritis with sores sitting on his spinal column. My son, at 34 should not have the exact same condition and diseases or the same mutated DNA as the father he had just lost, with no possible medical reason other than inherited mutations which didn't exist in either maternal or paternal relatives until Johnny came home from Vietnam. There should not be an entire cadre of men and women, my son's age, who suffered from learning disabilities in multiple forms and neurological impairments requiring special methods of teaching if education was going to be successful, whose only similarity is that regardless of where they grew up or what their background was, their fathers served in Southeast Asia and walked, swam, drank, ate and fought in poisoned air and land.

As much as I would like to say that there is a final chapter available to my memoirs that would be untrue because I will probably only be able to consider the finality of my work to be with my own death. The fight that I set out to win, has had some winning rounds, but for the most part the struggle seems to have no end. Until such time that wars and prisons are not as profitable to the rich and the corporations, there shall always be both. When and until, the elected officials are required to enlist and go to the front lines before they can send others into battle, there is no incentive for them to fear; and will always be old men sending young men to die for economic gain or by using the military and useless incarceration of millions of Americans as a way for the rich to thin the herds of poor, working and middle classes. Since there are constant cuts to education, welfare and research, those who cannot get a proper education, a warm place to live or an answer to their illnesses, throwing people into combat or incarceration will always provide the government, run by the wealthy, to fill their coffers over the bodies of those who do not fit in their blue-chip world. Agent Orange, asbestos, BZ, napalm and so many other chemicals have, as again, I remind the reader, were in my 1984 speech with depleted uranium and other poisonous elements following close behind, are all responsible for so much illness, paralysis, inherited annihilation, mutation, neurological damage and death. But still no party or agency is willing to recognize that the future of America has been thwarted and reduced to the beginning of a dumbed down population, which will be run and administrated by the wealthy and power driven who insulated their own issue from the harm that was done by robbing the working class of opportunity.

In the Presidential race of 2012, which was filled with over nine contenders representing the GOP, to try to unseat President Barack Obama and especially his Affordable Care Act, we saw the "know nothing" candidates of privilege. Earlier I had stated that President Bill Clinton actually did more for the Vietnam Veterans than any Head of the Executive Branch had ever done; but because it was too early to know what percentage of our children would be effected so dramatically by Agent Orange, nothing was accomplished. People like Johnny and I were, like so many of the vets we knew who had children with problems, regardless of our own superior educations and abilities, chose, especially after the "pre-existing conditions" regulations were put in place by the insurance companies, to make choices far removed from our non-veteran counterparts on where to spend our "disposable income". We made what would be considered upper middle class and possibly, in some cases, much higher incomes than could be seen by the lifestyles we learned to live with. Instead of buying second and third homes, some with elevators for our luxury automobiles, we used every cent we had to keep our children alive and provided with the care, equipment, educational standards and uncovered medical expenses necessary.

So in 2008, our country elected a President who, knowing that our children's health needs took precedence over monetary gains and privileges afforded only the rich, took action to stop the inequality. Agent Orange children in the United States make up about one-third of the people who had no, and could get no insurance because of the present practices of the incredibly wealthy insurance companies and their shareholders. The Republicans standing on the many stages for their many debates with each other, represented the T.A.D. worshipers and supposedly the best of the right wing political machine. How pathetic were those debaters in proving that even with probably very high priced college and university degrees, intellect and understanding of what was wrong and what was needed in this country? All I could recall thinking as I watched those political comedies, those debates, was that these people who wanted to be the most important person on Earth, the President of the United States of America, could not even remember the branches of government or what the Constitution actually said. It had to be that when a privileged family sent and paid the entire bill for their privileged child's golden education, it did not matter to the family or the student as to how high the grade point average was, just as long as graduation was achieved regardless of the beer parties and the fraternities. While, those students, of very limited means and no financial backing from privilege, who became President, had used higher education as a springboard for excellence and graduated with high honors and abilities that surpassed even their own original expectations.

The unfortunate reality of what I just put to paper, is that because there are not enough Bill Clinton's or Barack Obama's running and overseeing the management of this Nation, while the wealthy are providing first rate education to second rate students, who may never do anything of merit but Daddy's money will do them just fine; the government has very slowly created a system with overcrowded and understaffed schools for those students who, if encouraged and provided with an adequate education, would want only to excel. Adding to that sad statement of fact, that besides those who do not come from families of means, regardless of finances, children of Vietnam veterans, Iraqi vets and residents of places like Love Canal, New York and Ironbound, New Jersey, etc. are suffering from either learning disabilities, Autism Spectrum and/or severe medical problems in pandemic numbers, far higher than even the Bubonic Plague on a worldwide basis. In the past, before we even realized the actually high ratios of what just Agent Orange was going to create in this country, I used to stand at the speaking podium and explain what our projections were just here in the United States. My words, regardless of the audience makeup were always the same, "If one and a half million Vietnam Combat Veterans, who served during and after the spraying, each had three children and each of those children had three children, the total after only one and a half generations will be over 40.5 million births within the next twenty-five years, of which by our calculations, would have some sort of medical or educational maladies, and many having both." Just as the statements I made back in 1984, about what would happen when our children married the children of those who never served, have actually become reality, unless this government takes the Agent Orange Legacy seriously, now that it is perhaps too late to reverse the genetic mutations which have created two generations of special needs victims, then there really is no great hope for the "exceptional-ism" of the American citizens.

What is even more frightening is that we shall become the pawns of the ruling class of the ridiculously wealthy who never served in even a street fight, much less a war zone, and their pretty little rich kids that got into Ivy League schools because Daddy was an Alumnus or built a library, so that the school would welcome their children with open arms and never notice that a 1.5 or 2.0 average does not a President make. Just look at George W. Bush and how many new cases of Traumatic Brain Injury he felt that the average American families should have to deal with.

It truly is my hope and my intention in penning this book, that it shall not only open the eyes of those who read it, even if they think that they have no connection to the war in Vietnam or the wars which have taken place since 1975, but to let those millions of people whose lives have been effected by what happened in 1964 through 1975; that I feel what you feel and my family's hardships and nightmare experiences, are yours as well. It is not enough to just know that this one woman fought a good fight, because unless the government that caused such devastation, for the act of defending its ridiculous beliefs, finally does much more to change the plight of the Agent Orange Child and now his and her children as well, through research, care, treatment and compensation, even at this late date, the American way of life shall deteriorate more and more every year.

APPENDIX

VNAORRC, Vietnam Agent Orange Relief & Responsibility Campaign | 2009 Paris Tribunal Press Release

Vietnam Agent Orange
Relief & Responsibility Campaign

Justice for all Agent Orange victims

International Peoples' Tribunal of Conscience In Support of the Vietnamese Victims of Agent Orange

Press Advisory

May 22, 2009

Tribunal renders judgement against U.S. government and chemical companies – Hears testimony of U.S. Veteran and Vietnamese Agent Orange victims

For information, please contact:
Jearnne Mirer, Esq.,
Secretary General, International Association of Democratic Lawyers

On May 18, 2009, an international tribunal, sitting in Paris, ruled that the United States government and corporate manufacturers of Agent Orange are liable and responsible for the spraying of the dioxin laden chemical on the people and land of Vietnam during the Vietnam War. The judges decided that "*the use of Dioxin was a war crime because it was a poisoned weapon outlawed both in customary international law and by the Hague Convention of 1907*" and " *that that the use of Dioxin was a crime against humanity as defined by VI c of the Nuremberg Principles.* "

The Tribunal held that, because the use of Agent Orange was illegal under international law and its use "*produced so much pain, suffering and anguish to at least 3 to 4 million people and their families... [that] the effects of these crimes will be felt for generations to come... the time has come to provide an adequate remedy to the Vietnamese victims of Agent Orange and their families and to repair as much as possible the environment of Vietnam.*"

The judges ordered the U.S. government and chemical manufacturers of Agent Orange to fully compensate to compensate the victims and their families and to clean up the environmental contamination in and around dioxin laden "hot spots" in Vietnam.

American veteran **Frank Corcoran**, who served in Vietnam and later contracted cancer acknowledged by the Veterans Administration to be related to Agent Orange, testified that, while he received 100% disability for his illness, " *the US is denying the Vietnamese people the same justice*." **Rena Kopystenski** whose Vietnam veteran husband, John, died a year ago and whose son and grandson suffer from the effects of John's exposure to Agent Orange testified that when she looks at photos showing Agent Orange's terrible impact on the children of Vietnam she realizes that, "while the chemical companies maimed and destroyed a selected segment of the American population, it has totally devastated an entire population and future populations of the country of Vietnam." She concluded, "with the death of my husband comes a new dedication to force answers, treatment and compensation for those who have been left to relive the War in Vietnam."

The panel of international judges included Jitendra Sharma, President of the IADL and Supreme Court lawyer, India, Claudia Morcom, judge, Michigan and Juan Guzman, Judge, Chile, the judge who tried Augusto Pinochet. The judges heard testimony about the personal impact of Agent Orange from Vietnamese, U.S. and South Korean victims and from renowned scientists from May 15-16th.

The Executive Summary of the Decision of the Tribunal is attached, together with the full Tribunal Decision in pdf.

International Peoples' Tribunal of Conscience In Support of the Vietnamese Victims of Agent Orange

Press Advisory

May 22, 2009

For information, please contact:
Jearnne Mirer, Esq.,
Secretary General, International Association of Democratic Lawyers

VAORRC, Vietnam Agent Orange Relief & Responsibility Campaign

- **www.VN-AgentOrange.org**
- **info@vn-agentorange.org**

TESTIMONY OF RENA KOPYSTENSKI
©(RPK2009)
INTERNATIONAL TRIBUNAL OF CONSCIENCE
15 May, 2009
Paris, France

"Ironically, the last time that I spoke to an international forum, regarding Agent Orange, was another day in May, May 4, 1984 to be exact. It was on that day, in a Federal Courthouse in Brooklyn, New York, that Judge Jack Weinstein ordered the final rape of the Vietnam veteran in the form of a settlement of the Agent Orange lawsuit. The lawyers cleared upwards of 40 million dollars and the value of a dead vet was $3,800.00.

On April 6, 2008, my beloved husband, my soul mate of 40 years, passed away from the ravages of Agent Orange, which had plagued him continuously since 1971. My husband John Kopystenski was a remarkable man who worked hard for his family, loved his family, but also loved to help anyone who really needed it.

In 1971, John, who was a teamster, had to take a union physical, which in America was very thorough and very precise, if the teamsters provided it for their members. He underwent x-rays of his upper and lower back, which showed him to be in perfect condition. In 1976, only 5 years later, due to severe back and sciatic pain, he underwent the same x-rays and was found to have 75% of his spine involved in acute osteoarthritis, which was spreading without explanation. as well as disc deterioration that medical experts told us would eventually, in the near future, take away his ability to walk.

It was not until the summer of 1977, when I was 6 months

pregnant with our son, Alex that we learned of Agent Orange and the effects that some vets were experiencing as well as the numerous birth defects that their children were born with. I remember sitting in my living room, watching the 6 o'clock news and hearing what others were experiencing as a gift for their service in Vietnam. I still recall grabbing my stomach and crying as I whispered to my unborn son "you are going to be just fine"; but from that day in August until this day, nothing has been "just fine". Our son was born unusually jaundiced and had to stay in the hospital for nearly a month before he was well enough to come home. I stayed with him for nine days but then my insurance ran out so I went home, without my child. Every morning I drove John to work and then drove the 25 miles to the hospital and sat all day with my baby, drove home each night to cry myself to sleep, until I could take him home. When Alex was 3 months old, we rushed in a rainstorm to meet the pediatrician at the hospital because his little stomach was so distended that we thought he was going to burst. At first, the doctor told us, it was "probably gas", but after John went beau-koo dinky dou on the doctor, he ordered a barium enema for our son. When the doctor came out again, he was red-faced and extremely contrite in explaining that our little baby would never have lived for the trip home if he had not placated my husband. Our tiny baby was suffering from intususception, which was caused by an overlong and deformed intestine. He also explained that we could eventually have the entire intestine removed, cut and replaced properly, but, that, for such a young child, he wouldn't survive. We nearly lost our son at least ten times over the next three years from this deformity and he, to this day, suffers from intestinal problems. I shall talk about my son and now, my grandson, again, later in this testimony. But, I will tell you that it had always been our plan to have a large family and because of Agent Orange and our fear of what the outcome would be for any other children, John and I decided that Alex was going to be our only child.

While the private physicians blamed John's exposure to Agent Orange in Vietnam, for his rapidly increasing medical problems, the Veterans Administration blamed John. This man never drank, smoked or did drugs, but the VA treated him like a leper and a freeloader. He underwent the VA's "Agent Orange screenings" which were a joke; but the joke was on my husband and the other over 2 million servicemen and women who served their country valiantly, whether they believed in the war or not. He was never given a liver biopsy or any of the other tests which were found helpful by the scientists working with vets as part of the New Jersey Agent Orange Commission study, which John and I were instrumental in creating. The only compensation given to Vietnam vets was for Post Traumatic Stress Disorder and then only if they wet their beds or beat their wives.

Fortunately, for us, we had very good medical insurance and John was given the best care possible, but that was only until the insurance companies called both my husband and my son's problems, "pre-existing conditions caused by AO poisoning" and the financial burden became ours. How ironic is it that the VA wouldn't recognize my husband's maladies or what his chemically altered DNA had passed onto our son, but the insurance companies not only recognized Agent Orange but used it as an excuse not to cover my loved ones. By that time we had learned that Alex was neurologically impaired, had leukopenia, a highly challenged immune system which caused severe chloracne psoriasis; and our bills for his care averaged somewhere between $50,000.00 to $250,000.00 per year. John's medical care had to be handled more creatively since the VA would not care for him unless he had exhausted all of his assets, so a friend at the VA suggested that we divorce and I take him for everything so that I could afford to take care of Alex. We divorced in 1986 and remarried the day after he was granted 100% Agent Orange service connected in 1999, which means that the government's refusal to fix what they and the chemical companies had broken forced a middle class middle-aged couple to live in sin, for 13 years, just to keep our family alive.

Our son Alex was born with a deformed foot, which we had corrected; leukopenia, which meant that he had to grow up in a virtual "bubble existence", a deformed intestine, which was so elongated and enmeshed that he was never a good candidate for surgery and still has to live with digestive and intestinal problems on a daily basis. Dr. Bennett Shaywitz, who was the foremost pediatric neurologist in the country, at the time, found Alex to be of very high intelligence, but suffering from eight different learning differences (disabilities), all of which were severe, when he tested Alex at Yale University. We ended up home-schooling Alex, through his college courses, with me studying constantly to teach him different methods to learn, such as Korean ChismBop for math, and auditory learning to teach him to read.

When Alex began to mature, the skin problems that he had had since birth grew into the most severe psoriasis imaginable and nothing we did would calm this condition, which now covers the majority of his body and all of his extremities. We were finally told that it is a condition caused by his father's exposure to Agent Orange and that normal methods cannot cure it. We recently learned that Alex is showing all of the signs of Agent Orange diabetes, which is what killed his father, but Alex never went to Vietnam. This has been my son's life and these problems, I believe, are the reasons that he has never married. Because we took great care to raise him with a great self-image and he is a talented human being and is now a wonderful custodial single parent. Alex became a father in 2003, at 25 years of age, to a beautiful little boy, whom he named Giovanni, Gio for short. John and I were happy to help him with his son. When Gio was two years of age, we started to notice that he was talking less and less and losing interest in a number of things. We had him tested and he was diagnosed to be autistic. There is not enough time, in my life, for me to study and learn how to turn this child's life back to normal, however, I did start to question why autism is of epidemic proportions in the United States. If, as it was proven in the early 80's, 7 out of every 10 children born to exposed Vietnam veterans, had some form of dyslexia or other learning problems, would it not be more than possible that, if every offspring of a Vietnam vet, had children and the autism numbers went from 1 in 2500, ten years ago, to 1 in 90 now, that it is not inconceivable that there is a correlation between Agent Orange exposure in Vietnam to autism in the 21st century?

In the speech that I gave in August of 1984, I stated, "by taking the best and the brightest to fight in Vietnam and then spraying them with liquid poison, America has broken its own backbone". It is with humility, that I look at the stories and pictures of what Agent Orange's legacy has done to the population and especially the children of Vietnam and realize that, while the chemical companies maimed and destroyed a selected segment of the American population, it has totally devastated an entire population and future populations of the country of Vietnam. As hard as my family's life may be, we were blessed to live in the United States and were able to afford the best medical care available, but I do not see those alternatives available to the majority of the effected families in Vietnam.

The monies paid by the chemical companies in 1984 really only benefited the attorneys and the insurance company that managed the monies. Any Vietnam vet who had found an alternative method to assist with the medical bills, such as social services, social security, Medicaid, etc., could not even take the meager $1,000.00 or so dollars available to them under the settlement agreement because any "windfall" would make them ineligible for the assistance they were getting. Moreover, the VA, at that time was providing no help, care or assistance for anyone exposed to chemical defoliants.

Our grandson Gio, by all evidence seems to be medically healthy, however, his autism creates enough of a challenge and I worry constantly about his future and how he will survive as a grown-up. We are doing all that we can to pull him out of the autism window in order to insure that he can cope and succeed as time takes its toll on his support system. I have written to the CDC and anyone else who might have any influence in forcing the powers that be to look into the relationship between the changing DNA of the Vietnam combat veterans and the epidemic of autism in America; but I might as well simply yell into the wind.

I do not believe that any man or woman who fought in Vietnam, be it those who lived in Vietnam, or those who were sent by their governments to "spread freedom and democracy", actually had any animosity for or knowledge of the lives they were forced to take. How damning is it that both sides were sprayed and betrayed by chemical companies whose only agenda was profit and wealth? To realize that now, over 30 years later, the chemical lobby is still so strong that it arrogantly takes no interest or responsibility for the damage that it has done.

I recently heard of a park in the State of Michigan that was polluted with dioxin and that Dow Chemical had been ordered to clean it up; however, under the Bush administration, the chemical companies did nothing and nothing was done to the chemical companies. Ironically, within the first 50 days of the Obama administration, an order was issued to Dow, and the work began, with haste. It is because of things like this, while I may be sadly mistaken and naïve, I believe that the Vietnam combat vets, their children and their grandchildren, as well as the people of Vietnam, may stand a chance at some sort of acknowledgment and repair for what has been done. It is important that we work together, as an inclusive entity to make this happen.

In August of 1984, the New York Times editorial stated that, "Rena Kopystenski states that the Vietnam veteran does not want money, they want answers"; however, now, more than 20 years later, what has happened to our children and the children of Vietnam still remains, for the most part, unanswered and flagrantly ignored. If this is not a crime against humanity, I, whose ancestry includes the Holocaust, do not know what is. The damage done to future generations is not without cause or reason, but it does not have to be without treatment and cure. I believe that even in these scary financial times, the chemical companies that created this monstrous problem are not financially without the resources to fund the health care and treatment to cure what they do not have to study to find out what they have done THEY ALREADY KNOW EXACTLY

WHAT THEY HAVE DONE.

The loss of my beloved husband John, who was only 63 when he passed, was and is the worst thing that could have happened and yet, because of my anger, he is the reason that I am here today. John was sentenced to death in 1966 while serving as a door-gunner on a Medivac chopper in the area around An Khe. He never knew that what he did was “heroes’ work” until vets came up to hug and thank him, as a symbol of all door-gunners, well after he had returned home. He never believed in the Vietnam War, but, he was an American and he was drafted, so he served his country to the best of his ability. John also made an impact on the Vietnamese people and we sent money to an orphanage every single month until that day in 1975 when the priest that ran the orphanage wrote and told us that it was gone. He was the strongest, most decent and kindest man I have ever met and he did not deserve to spend so many sick and painful years. Even in his worst times, Johnny stayed with us longer than he should have just because he was worried that if he took the peace that death would bring, he would leave his wife, sons, his small grandchildren, and us without his physical presence and I suspect his pension income. This man took in other peoples’ throwaway children and refused to take a dime for their care, because “you can’t teach a young man that he’s worth anything if he knows you are being paid for his care”. This was my husband, my friend, my mentor and he died from the effects that Agent Orange visited upon him and that the chemical companies allowed to persist.

How ironic is it that the VA has finally named “diabetes” as an aftereffect of Agent Orange and will now compensate any veteran who served in Nam and has developed diabetes? How sad is it that it took so long and that Agent Orange diabetes is a killer, no matter how careful one watches their diet and sugar count? At first the only problem that was acknowledged was cancer, soft tissue sarcoma and the skin condition known as chloracne, which not to minimize in any way, were not the only problems. John, like so many of his brethren developed sebaceous cysts which our doctor removed, only to have them return. The doctors finally told us that somehow John's DNA had been altered and no matter what we did, those cysts would keep coming back.. Should that not have been a sign for the VA and those researchers who were supposedly doing their jobs, to realize that if DNA had been altered and immune systems had been compromised, that offspring didn't stand a chance? The number of vets who suffer from neuropathy is staggering and men in their 60's have medical conditions of men in their 80's when their only commonality is that served in Vietnam.

In the early 80's we received over 100 calls each week from vets all over the country who, regardless of their backgrounds and environmental surroundings were all suffering from the same illnesses and medical problems. The only common denominator, once again, was their service in Vietnam. It is not that no one realized it then as opposed to what was recognized back then has been ignored since then. A friend of mine wrote a book entitled "Waiting for an Army to Die", which was written right after the Agent Orange settlement. The reality is that, just as in the 1980's when things might have been able to be turned around, now in the year 2009, the government of the United States is still waiting for that Army to die.

I truly believe that the only lawsuit that may stand a chance is one that is on behalf of the children and grandchildren of both the American vets and the Vietnamese people. I also believe that enough of our children have already married into families that were fortunate enough, back in the day, to avoid any involvement in Vietnam, so that my original prediction that our children would eventually marry those of offspring of the law, medical or corporate citizens has come to pass and they now have a reason to feel anger, to become involved in our fight. I do not think that I am being idealistic to think that if we, as a collaborative effort, bring suit, simply by the exhaustive number of our effected victims, we will be hard to be ignored and I further believe that no suit should be brought in New York Federal Court, since Judge Weinstein's bias is not only well recognized but should be a valid reason for his voluntary exclusion. With age should come wisdom, but, in this instance, sometimes age creates an unyielding refusal to see the damage you have done and an inability to admit that damage even if you do recognize the error. All of this, for an old man to save face, directly in the face of the horrendous birth defects and illnesses that an uninformed decision allowed to happen, twenty-five years ago by a judge that kept dozing off during the testimonies given during every court date that I attended, which was every one of them. In my early 30's, I was not yet aware that everything that goes on in a courtroom has already been decided and choreographed in a backroom. But, just because that was the crime against us then, does not mean that this crime should be allowed to continue.

I have known many vets who died before their time, amongst them: Frank Delaney of New Haven, Conn. who passed away from cancer of the brain in 1984; Stephen Drake of New Jersey, 1982 of cancer; Dave Cline, who spent his entire grown life fighting for the rights of both American and Vietnamese Agent Orange victims, in 2008; Bill Davis of Chicago, Ill., in 2008 and of course, John Kopystenski in Las Vegas, Nevada in April of 2008, just to name a few. I have also known many vets whose children bore an even greater burden than their own and who deserve answers and recognition for the maladies and horrors they have and are suffering from. I have requested that vets and vet group leaders from throughout the United States, send me lists of their Agent Orange victims and Agent Orange children and I shall be more than happy to make those lists available to anyone who has an interest. It is for those men, women and their children, that I have traveled so far from my home and family.

I am not a scientist, nor am I very knowledgeable with regard to the scientific data collected regarding Agent Orange. I am, above all else, a wife without a husband at my side and a mother and grandmother who has no answers for why my son or his son is so afflicted. I come before you today because I was told that this tribunal wanted to hear from someone who could give them a better understanding of what it is to live in the shadow of Agent Orange. It seems to me that there is not enough directed anger on the part of those who make up today's social conscience to bring forth the changes that are needed, and that is very sad. I am a voice from the past, a part of the beginning of a fight that never seems to end, but my anger has never subsided and with the death of my husband comes a new dedication to force answers, treatment and compensation for those who have been left to relive the War in Vietnam every time they look in a mirror or try to live what is deemed "a normal life".

International Peoples' Tribunal of Conscience In Support of the Vietnamese Victims of Agent Orange

Thứ ba, 28 Tháng 9 2010 22:29 Lương Nhung 487

International Peoples' Tribunal of Conscience In Support of the Vietnamese Victims of Agent Orange

EXECUTIVE SUMMARY OF THE DECISION Paris, May 18, 2009

Read the full Tribunal Decision in pdf (2.7 MB)

The International Peoples' Tribunal of Conscience in Support of the Vietnamese Victims of Agent Orange met on May 15 to 16 2009 in Paris to hear evidence of the impact of the use of Agent Orange by the US military in Vietnam from 1961 and 1971. A summons and complaint announcing the Tribunal was sent to the United States Government, and the Chemical Companies which manufactured Agent Orange. Despite notice neither the Government nor the firms responded.

The Tribunal was constituted by the International Association of Democratic Lawyers (IADL). The Judges of the Tribunal came from every part of the globe: Jitendra

Sharma, India; Judge Juan Guzman, Chile; Judge Claudia Morcom, USA; Professor Marjorie Cohn, USA; Dr. Gavril Chiuzbaian, Romania; Prof. Adda Bekkarouch, Algeria; and Attorney Shoji Umeda, Japan.

The Tribunal received evidence and testimony from 27 people including victims and expert witnesses. The testimony from the victims was very compelling and the testimony of the experts tied the damages that these victims suffered to their exposure to Dioxin. Testimony also described the extent of the spraying, the millions of persons exposed, the jungles and forests destroyed and families devastated.

After examining the evidence the Tribunal found that the United States Government and the Chemical manufacturers were aware of the fact that Dioxin, one of the most dangerous chemicals known to man, was present in one of the component parts of Agent Orange; yet they continued to use it and in fact suppressed a study which showed in 1965 that Dioxin caused many birth defects in experimental animals. It was not until the results of that study were released by a leak from concerned citizen that the use of Agent Orange was stopped.

Considering that this Tribunal finds:

1) that the evidence presented to the Tribunal has established that during the war of USA against Vietnam, from 1961 to 1971, military forces of the United States

sprayed chemical products which contained large quantities of Dioxin in order to defoliate the trees for military objectives;

2) that the chemical products which were sprayed caused damages to the people, the land, the water, the forest, the ecology and the economy of Vietnam that this Tribunal can categorize as:

a. direct damages to the people: The illnesses produced directly to the people who have been exposed to Dioxin include cancer, skin disorders, liver damage, pulmonary and heart diseases, defects to reproductive capacity, as well as nervous disorders;
b. indirect damages to the children of those exposed to Dioxin, including severe physical deformities, mental and physical disabilities, diseases and shortened life spans;
c. damages caused to the land and forests, water supply, and communities. The forests and jungles in large parts of southern Vietnam have been devastated and denuded, and may either never grow back or take 50 to 200 years to regenerate. Animals which inhabited the forests and jungles have become extinct, disrupting the communities which depended on them. The rivers and underground water in some areas have also been contaminated. Dioxin will persist in the environment for many years; and
d. erosion and desertification necessarily will change the environment contributing to warming the planet and

the dislocation of crop and animal life.

Considering also that this Tribunal finds:

1) that the US war in Vietnam was an illegal war of aggression against a country seeking national liberation: the illegality is based on Articles 2(3) and 2(4) of the Charter of the United Nations which require countries to peacefully resolve their disputes. The massive spraying of Agent Orange/Dioxin on the southern part of Vietnam and the massive bombardment of the northern part of Vietnam clearly demonstrates that the United States violated the UN Charter mandate to refrain from the use of force in international relations;

2) that the Nuremberg Principles define a war of aggression as a *crime against peace* punishable under international law;

3) that the use of Dioxin was a war crime because it was a poisoned weapon outlawed both in customary international law and by the Hague Convention of 1907. [Hague Convention 23(a)]. Violations of the customs and laws of war are considered war crimes under Principle VI b of the Nuremberg Principles. The Chemical companies knew how their Dioxin- laced products would be used in Vietnam; yet they continued to manufacture and supply these agents with very high levels of Dioxin to the US government. By providing poison weapons the companies were complicit in the war crimes committed by the US government;

4) that the use of Dioxin was a crime against humanity as defined by VI c of the Nuremberg Principles, because it constituted an inhuman act done against a civilian population in connection with a crime against peace and war crimes;

5) that the use of illegal weapons in an illegal war has caused the devastation described above. These crimes have produced so much pain, suffering and anguish to at least 3 to 4 million people and their families. The effects of these crimes will be felt for generations to come; and

6) that the time has come to provide an adequate remedy to the Vietnamese victims of Agent Orange and their families and to repair as much as possible the environment of Vietnam.

CONCLUSIONS:

This Tribunal finds:

1. that the United States Government is guilty of the offenses listed above and determines that the damage to the environment of Vietnam can be defined as "ecocide";
2. that the Chemical companies who were charged in the summons and complaint are guilty of complicity in the offenses listed above; and
3. that the United States Government and the Chemical companies which manufactured and supplied Agent Orange must fully compensate the victims of Agent

Orange and their families. The US Government and the Chemical companies must also repair the environment to remove the contamination of Dioxin from the soil and the waters, and especially from the "hot spots" around former US military bases.

To complete the above task of compensation and repair, the Tribunal recommends that the **Agent Orange Commission** be established to assess the amount of compensation to be allocated to each victim, family group, and community.

The Agent Orange Commission will also determine the amount necessary to provide specialized medical facilities and rehabilitation and other therapeutic services to the victims and their families.

The Agent Orange Commission will also estimate the costs of the necessary studies of contaminated areas and the cost of environmental repair in the future.

The Agent Orange Commission will also determine the amount to be paid to the State of Vietnam to indemnify it for monies it has expended to support the victims and repair the environment.

The Tribunal urges the Government of the Socialist Republic of Vietnam to forthwith constitute such Agent Orange Commission of people of eminence in the fields of medicine, science, engineering, law, epidemiology, agriculture, toxicology, ecology, public administration, and representatives of civil society. The Agent Orange Commission shall make its recommendations within one year of its constitution.

Once the Agent Orange Commission has established the requisite amounts, those monies shall be paid by the United States Government and the Chemical companies jointly and severally to a trust fund specially created for present and future victims and their families, and repair of the environment. The amount of $1.52 billion a year being paid by the United States Government to the US Vietnam veteran victims of Agent Orange can be employed as a guide for the calculations performed by the Agent Orange Commission.

The full report of the Tribunal along with this Executive Summary shall be submitted to the Vietnamese Government within 4 weeks and will be published in full and widely distributed in the International community.

JUDGMENT OF THE INTERNATIONAL PEOPLES TRIBUNAL OF CONSCIENCE IN SUPPORT OF THE VIETNAMESE VICTIMS OF AGENT ORANGE

MAY - 2009

WARS DO NOT END when the bombs stop falling and the fighting ceases. The devastation continues long after, in the land and in the minds and bodies of the affected population.

Today, three million Vietnamese suffer the effects of chemical defoliants used by the United States during the Vietnam War.

In order to deny food and protection to those deemed to be "the enemy," the U.S. defoliated the forests of Vietnam with the deadly chemicals Agent Orange, White, Blue, Pink, Green and Purple. Agent Orange, which was contaminated with trace amounts of TCDD dioxin – the most toxic chemical known to science – disabled and sickened soldiers, civilians and several generations of their offspring on two continents.

In addition to the millions of Vietnamese still affected by this deadly poison, tens of thousands of U.S. soldiers are also affected.

It has caused birth defects in hundreds of thousands of

children in Vietnam and the U.S. – that is, the second and third generations of those who were exposed to Agent Orange decades ago. Medical evidence indicates that certain cancers (for example, soft tissue non- Hodgkin's Lymphoma), diabetes (type II), and in children spina bifida and other birth defects, are attributable to the exposure.

The deadly mark left by Agent Orange on the natural environment of Vietnam includes the destruction of mangrove forests and the long term poisoning of soil and crops.

Photos, right: Edwin Martini/courtesy of the

National Archives, College Park, MD

JUDGMENT OF THE INTERNATIONAL PEOPLES TRIBUNAL OF CONSCIENCE IN SUPPORT OF THE VIETNAMESE VICTIMS OF AGENT ORANGE

VIETNAM AGENT ORANGE RELIEF &
IADL
International Association of Democratic Lawyers
is a Non-Governmental Organization (NGO) with consultative status to ECOSOC and UNESCO

Website: **www.iadllaw.org**
Book design: Barbara Barefield DesignWorks, Detroit, MI

THE INTERNATIONAL ASSOCIATION of Democratic Lawyers (IADL) has convened this Tribunal of Conscience in Support of the Vietnamese Victims of Agent Orange in coordination with the supporting French committee composed of IADL affiliate Droit Solidarité, along with Association of Friendship Franco-Vietnamean Association, Republican Association of Veterans, International Committee for Village of Friendship Van Canh, French Peace Movement, International Association of Humanitarian Law, General Union of Vietnamese in France, and Committee Vietnam-Dioxin.

IADL has committed itself to the campaign for justice for these victims as it had committed itself to opposing the war in Vietnam in the 1960's and 1970's.

The Tribunal is comprised of the following lawyers and Judges:

1. Sr. Advocate Jitendra Sharma, India

2. Judge Juan Guzman Tapia, Chile

3. Dr. Gavril Chiuzbaian, Romania

4. Judge Claudia Morcom, U.S.

5. Professor Marjorie Cohn, U.S.

6. Professor Adda Bekkouche, Algeria

7. Attorney Shoji Umeda, Japan

Brief Biographical notes of members of the Tribunal are attached as Exhibit A.

Judgement of the International Peoples' Tribunal of Conscience in Support of the Vietnamese Victims of Agent Orange

JUDGMENT OF THE INTERNATIONAL PEOPLES TRIBUNAL OF CONSCIENCE IN SUPPORT OF THE VIETNAMESE VICTIMS OF AGENT ORANGE

MAY - 2009

ON APRIL 4, 2009 the United States Government and the firms which manufactured Agent Orange were served with a summons and complaint advising them that the International People's Tribunal of Conscience would convene in Paris on May 15-16, 2009, to take testimony, investigate and opine on the effects of the use and manufacture of Agent Orange on the Vietnamese people, and to determine what remedy is required. The summons and complaints are attached as Exhibit B.

Despite having been properly served with the summons and complaint, none of the respondents entered an appearance or filed any statement. The Tribunal thus proceeded ex parte against the respondents.

The Tribunal was assisted by Advocates for the Claimants, Mr. Roland Weyl, Ms. Jeanne Mirer, and Mr. Jonathan Moore who facilitated the presentation of the evidence.

The President of the Vietnamese Association for the Victims of Agent Orange

(VAVA) Senior Lieutenant General Nguyen Van Rinh (Ret.)

opened the Tribunal by thanking the the Tribunal organizers, and judges for their willingness to hear from the witnesses and consider the plight of the Vietnamese Victims of Agent Orange.

The Tribunal heard the evidence presented, both written and oral, from victims, from interested parties and experts. It makes the following findings of fact and conclusions of law.

Findings of Fact:

1. Nature of Agent Orange:

Agent Orange was the name of the chemicals used by the U.S. government during the war in Vietnam. It is a 50-50 mixture of two chemicals known as 2,4,D and 2,4,5,T which was packed and shipped to Vietnam in barrels containing an orange painted band. This is how the name Agent Orange was acquired.

If 2,4,5,T is not manufactured properly, Dioxin as an impurity appears. Dioxin is one of the most harmful chemicals ever known to man. (See Testimony of Dr. Tran Xuan Thu)

2. Suffering of Affected Individuals, Impacts on Second and Third Generations

A. The Tribunal heard from the following individual witnesses who spoke of the personal impact exposure Agent Orange had on them, their children, families and communities. 2 A synopsis of the testimony from these individuals

is set forth below:

1. MR. MAI GIANG VU

A Vietnamese living in Thoi, Precinct 9, district 11, Ho Chi Minh City, testified that he was exposed to Agent Orange while a member of the Army of South Vietnam (RVN) from June 1968 to February 1974. During that time he helped other soldiers carry barrels of the chemicals to spray in the jungle.

He continuedto do this work until he lost an eye in battle. Prior to his exposure he had two daughters who were healthy and remain so. After his exposure he and his wife had two sons, one born in April 1974, the other in April 1975. Both of his sons appeared healthy at birth and in their early years. By April 1980 his eldest son began to show unusual symptoms.

His second son also started to present the same symptoms. At first they were no longer capable of walking or functioning normally, then their limbs gradually "curled up" and they could only crawl. By the time they were 18 they were confined to bed. One died at the age of 23 the other died at the age of 25. The doctors had no explanation for his son's illnesses until he explained his exposure to Agent Orange. At that point he was advised of the relationship of his exposure to their illnesses. In addition to his children, his own health is very bad. He had prostate surgery. His nose and throat are constantly infected. He reported that many families suffer tragedies similar to his, and they need help from all the possible sources.

2. MR. PHAM THE MINH

A Vietnamese who resides in An Duong district, Hai Phong City, Vietnam. He was born on December 16, 1979. He testified that both his mother and father were soldiers in the Air Defense Forces during the U.S. War in Vietnam. They were contaminated by Agent Orange chemical when they were serving in the battle field of Quang Tri Province, south of the DMZ, where the spraying was very intense. Mr. Minh stated that both he and his sister have suffered harm due to the exposure of his parents to Dioxin. His sister was born prematurely with congenital heart and lung diseases. He has deformities of his lower limbs and very harsh pains all over his body. He has to take many medicines to be able to continue with life. He has digestive problems and is prone to pneumonia and lung diseases. He has had his deformities since birth.

He cannot walk without the aid of a walking stick. He showed both legs to the Tribunal. Both are crooked and very skinny. He told the Tribunal that he is single, without any children. Because most of the men who suffer deformities are not understood or accepted by women, their life is very difficult. They suffer both physically and emotionally. He indicated that in his community there are more than 17,000 persons who suffer deformities and other illnesses that are the consequence of Agent Orange. Many suffer from cancer. He knows that these victims burden their families for care and medical help, which is not available to the victims as much as is needed.

3. MR. HO NGOC CHU

a Vietnamese from Group 3, Tran Phu, Quang Ngai City, Vietnam. He testified that he was born in 1937 and that he joined the liberation forces of South Vietnam in the 1960s. He served in the vast areas of the mountain Mr. Minh (above) stated that both he and his sister have suffered harm due to the exposure of his parents to Dioxin.

His sister was born prematurely with congenital heart and lung diseases. He has deformities of his lower limbs and very harsh pains in all his body. He has to take all sorts of medicines to be able to continue with life. ous regions along Truong Son, and Quang Nam in South Vietnam where the U.S. sprayed regularly and intensively. He was told the products sprayed were simply herbicides and not harmful. He was sprayed four to five times. He tried to stay in his tent most of the time when the spraying occurred but on one occasion he was directly sprayed when he was carrying a bag of rice back to his base. His whole body was sprayed as was the bag of rice. As a result of the spraying, vegetables died and the jungle became defoliated.

The cassava, their regular food, was killed also. To survive they had to continue eating cassava roots and drinking water from the contaminated streams. He started having various physical troubles thereafter. His eyes became weak, his teeth fell out, and he had other problems related to his prostate, incontinence, and a disorder of the large intestine. He married in March 1977 and in November his son was born prematurely and extremely weak. His son did not develop normally. He only started to speak and to walk at the age of 4. His limbs did not function normally and he was not able to learn at school. The doctors said that he was suffering retardation. Sometimes his son had severe convulsions. Now his son is over 30 years old, but is unable to support himself.

According to the doctors, his son's illnesses are the result of Mr. Chu's own exposure to Agent Orange. Although he receives a small indemnification from the government to assist his family, it is insufficient to cover all his medical expenses. Mr. Chu noted that the part of the country where he and his family lived has been ruined by this pollution from Agent Orange.